EQUITY AND LOAN FINANCING FOR THE PRIVATE COMPANY

To those who spent so many hours of blood, sweat, toil and tears in the production of this book, the first on this subject – and to those who read it!

Equity and Loan Financing for the Private Company

Michael Springman

Gower Press

First published in Great Britain by Gower Press Limited 1973

Reprinted 1977 by Gower Press, Teakfield Limited,
Westmead, Farnborough, Hampshire, England.

ISBN 0 7161 0159 9

Printed and bound by Ilfadrove Limited,
Barry, Glamorgan, S. Wales.

Contents

Illustrations

Foreword

By J.O. Hambro MC, Chairman, Hambros Ltd

How does a private company interest a merchant bank in taking a part of its equity? At last, we have a book which describes the investment policies and vetting procedures, adopted by the banks when they are negotiating minority equity stakes in private companies.

Michael Springman examines the many factors involved in a successful approach to a bank. A full and well-timed proposal is the first step towards a strong bargaining position. Normally, if a decision is required immediately, the answer is nearly always no. Therefore, sufficient time must be allowed, before the finance is actually required, for completing the investigations and negotiations, including the gathering of any missing facts.

The author describes the many obstacles the applicant has to surmount before obtaining finance. Most companies, seeking finance from merchant banks, do not have a long record of past earnings. Great weight has therefore to be given to the probability of their achieving their future potential earnings and the relationship of this forecast to past achievements. This judgement requires the evaluation of such intangibles, as the quality and the capability of the management, and its ability to run the company profitably, after and during its planned expansion. Bankers not only require a profitable investment situation, but also a management that can be trusted with their money. Lacking both time and full information, they have often to rely on a 'nose' or 'feel' for a profitable or unprofitable investment.

After investment, comes the working relationship. The book sets out the dynamics of partnership between the directors and the bank, usually represented on the board by a non-executive director. The difficult path through rapid expansion to, perhaps, public issue or takeover, is also analysed.

This book is essential reading for the ambitious private company management which cannot afford to be uneducated in the ways of obtaining long-term finance. In addition, an increased understanding by private companies of the objectives of the financial sector, may also allow the banks, in their turn, to handle a greater quantity of applications from this important market sector – the private company.

Acknowledgements

I have to make the following achnowledgements and thanks.

To Mr. John Bolton, CBE, DSC, who lent me material and also commented on the format of the book.

To Mr. J.F. Staddon, FCA, the Secretary of the Institute of Directors, who read through the manuscript and made useful comments.

To Mr. Peter Baynes, past Director of the Society of Long Range Planning, and now Strategic Planning Manager, British Tourist Authority, for commenting upon the chapter on forward planning.

To Mr. Michael Levete, past Chief Marketing Executive, Charterhouse Finance Corporation Limited, and now Managing Director, London Broadcasting Company, for his comments on the chapter on public issue.

To Mr. P.B.D. Bunyan, the Librarian and Information Officer of the Institute of Directors, for supplying me with original information from the library on the functions of non-executive directors and also for checking my bibliography.

To Col. G.A. Shepherd, MBE, the Librarian of the Royal Military Academy, Sandhurst, for allowing me, as an ex-cadet of the RMC, to consult some books from the library on Napoleon.

And to those other people who have not been named, but who have assisted me in the preparation of the book or lent me material.

Acknowledgments

[illegible]

1

Introduction

LONG-TERM IMPORTANCE OF SMALL COMPANIES

The publication of the Bolton Report on small firms and the research reports, commissioned as a result of the inquiry, have highlighted the importance of small firms in our economy and their declining share of the country's output. Despite this fact, small firms account for one fifth of the gross national product, and employ more people than the public sector.

They provide a productive outlet for the energies of that large group of enterprising people who set great store by economic independence, and who are unwilling to work for large corporations, but who still wish to exercise their vigour, ambition and enterprise to the benefit of themselves and the country.[1] In addition, small firms make an important contribution to the export trade, both directly on their own account and also indirectly as suppliers to large firms.

Although the report finds that this sector is vigorous enough to fulfil its function in the foreseeable future, the report concludes by stating[2] that 'Benign neglect is no substitute for a policy'. The Department of Trade and Industry has already formed a Small Firms Division, as recommended in the report, and, now that this organisation exists, increasing attention will be paid by the government to the role of small firms in the economy. This may lead to greater opportunities for small firms in the fields of governments contracts. Should the monopoly legislation be strengthened and more closely applied by the government and the European Economic Community, large firms may find it expedient to work in cooperation with their brethren, as proof that their actions are not monopolistic.[3]

Furthermore, this interest in the small firms sector has resulted in the formation of specialist financial organisations to assist small firms to capitalise on these opportunities. The report also found that there was no 'Bolton gap', and that, in general, small firms, with good growth potential, and which are well advised, normally obtained external finance.[4]

RECOMMENDATIONS OF THE BOLTON REPORT

On 19 August 1971, the government announced their acceptance of the report's recommendations for the formation of Small Firms Advisory Bureaux in principal industrial centres, to signpost and to provide introductions to suitable sources of commercial advice on finance and other matters. The following points have been made in the report itself and in the research reports on finding suitable sources of finance.

Advice Gap

One of the conclusions of the research report, *Financial Facilities for Small Firms,* was that an 'advice gap' existed in the quality of advice given to small firms by their professional advisers. This covered sources of capital, types of loan finance suitable for various situations, and the normal conditions that would be imposed for these various types of finance (for example the long-term rate of interest).[5]

The institutions also complained of weak management of small firms, which was often the result of bad professional advice.[6]

In another report, it was stated that small firms simply distrust financial institutions, as they threaten their independence. For provincial businessmen, this particularly applied to London-based institutions.[7] Furthermore, there was a formidable barrier of prejudice against borrowing of all kinds.[8] If small firms were better advised and informed, they would decide it was in their interest to take institutional equity finance, and thus to use the full range of facilities available to them.[9]

Preparing Applications for Finance

One very significant finding of one research report is that managers of small firms need education in techniques for evaluating their proposals to financial institutions.[10] This report also emphasises the importance of having up-to-date audited accounts, when presenting applications for finance, in a format suitable for a potential lender. When insufficient and possibly inaccurate information is presented, the finance house will place the least favourable interpretation on the information provided.[11]

Institutions require information on forward projections of earnings and therefore managers of small firms should be able to use this technique.[12] Managements should also understand that lenders must know enough about the background and prospects of the firm to be able to form a balanced opinion of the risks involved.[13] The Bolton Report suggests that banks should impose, as a condition of their loan, the requirement that cash-flow statements be made available to them at regular intervals, and that proper techniques for estimating and budgeting be employed by the company.[14] All who were consulted in the course of preparing the Bolton Report thought that small businessmen are unskilled in presenting a financial case to potential lenders and investors.[15]

Equity, Loans and Security

The research report notes a reluctance to accept external equity finance, but suggests that this tendency is less marked than in the past. The level of taxation and inflation has made firms more willing to listen if proposals are carefully explained.[16]

Given the difficulty of financing 'start-ups' and growth from personal wealth or retained earnings, such developments in future are likely to depend increasingly on external finance to supplement the founder's initial investment.[17] Many small firms expect to borrow long-term funds at well below the economic rate. In addition, managements are often unaware of the borrowing conditions they must expect to meet, especially in terms of collateral required and the level of equity stake required.[18]

Lack of adequate systems of costing and financial control is seen by potential lenders as a symptom of poor management. The research report finds that this is one of the major reasons for refusal of finance.[19]

To summarise, the management of any small firm which requires finance for growth must be completely familiar with the conditions likely to be attached to any institutional financing. They must know how to put together a proposal containing all the information required for the institution to be able to evaluate the risk. Without institutional finance, small firms may find that it will not be possible for them to retain or improve their present position in the market.

PURPOSE OF THE BOOK

General

The purpose of this book is to make the managements of private companies familiar with the processes which take place before an institution will agree to provide long-term loan finance or equity capital. As many managers may have no experience in this field, a discussion of the points involved will give them prior knowledge of some of the obstacles they will have to surmount. They will then know which contract conditions are standard, even for public companies, and which are onerous and, therefore, to be resisted. But, above all, they will have prepared in advance, it is hoped, nearly all the information required. This will not only speed up the negotiations, but also raise the reputation of the management in the eyes of the lender.

The specific objectives of the book are as follows:

Financial Institutions Attitudes and Methods

1. To outline the investment policies of financial institutions and their aims and objectives for any investments they make in private companies.
2. To describe the profile of a successful company and the possible dangers, to both the company and the investor, which can follow any investment.

The Information required for Company Evaluations

1. To describe the information likely to be required by an investor or lender, both on the past performance of the company and on future expectations.

2 How to brief and work with the company's professional advisers.
3 To list the information required in an investigation by reporting accountants.

Methods of Investment and Agreement

1 To explain how investments are made in private companies.
2 To describe the initial negotiations, the letter of offer, the method of valuing the equity capital of a company, and how shares can be made available to institutions.
3 To outline the normal terms of the shareholder's agreement, including warranties, indemnities and covenants required.
4 To explain the terms of a debenture deed, and how a company can calculate the levels of secured and overall borrowings, which are normally permitted by a lender.

Monitoring after Investment

1 To state the functions of the board of directors and the responsibilities of the directors.
2 To outline the functions of a non-executive director in a private company, and how board meetings should be conducted.
3 To explain how investments in private companies are monitored and what methods of reporting are required.

Public Issues and Mergers

1 To explain the preparatory work to be carried out prior to a public issue.
2 To list the points to be considered in a takeover of a private company, the agreement, the integration plan and the dangers to both parties.

LIMITATIONS

General

1 Although the points discussed relate to manufacturing companies, some of the points would also apply to companies selling services and to those who act as distributors.

2 In each case, the management must select the points that are applicable to their own industry and add any other points which are not covered by this book.
3 No book on this complex subject can ever be exhaustive, but it can indicate a line of approach to solving specific problems.

Advisers
In no case should managements try to use this book without closely consulting their advisers, solicitors, auditors, valuers etc., for taxation and company law change rapidly. It is hoped that this book will enable managements to work more closely with their advisers and enable all concerned to draw up a concerted plan of campaign. There is an old adage that 'a man who acts as his own lawyer, has a fool for a client'.

WHO SHOULD READ THIS BOOK

This book is intended for the directors of private companies, who wish to find out how to make an application to a financial institution for long-term loan or equity finance. It can also help their advisers, who are not fully familiar with the way in which institutions handle this type of finance, to know how these investments are made. It may also be of interest to those institutions which are starting to provide risk capital to private companies, by assisting them to evaluate the risks attached to such investments and thus to increase the number of cases they can accept.

CONTENTS AND USE

This book should be used as a handbook. It describes background institutional investment policy and the type of private company considered suitable for investment; the preparation work required prior to approaching an institution is then discussed. An outline is then given of the legal terms used in agreements and how negotiations are likely to be conducted, so that, prior to an approach, the borrower can have calculated exactly what he wants from an institution, and the maximum he is prepared to give in return. Finally, it describes the function of the board of directors, the monitoring of investments, public issues and takeovers of private companies. Thus the book outlines in a logical manner a method of approach to be adopted in obtaining long-term external capital. At the end of most chapters there are checklists describing information required or work to be carried out.

The book is intended to help speed up and simplify negotiations between financiers and private companies. If it helps to set standards in a field where few exist, its purpose will have been achieved, for in doing so, investment in private companies may well be made easier for companies that deserve such support. No book can turn a bad investment into a good one but it can help a potentially good investment to obtain the funds it needs and show bad investments the goals at which they should aim in order to obtain new funds.

REFERENCES

1 Report of the Committee of Inquiry on Small Firms, Chairman J.E. Bolton CBE, DSC, *Cmnd.* 4811, HMSO London 1971 (In future referred to as the Bolton Report) 342-344, sections 19.2, 19.4, 19.5, and 19.7.

2 *ibid.* section 19.20

3 As defence against an anti-trust action in 1950, Dupont cited their assistance to small firms in building up their business in converting nylon and Dupont's policy decision not to engage in this activity as positive proof that their actions were not monopolistic.

4 Research Report No. 4, *Financial Facilities for Small Firms,* HMSO, London 1971, pp 68-74.

5 *ibid.*, p. 69

6 *ibid.*, p. 148 (c)

7 Bolton Report, section 12.3 (ii)

8 *ibid.*, section 12.96

9 *ibid.*, section 12.60

10 *Financial Facilities for Small Firms,* p. 74 para 6 (a)

11 *ibid.* p. 165.

12 *ibid.* p. 74, para 6 (a) and p. 147 Suggestions for improvement (c)

13 *ibid.* p. 68 (c) and 69 (c)

14 Bolton Report, section 10.14

15 *ibid.*, section 10.5 (i)

16 *Financial Facilities for Small Firms,* p. 148 (e)

17 Bolton Report, section 12.5

18 *ibid.* sections 12.60/61

19 *Financial Facilities for Small firms,* p. 70

2

Investment in Private Companies

INTRODUCTION: FINANCIAL INSTITUTIONS

Any company coming to the City for risk capital must understand the policies and capabilities of merchant banks and other financial institutions, which are expert in financial markets and in borrowing and lending out money. Even when they have close associations with certain industries, these institutions do not have either the time, qualifications or experience to become too closely involved in the day to-day running of a company. They back situations and people that have the capability to make money for all parties in the venture.

In addition, merchant banks are traders who earn their profits by a quick and profitable turnover of their capital. They aim to realise their investment in three to five years, either by means of a public issue or a takeover.

The organisations which offer such risk capital are banks, merchant banks, investment trusts, insurance companies, pension funds, or special venture capital funds. For convenience, these organisations are referred to in this book as banks. Although some may not be banks, the vast majority are subsidiaries of banks.

GENERAL

A bank invests in a private company which can, within a three to five year period, either be floated or merged with another company, thus producing a capital gain for all the shareholders, including the bank. Normally, minority equity stakes are taken, backed up by loan capital. Majority holdings are usually taken by industrial holding companies operating in selected fields of industry.

The service by the bank to a company is allied with other normal banking services, e.g. overdraft facilities, hire purchase, leasing, foreign exchange, acceptance credits and other methods of export financing. A private company needs all these services, thus a bank that provides a complete range can satisfy a company, which then has no need to go to a potential competitor of the bank for other such services.

The various stages are investigation, negotiation of terms, accountant's report and the agreement. At any of these stages a project can fail through disagreement or because the investigation reveals an unsatisfactory and hitherto undisclosed situation. A bank would not wish to weaken its position by lending monies to a company prior to signing an agreement, and thus lessen the company's desire to complete the negotiations.

The bank will need to offer an efficient monitoring service to the company, in order to protect their own and other shareholders' investments in the company. They will often appoint consultants or advisers to sit on the board of a company and guide the company through the difficult stages of growth.

THE BANK'S INVESTMENT POLICY

A bank will make the following decisions before investing in any company:

Objective

A bank will aim to achieve a capital profit of two to four times the initial investment, over a three- to five-year term by means of a public issue or takeover, realising that the period is often more likely to be seven years.

Funds

A bank will decide whether to provide funds from its own resources, or whether to raise them by means of a joint company with other institutions and private investors. A decision will be made on the maximum level of investment in any one company.

Main Characteristics

The main characteristics are outlined in Chapter 4. Companies in which a bank intends to take a direct investment should have the following characteristics:

Good Management
Directors who have proved that they have been able to earn profits over a period. There should also be a good second line management. In smaller companies with pre-tax profits under £20,000-£30,000, there are usually only one or two managers, and therefore management gaps will almost certainly exist. Such gaps are preferable in the financial field, since they can be filled by an accountant with industrial experience, rather than in sales, research or production, which may require men of very specialised experience.

Type of People
As the bank will normally take a minority equity position in any company, the management must be men of integrity, who are easy to work with, honest and trustworthy. The directors should be willing to discuss their business objectively with a bank, even in times of difficulty, and to be able to accept constructive criticism. It is important that the investigations are carried out in an honest and frank manner.

Merchant banks have money and a good reputation; they must be able to work with the people who they have backed. In short, a bank will only back people who will be good stewards of the funds entrusted to them, and who have shown, over the last few years, that they can make money even under difficult circumstances.

Profits
The company must have a consistent profit record with a good upward trend over the period. Ideally, the company will have

expanded beyond the stage where it can be financed by overdraft facilities and finance from family and friends.

A minimum level of pre-tax profits is £30,000 to £50,000. Larger situations with profits over £100,000 may occur, since the shareholders may wish to maintain control in a period of fast growth, or where a reorganisation has to be given time to settle down before a public quotation can be obtained. Companies with pre-tax profits below £30,000 may only be considered if their growth potential is great enough to achieve a flotation in a reasonable period. Often there is as much, if not more, work investing in a small company, rather than in a larger more sophisticated one.

Growth Potential

The company should have potential for growth in sales, and profit margins; it should be operating in fields which are expected to expand, or it must be able to expand and maintain its share of a static market. The competitive position will be assessed, since the company must be able to improve its position in the face of tougher competition from larger firms. Ideally, a company will be a market leader in a small field with prospects for expansion. Often a small company creates a market, which as demand grows, is satisfied by a larger company which copies its ideas. Too great a dependence by a company on one customer is dangerous and can produce a serious fluctuation in the company's profits.

As the bank's investment will increase the equity and water down the earnings, the company's expansion in profits must be sufficient to return earnings per share to the previous level. The expansion in profits required should be achieved within the period decided upon by the company and the bank.

Financial Position

A company must be able to earn sufficient profits over a period, to finance the replacement of fixed assets and the development of new products in order to remain in business. The bank will only use its funds to support growth and not just to maintain the existing position. It is unwise for a company to require a decision from a bank on investment at short notice, since this does not imply careful or far-sighted management. On the other hand, a company's growth may be seriously limited by a bank which under-finances a project. Provision should also be made by a bank for a company that grows faster than was envisaged.

Period

A bank will aim for a quotation in three to five years, although the actual period may be longer. The company must accept that a bank will expect to realise its investment within a specified period in order to avoid the capital being 'locked in'. No bank likes to be seen to have made a bad investment. Several merchant banks, which have lost money after making a large speculative investment in a new company, have complained bitterly when the company has failed. This is not the fault of the venture capital operation in itself, but is the fault of the bank concerned. Either they did not carefully weigh the risks, or they did not fully investigate the company concerned. Any investment made by a bank should be proportional to the possibility of total failure.

A bank will therefore investigate the 'downside' potential as well as the possible growth of the company and trim its stake accordingly. If there is an equal possibility of four times growth or total failure, then the investment is 'racing money' which the bank should be prepared to lose completely.

Equity Holding

The most critical parts of any negotiation between the company and a bank are the percentage equity to be acquired by the bank, the price to be paid, and the level of director's salaries which should be in line with the current market rates. The equity acquired is usually between 25 and 35 per cent, but could be smaller if the company is of a substantial size. The equity stake will need to be sufficient to make the effort worth while and can be acquired by direct subscription, an option to subscribe or through a convertible debenture.

The bank will usually require the directors to either merge, or sell their outside interests in other associated companies in order to prevent a conflict of interest. Normally, directors of a company are required to have a substantial amount at risk, thus, increasing their incentive to improve the profitability of the company and the value of the shares. For this reason the bank will normally take a minority interest.

The bank's valuation of the shares to be purchased will be below any potential flotation price for the following reasons:

1 The company has not achieved a public quotation.

2 The investment is not freely marketable.
3 There may be no proven record of growth.
4 There are usually unsolved problems – management, marketing etc.
5 A bank is carrying the risk as a minority shareholder since it is not acquiring control.
6 Any loan is often risk money.

New shares are normally subscribed since:

1 New money is invested in the company.
2 A bank does not like buying out existing shareholders, unless they are taking a small interest in a large company prior to flotation.
3 The bank may convert part of its debenture into ordinary shares and thus reduce the loan capital outstanding.

Where equity is owned by directors and their families, there is no objection to the bank's loans gearing up the value of their shares. Where, however, there are outside shareholders not working in the business, their equity will be heavily geared by the bank's loan. There are several alternatives: they may – be bought out, – have their equity heavily diluted or – be given the opportunity to match the loan capital *pro rata* to their equity holding.

Directors' or other shareholders' loans are normally frozen or converted into equity.

Security

The bank will aim for four times interest cover. Maximum overdraft facilities will not be obtained unless the bank's loan is in proportion to the equity (See Chapter 14).

THE BANK'S MARKETING PLAN

Once a bank's investment policy has been decided upon, the policies are put into effect by drawing up a marketing plan. The general aims would be as follows:

1 To analyse and define the growth sectors of the market.

2 To keep under review the services the bank would need to provide for the company.
3 To clarify the potential increase in company profits required, and to relate the level of the investment requirement to the risk the bank is prepared to accept.

Analysis by a Bank, by Industry and customer

A bank will use the knowledge of the investment department and, if required, outside consultants, as well as general industry surveys prepared by stockbrokers, in order to define by industry areas of growth in the economy. Any survey will cover the effects upon industry of such major factors as:

1 The EEC and any changes in import duties.
2 Government regulations expected, such as pollution control.
3 Major changes in technology.
4 Levels of demand.
5 Levels of supply from within and from outside the EEC, e.g. USA and Japan.
6 Expected changes in the structure of industry.

Note
Such studies are often made available to companies who are customers of a bank.

Companies which are potential direct investments, and which could either be floated or merged with another company within a three to five year period will be identified.

A bank will decide which product group to avoid, because of a conflict of interest with similar companies in the same product field.[1]

Any bank which has an investment business advising unit trusts, institutions and private clients, will already have this information on the economy and the growth sectors in the economy to function efficiently, as investment bankers.

Sales Appeals

With the advent of the Common Market, many more continental banks may wish to follow their existing policy in Europe, and take direct investments in British industry. A bank will therefore be in competition with any other firms offering similar services to a company. The company will come to a bank which best understands its problems, and is able to offer a solution that is acceptable to the company.

Between industry and banking there is a dichotomy, since industrialists are not often bankers and bankers are seldom industrialists.

Sidney Smith, the Victorian wit, once saw two charwomen hurling abuse at one another while scrubbing the steps of adjacent houses. He turned to his friend and said, 'Those two will never agree – they are arguing from different premises!'

Bankers have been described in the United States as men who neither sell nor produce, but are merely 'coupon clippers' (i.e. collect dividends). This view is true in part, as bankers are experts in financial markets and financial situations. Industry therefore feels that banks tend only to analyse a company's accounts, since they cannot evaluate the company as a whole as it is now, or as it may be in the future.

Small companies frequently seek joint stock branch managers as advisers, as the directors are often in touch with their bank managers.[2] Merchant banks usually tend to be associated with large companies and toughly fought 'takeover' battles.

On their part, bankers often complain that financial management is neglected in both large and small firms. Out of date accounts, a complete lack of adequate costing information and little idea of how to forecast cash flow, are serious charges that are legitimately levied by bankers, at very many companies.

Small firms would certainly benefit from a closer association with the City. They would gain from the expertise available in suiting sources of finance to their various requirements, and from bankers' knowledge of current economic conditions both in the UK and in their export markets.

In the long run, owners of a company may wish to realise their investment and sell out to a larger firm. If so, they are likely to obtain a far higher price when acquired if they are already a successful public company, for their company's shares will then have a market price. There is also the possibility that other bidders may offer a higher price for the shares.

A small company needs more equity (i.e. risk capital), if its cash requirements are expanding faster than can be financed through retained earnings. Unless, of course, the company is able to obtain further secured borrowings by pledging their fixed assets.

Provided the board of the company wishes to expand its markets and profits, the shareholders should consider seriously whether they have more to gain from parting with some of the equity than from holding on to it all. The possibilities, should no more loan capital be available, could be as follows:

1 Preserve the 'status quo' and risk losing a competitive position.
2 Expand, and seriously risk the dangers of 'over-trading', and the possibility of receivership or the forced sale of the equity at a low price.
3 Sell part of the equity before the expansion is put into effect.

Advantages from Bank Investment

When a small and a large company are in competition, the large company can always draw its customers' attention to its assets and financial standing, then contrast them with those of his much smaller competitor. An investment by a merchant bank can go a certain way to correct this image, thus making the small company appear more viable to both suppliers and customers. The company should look for a merchant bank with a good consultancy service, with men of wide industrial experience. Such men would advise the companies in which the bank invests on the problems of expansion. They can become catalysts, enabling both parties to benefit from the association.

Sales Promotion by the Bank

As advertisements tend to produce a mountain of rubbish which takes time to sift, a bank will rely upon its reputation in order to obtain new business. Existing customers, provided they are satisfied, can be a profitable source of contacts.

The bank's policy in handling customers is critical to achieving a follow on of further companies for investment. A small businessman's worst fears are confirmed if a bank tries to 'put the boot in' as soon as trouble looms ahead. Institutions will not lose face if they deal fairly with their customers and only resort to liquidation when a company does not appear to be a viable concern. It is in the interests of a company looking for investment to find out how successful a bank has been in helping other companies to overcome their difficulties. An investment will only be successful if both parties feel, and continue to feel, that they have received a fair deal. Care should be taken by both the company and a bank to ensure that their actions will not prejudice their working relationship and the success of the project.

The Bank's Organisation and Direction

The company must expect a bank to use banking staff for the initial meetings to analyse the accounts of the company and to negotiate with the directors. A consultant may be appointed, after an investment has been made, to sit on the board of the company. He can also be brought into the negotiations at an early stage to advise the banking staff whether the company's objectives are reasonable, and on the steps the company should take to meet these objectives. These objectives were, of course, the criteria on which the bank's investment decision was made. Any final decision on making an investment, and on the valuation for the shares, is a banking decision. When a bank uses both types of staff, the management are aware that there is not only a financial appraisal, but also an industrial evaluation by someone who speaks their language and understands their problems. Once the bank's investment and sales promotion policies are decided upon, a bank will need to carry out the following operations:

1. Set out standard procedures, implementing the bank's investment policy and objectives.
2. Devise an investigation procedure.
3. Decide on the content of the investigation, and the period of time that it should take.
4. Lay down the procedure for agreeing the investment terms, and then offer these terms to clients. Normally, an offer is discussed with a company after initial approval by either the investment committee or the board of a bank. A letter of offer will then be issued, subject to a satisfactory accountant's report on the company, and to the completion of the agreement.
5. When the terms are agreed by both parties, the agreement is negotiated and the documents are signed. A bank may then appoint a nominee director, who must be acceptable to the management of the company.

THE BANK'S REPORTING AND MONITORING

After an investment has been made in the company, the consultant or nominee director, if he has been involved in the initial investigation, will have a fair knowledge of the company, the management and any outstanding problems.

Consultants, although they are bank nominees, join the board of a company to help the company improve its profitability and efficiency, and to advise on future policy. They often negotiate their fee directly with the company, but are normally guaranteed a minimum salary by the bank. They are sometimes lent money by a bank to purchase an equity stake in the company. As consultants, they are not employees of the bank, and they will thus, take an independent line and recommend what they consider is the best policy for the company.

When any changes in the agreement are suggested, or any requests for fresh capital are made, these proposals will be discussed with the bank. The consultant can, of course, give the bank a clear idea what the money is wanted for and why. He will also see that the company's requests are properly though out and documented.

A consultant will attend monthly board meetings, see that any improvement plans are carried out, and ensure that the reporting system meets the company's and the bank's requirements. Ideally, among these consultants, the techniques of marketing, production and technical management should be represented, as well as financial skills.

At all costs, a bank must avoid smothering the company. If a bank invests in management, it cannot attempt, like the Admiralty in the case of the ill-fated PQ 17 convoy, to issue 'bridge instructions' when it is far removed from the scene of day to day operations. Should this occur, it is time for the company to change either its management or its bank!

Bad Investments

The perfect company with no financing problems is unlikely to need equity capital, since it will generate sufficient cash flow to finance its operations; but well managed companies may need cash for new acquisitions or for new ventures. Most companies, in which a bank invests, even though they may be well managed at the time of investment, will have to meet problems arising from growth.

A bank can undertake rescue operations on an unprofitable company, provided it has consultants with the experience and time to devote to these lengthy situations. However the company should have good asset backing.

A bank will recognise that a proportion of the investments it makes will be unprofitable. One of the appendices to the Bolton Report[3] gives the following figures: 'In most cases, institutions achieved one success, one 'plodder' and three failures out of five; and in another case, one success, one failure and three 'plodders' out of five is mentioned.' Some of the failures might have been avoided by a more thorough initial investigation into the company.

CONCLUSION

Perhaps, like the elephant's child, a bank, 'best beloved', will learn from being bitten by the crocodile, and develop a longer and more sensitive nose!

REFERENCES

1 Some dislike films, others like or dislike high technology, and several shy away from service companies like distributors with little asset backing.

2 Report of the Committee of Inquiry on Small Firms. Chairman – J.E. Bolton CBE, DSC, *Cmnd.* 4811, HMSO London 1971, p. 116.

3 Research Report No. 4, *Financial Facilities for Small Firms,* HMSO London, 1971, p. 139.

3

Small Companies: Scope, and Reasons for Refusal of Finance

SMALL FIRMS

Type of Business

In one of the research reports, commissioned by the Bolton Committee, small firms are classified under the following headings:[1]

Competitors
Small companies in direct competition with large firms, and who enjoy a small product sector or local supply position which large manufacturers have failed to penetrate or which they have no desire to enter. The survey found that, although the fastest growers were in this category, half the firms studied had failed to reach the mean growth rate for the manufacturing sector as a whole.

Satellites
Companies which were dependent on one or two large customers for a large (more than 50 per cent) proportion of their business. In many cases this role was combined with the specialist role described below.

These firms were often able to ride on the backs of large firms in an expanding market. They could be placed in a difficult position if demand fell in their major customers' markets, and they were unable to find alternative outlets for their skills. The danger of this role is that there is a tendency to pay insufficient attention to the marketing function and to rely on the large firm for this activity.

Specialists
Small companies which carried out a function a larger firm could not, or did not, wish to perform. In many cases they produced and marketed one major line to provide a base for the business, and also made products to customers' specifications.

Jobbers
Small companies acting as producers of products made to the customer's specification. The growth rate of this sector was far lower that that of the next sector.

Marketeer
Companies producing products to their own design, which they marketed to all-comers. Half of the sample failed to reach the mean growth for the class, but a quarter achieved a growth rate of 117 per cent over seven years (1963-1970). This suggests that the sector is volatile, but, where fast growth is achieved by a marketeer, it is significant. In the jobber category, only a quarter grew by more than 60 per cent in this period.

The Role of Small Business

Although small businesses produce 21 per cent of the net output of this country, there are powerful forces making for greater industrial concentration, and thus a reduction in the number of small firms. 'Technological creep' continues to raise the optimum size of plants in most branches of industry.[2]

The Bolton Report analyses the types of activity, where small firms can operate to advantage, by using their flexibility and speed of movement, and where size can be a hindrance and not an advantage.[3]

Small Optimum Size
Where the optimum size of the production and sales unit is small, as in the batch production field, where there are often frequent design changes and the operations are labour intensive with low capital

investment, fluctuations in demand or supply are met by shortening or lengthening hours of work. This method of adjusting to changes in demand is not suitable for a fully automated factory, which needs a high volume of standard products to produce the economies of scale which justify this investment. Small companies should avoid the mass production field, as success comes from a low unit cost, which demands high output and substantial funds to finance stock and debtors. Local production units are competitive, if they are handling perishable goods, or those products which are bulky and expensive to transport to a central production unit, e.g. some building materials.

Limited or Specialised Markets

There are markets for a wide variety of luxury goods, often specially made for a customer, which are unsuitable for mass production. Especially in the fashion world, flair, imagination and the ability to adapt to rapidly changing tastes are more important than price. The flexibility of small firms is very suited to this activity, as quality, design and personal contact should take precedence over cost. Local printers continue to exist, as they offer a service giving fast delivery of small batches of printing, which would be uneconomic for large firms.

Specialist Suppliers

Small firms act as specialists to large companies by providing parts and sub-assemblies at a lower cost then they can be made by larger firms. In the case of metal trades in the Midlands, it is not economic for large companies to centralise such services. Jobbers in metal manufacturing, in engineering and in wood products exist because they produce tenders quickly, cooperate in the design of products, and have low minimum order quantities with flexible delivery dates. In all, they try harder than the larger firms to fulfil their customers' special requirements. In the opinion of their owners, their main competitive advantages are as follows:[4]

Service	26.8%
Flexibility	24.0%
Design or quality	24.0%
Price	16.7%
Prompt delivery	8.4%
	100 %

Competition

Small firms compete with large multi-product firms, and in doing so provide a check on monopoly profits and inefficiency. In these mass markets, the few existing suppliers compete against one another by cutting prices. Profits are maintained by rationalisation and standardisation to give maximum output per product at the lowest cost. This elimination of low volume products naturally reduces consumer choice, so small firms can increase consumer choice by finding gaps in the product range of multi-product groups. They also provide price comparison where large firms tend to keep profits on low volume items at too high a level.

Innovation
Small firms, despite their low expenditure in research and development, are important innovators of new products, techniques and services, especially where the capital investment required is low.

New Industries
The most vital field for the small firm is in new industries, where demand is small and the products are complex. Often these fields are outside the notice of the larger companies. In such markets, the small company can grow with the industry, gaining a reputation for quality and high technology, and later adapting its know-how to carry out other applications. Often, the fast development rate of new technologies or market expansion makes rapid growth possible. This is described in the Bolton Report, for these new firms may challenge large firms of the future.[5] Without this challenge from new firms, the economy could ossify and decay, for managers of large firms are often unwilling to take risks which could reduce their profits in the short term, especially if they are paid a bonus on results. In these new industries, it is well qualified, competent and ambitious young men starting new firms on the basis of a sound marketable idea, who are of interest to the banks.[6] The problem is to decide whether they have achieved sufficient commercial success in exploiting their new ideas, and have enough potential for growth to justify further investment. The problem of identifying the high fliers in these new technologies or in rapidly expanding markets, needs more than an analysis of past financial results; it requires a technical view of the prospects of the firm within the industry concerned.

DEPENDENCE AND ITS DANGERS

Even though a small company may be independent in the legal sense, it may not be free commercially. For the large company can often define the conditions under which the small company can survive. The smaller firm's freedom can be restricted in the following ways:[7]

Suppliers
A large supplier can give extended credits, and/or special discounts, which increase over a long term period, or offer technical assistance, provided that all the materials are bought from them for *X* years. The supplier is, in effect, integrating forward without acquiring the smaller company.

Joint Promotion Activities
Manufacturers and suppliers cooperate on joint marketing promotion campaigns, with the supplier providing the greater share. Thus, suppliers gain effective control over their customers, and this outcome can only be avoided by the most wary and successful small firm.[8]

Customers
Where there are only a few customers for a product, a small firm may have to sell a substantial part of its output to one firm. In this case, the larger firm may use its superior bargaining position to set the goals, and programmes for the smaller firm.[9] In effect, to keep the business, the smaller company may be concentrating more on maximising the profit of its customer than on maximising its own earnings.

Sub-Contracting
The small firm becomes the reservoir of capacity available when required, but the first to be shed in a recession. In this case, the management of the small firm are merely acting as branch production managers for the larger company.

Product Development
When products are made to the customer's specification, the subcontractor tends to rely on the customer for product development. Apart from the unfavourable bargaining position of the smaller company, it is dangerous to be so concerned with satisfying a

customer, that new products and markets are completely forgotten. If a small company designs a product to its own specification to fill a customer's needs, it is more able to enter alternative markets than firms which are completely dependent on a customer for product specifications and development. The greater the product responsibility, the less the dependence on a large customer and the greater the freedom of movement for the small firm.

Continuity

Lack of continuity in demand from a major customer forces a firm to keep in contact with its markets and to develop new customers. Market development is often forgotten if the company can rely on a continuous demand from a customer. For this reason, jobbing firms, serving one or two customers, often have no marketing organisation and thus are out of touch with market developments. If they lose their principal customer, it is often hard to find a replacement. Firms who are dependent on their customers for product development lack the ability to launch new products. (70 per cent of small firms would find it difficult to replace their major customer.)[10]

To summarise therefore, the independent small firm, which develops and markets its own products, can shape the future by reacting to changes in technology, to changing market conditions, to opportunities and threats. A firm acting as a satellite to a major customer is not only in an unfavourable bargaining position, but it is not in control of its own destiny.

REASONS FOR FAILURE

In the United States

An extensive investigation was undertaken by the Temporary National Economic Committee[11] on the problems of small business, as part of their investigation into the concentration of economic power. The report, published in 1941, considers that the principal reasons for the failure of small businesses are as follows:[11]

1. Managerial competence
2. Adequacy of capital
3. Control over assets and liabilities

4 Control over costs of operation
5 Control over sales, markets and products
6 Granting excess credit

1 *Managerial Competence*

Lack of managerial competence is seen to be the principal reason for business mortality, accounting for half the failures. Most proprietors lacked even the elements of knowledge of management control, and their firms' records were quite inadequate for their managers to exercise proper supervision. Most managers of firms that failed had little experience in trade, finance and marketing. Their optimism exceeded their understanding in the case of about two-thirds of the new entries into business. In most cases, their incompetence and inexperience were discernible at the time of assuming managerial responsibilities, for they were ignorant of the requirements needed for success, and of the problems they had to surmount.

2 *Adequacy of Capital*

The higher the proportion of capital provided by the owners, the more likely the firm was to survive. For, if companies lacked capital at their inception, they had no reserves to meet emergencies, and had to live on credit and short term loans. Many were felt not to be viable at the time they were formed. Others had dissipated their capital by speculating unsuccessfully in stock, which later proved to be unsaleable. Great importance therefore, is attached to building on a firm financial base.

3 *Control over Assets and Liabilities*

The report emphasises the importance of financial ratios, as the measurement of the financial position of a company (see Appendix to this chapter); these ratios can reveal where and when a company is becoming unbalanced. Particular emphasis is placed on the current ratio (current assets / current liabilities). For, in many cases, failure occurred through over investment in fixed assets, which reduced current assets below a safe margin. Often a company mistook a fortuitous event for a long period of vigorous growth in demand. By increasing its investment in fixed assets, the firm reduced its working capital. If the expected demand did not arise, or was not sustained, there was excess capacity and a shortage of working capital to meet current obligations. As insolvency approaches, there is naturally a lack of working capital free from obligations. More credit from suppliers is sought, and fixed assets rise in relation to current and total net assets. Therefore, decisions on investment in fixed plant should only be made after a careful analysis of the market (see Chapter 6). Small firms need to be as proficient as sophisticated large companies in the techniques of forward planning, for, with their limited finances, there is little margin available for error.

4 *Control over Costs of Operation*

The report felt that in certain cases, the directors of a firm were parasites, living on a parasitic enterprise, making heavy losses and paying their salaries through credit from suppliers. There was often a failure to control overheads, and little attempt had been made to relate total overheads to net sales. Prices were not fixed after considering costs and the normal profit required, as no proper records existed. They were often dictated by the firm's poor location and by cut-throat competition. The ratio of rent to sales was considered a significant factor; for going concerns it was on average 4.7 per cent and for failures 10.6 per cent.

5 *Control over Sales, Markets and Products*

The sales effort of small firms was frequently misdirected. They either disregarded market potential, were unwilling to modify their products to meet future customer's needs, or they concentrated on low volume customers which are frequently unprofitable. The proprietors were often over-optimistic in estimating future income, and when their forecasts were not achieved they found that they had taken on unwarranted obligations. Sometimes, through lack of careful assessment of the market conditions, new firms had found that they were unable to overcome the existing competition. On the other hand, existing firms declined if they were unable to match the progressive activities of new and better qualified competitors.

6 *Granting Excess Credit*

When making credit inquiries, suppliers frequently failed to vet a firm's antecedents, to find the history of the firm and its directors. The report mentions previous failures, fires, frauds, cancellations of contracts, inaccurate financial statements, and gambling proclivities as reasons for bad debts. Unless the company has a sound financial structure, it is unable to take advantage of trade discounts, and must often pay exorbitant interest for any loan capital. To be successful, a company needs a progressive, well trained and experienced management, which has adequate records, showing the cost of doing business and the financial status of the enterprise. In many cases, the capital which the firm controls is not the manager's personal property, and this responsibility should not be entrusted to amateurs. The report gives the following statistics for the failure of new companies: three out of ten do not survive the first 12 months; two out of ten do not survive the second 12 months. Thus 50 per cent of all failures of new firms are caused by infant mortality. When a firm weathers the early years successfully, its chances of continued existence are greatly enhanced.

In the United Kingdom

Dunn and Bradstreet analysed the reasons for failure for 100 companies wound up compulsorily in 1965.[12] They found that over half these companies had a capital of £100 or less. The estimated deficiencies, however, were £20,000 or over in nine cases, and between £5,000 and £20,000 for 18 others. Only in three cases was the liability less than £1,000. The number of companies trading with a realistic paid up capital of above £5,000 was only 11. The breakdown by industry was: manufacturing 23 per cent, building and contracting 30 per cent, and distribution 29 per cent. According to this survey, the failure rate within the critical 2 year period was within 1 per cent of the 50 per cent rate quoted earlier for the USA. In the UK, more than one quarter of the companies failed within 2 years, 24 per cent failed within 1 year, and 65 per cent of the whole sample failed within the 3 year period. It is interesting to compare the reasons given by the directors and the official receivers for the failure of their company (Figure 3:1). The official receivers give mismanagement or gross mismanagement as reasons in 45 per cent of the cases, whereas the directors completely fail to give this as a cause in any of the cases. Instead the directors give other reasons, poor labour, excessive competition, ill-health, too rapid expansion, material shortages etc. Although, both parties agree that for 51 companies, the reason was insufficient working capital, they were not always the same companies, as 67 companies were mentioned in all by both parties. Bad debts were given as a reason by the directors in 18 companies, whilst the official receivers only give

	Official receivers' opinion	Directors' opinion
Mismanagement	67	–
Insufficient capital	31	23
Insufficient working capital	20	28
Poor labour and poor supervision	–	10
Keen competition	–	9
Ill-health	–	9
Excessive renumeration to, or drawings by, directors	7	–
Inadequate accounting	5	3
Inexperience	5	10
Expansion too rapid	–	6
Gross mismanagement	4	–
Bad debts	4	18
Under-estimating	4	7
Pilfering or fraud	4	4
Shortage of materials	–	4
Bad weather	–	4
Over-trading and expanding too rapidly	3	–
Increasing overheads	3	3
Customers dissatisfied	–	3
Let down by customers	–	3

Figure 3:1 Principal Causes of Failure of Companies

this reason in four cases, possibly because, with proper credit control, these losses would have been avoided. An article in *The Scotsman* gives the following reasons for business failure:[13]

1 Seeking turnover not profit. Fixed price contracts, taken at wafer thin margins, do not allow for inflationary increases in costs.
2 Faulty estimating, because correct financial information is not available to allow management to make correct decisions.
3 Overtrading, which is taking on more work than the firm can finance, often without due regard to the potential profit.
4 Starting on a shoestring, and picking up bits and pieces of failed businesses.
5 Forgetting that Government Grants come through after the factory is built, and that creditors may not be able to wait.

Companies often feel that they have only one more corner to turn before prosperity. Banks know that their borrowers cannot see round corners, and that the next corner may be even sharper than the last.

Borrowers should remember that banks have a duty to protect the money their depositors place with them.

REASONS FOR THE REFUSAL OF FINANCE

In the United States

The TNEC also examined the reasons why small firms were refused finance by banks.[14] The reasons for refusal are as follows:

Inadequate net worth; i.e. too high a debt-to-equity ratio (proprietors' equity too low)	40.3%
Inadequate working capital; a current ratio of 1½ to 2 was required	36.8%
Existing loan too slow; unable to repay existing loan	19.5%
Earnings too low; the firm would be unlikely to be able to pay the interest and repayments out of current earnings	19.1%
Collateral unsatisfactory; i.e. security insufficient	16.1%
Character of Management; not competent	14.5%
Unsatisfactory customer relationship; i.e. a lack of trust	12.5%
Too speculative; risk too high	9.6%
Not an existing customer	6.1%
The loan policy of the bank	4.9%
Past insolvency	5.7%
The character of the business	2.5%

In many cases, loans were refused for many reasons. However the report makes it clear that the higher the working capital and the net worth, the fewer the refusals. Where loans were refused because of inadequate earnings, this was because the firm would be unlikely to be able to pay the interest and any repayments out of current earnings. The banks found that working capital loans tended not to be repaid, as small companies' reserves were depleted after the recession. Long term capital was expensive and banks were unwilling to invest in fixed assets which were subject to depreciation. However, during a credit squeeze, short-term loans were likely to be called in by the banks, and, in addition, suppliers tended to cut credit to small firms.

In the United Kingdom

A recent survey, which was carried out for the Bolton Committee, examined the problems faced by small firms in raising external finance.[15] Some of the factors a financial institution will consider when deciding whether or not a loan should be granted are discussed below:

1 Reasons for seeking external finance.
2 Reasons for unsuccessful applications.
3 The main characteristics of companies requesting finance.

1 *Reasons for Seeking External Finance*

A high correlation was found between the number of successful loans which were for aggressive rather than for defensive reasons. The reasons why finance was required in the sample survey were as follows:

Aggressive

(a) For the purchase of plant, factories or other fixed assets, because of an actual or expected increase in demand.

(b) To improve liquidity or to meet commitments arising from expansion and/or product diversification.

(c) For the purchase of machinery or plant, to take advantage of technological developments and/or to produce at lower cost. (*Note.* This could be a defensive action if competitive pressures were forcing the company to cut costs.)

Defensive

(d) To improve liquidity, adversely affected by economic conditions, e.g. inflation, taxation, especially an enforced dividend,[16] debtors taking longer credit and suppliers restricting credit.

(e) For special reasons, such as the payment of estate duty, or to

increase or regear the capital of the company, e.g. refinancing a medium term mortgage by means of a long term loan.

2 *Reasons for Unsuccessful Applications*

The following reasons were given for refusal of finance:[17]

(*a*) Profit record unsatisfactory: it was felt that the company would be unable to pay the interest and redeem the loan out of net profits.

(*b*) Unfavourable capital structure: the loan was too ambitious for the company's record of earnings and its asset cover. Another reason given was that the owner had too low an equity stake in the business.

(*c*) Poor management: the quality of management was too low. One case mentioned was where the existence of a management development programme was probably responsible for a very favourable reception being given to a loan.[18] The experience of the company and its staff is always considered, when a decision on granting a loan is being taken, for poor management affects profits, and thus the ability of the company to repay the loan.

(*d*) No proper security: a company with insufficient security may be too ambitious in the amount it is requesting for a loan. The recent financial performance of the company may be such that it is already overborrowed, as the interest cover on the existing loans may be below the accepted level.

(*e*) Unwillingness to consider equity participation: the loan ratio to equity may be too high already. Until the net worth is increased by retained earnings, the company will not be able to borrow further monies. If, however, additional equity is subscribed for, this increase in funds will enable the company to borrow further monies (see Chapter 14).

(*f*) Unfavourable prospects for the industry in which the firm is operating: the institution may feel that the company's existing earnings may fall in the future, and thus the repayment of the loan at the due date may be uncertain.

(*g*) Insufficient accounting data: this reason is also given in another report.[19] 'Where accounts are out of date and not properly audited, the least favourable interpretation is placed upon the information provided'.

(*h*) The period of the loan was too long: the institution did not wish to be committed for this period. This decision would, of course, be affected by the asset and interest cover available as security for the loan.

Companies also refused loans offered to them because the rate of interest was too high, the loan was considered inadequate for the company's needs, equity was required, or because the terms were otherwise not acceptable. In a number of cases, the report considered that the terms offered were reasonable.

3 *The Main Characteristics of Companies Requesting Finance*

The survey distinguishes the main characteristics of those firms which were successful, and those which were unsuccessful in raising external finance.[20]

(*a*) The successful firms had a profit/sales ratio and growth performance for the years 1965-1969 which was generally above the average for all firms in the sample. The unsuccessful firms were generally less profitable than the average firms in the sample.

(*b*) The successful firms required finance for expansionist reasons and usually for specific purposes. The unsuccessful were either unclear why they wanted finance or wanted it for defensive reasons.

(*c*) The successful firms knew where to find finance, while the unsuccessful complained of an information gap and of poor availability of funds.

(*d*) The successful were well versed in, and well advised on, financial matters; the others were managerially and financially unsophisticated and did not appear to be well advised by their accountants and bank managers.

(*e*) The successful were not over-ambitious in their requests for finance, and persisted in their attempts to obtain finance on the most favourable terms. The unsuccessful were sometimes over ambitious, but they often failed to make another application when one had been turned down, or when they found the terms were not favourable.

(*f*) The successful took the recent government fiscal measures and the credit restraints in their stride, whereas the others seemed to be particularly badly affected by these measures.

Overall the report stresses the importance of knowing the prevailing market terms for loans. Many firms were surprised by the difference between the interest rate on long-term loans and that on bank overdrafts. Some approached the wrong institutions or did not shop around. Others did not present the best possible case and were uncertain as to what terms they wanted. Where institutions allowed successful applicants a certain option on the terms, the applicants had a clear idea of what they wanted.[21]

Actions if Finance was not Obtained
In the survey, the firms unable to obtain finance adopted one of the following remedies:[22]

1 They tried to obtain finance from other sources, such as suppliers, customers or from the banks.
2 They attempted to improve their competitive position and/or profitability, by operating more efficiently.
3 They cut back their output, or postponed their expansion plans.
4 They increased their short term debts, particularly with trade suppliers and customers.
5 They went into voluntary liquidation.

APPENDIX 1: MANAGERIAL APPRAISAL

Entrepreneurial performance

Industrial Experience
Does he have a good knowledge of the broad problems of the industry and a recognised position in it?

Technical Experience
1 Is he up to date in the technical fields in which the company is interested now and in the future? Give details of technical achievements, e.g. patents.
2 R and D programmes – have these produced profit to the company under this direction?

Market Knowledge
1 Is he aware what customers will buy and at what price? Does he have good customer and industry contacts?

2 Is his attitude towards competition satisfactory or complacent?
3 Is his applications knowledge good – can he see new developments in overall profit terms or merely from a technical point of view?
4 Does he work on facts or on wishful thinking?
5 Is there an overall marketing view – does he sell on specification or on expenses?

Growth

1 Is he growth conscious, and have companies under his management achieved growth? Examples.
2 Does this extend down to all the organisation sales vigour?
3 Is he aware of the problems growth brings and can he organise to achieve growth?
4 Does he plan realistically for growth?
5 Does he exhibit any tendency to overtrade?

Profit and Cost Consciousness

1 Has he a good profit record and a good record for use of funds in his present company and in others?
2 Are there unprofitable products in his product line?
3 Is the whole organisation profit conscious, especially the technical branch?
4 Does he meet his budget on profits?
5 How quickly are unprofitable situations sensed?
6 Cost reduction – has this been carried out and how?

Sensitivity to Critical Situations and Change

1 Has he performed well in adversity and under pressure?
2 Does he anticipate changing conditions and plan to organise either to earn profits or avoid losses?

Summary

1 Is he a good entrepreneur?
2 Is he a good negotiator with an honest record?
3 Will he be a responsible steward for the funds entrusted to him?
4 Does he carry through programmes from inception to completion?

Operating Management

Management Techniques

Does he have a knowledge of up to date management techniques and does he keep himself up to date?

Administrative Skills

1 Are objectives set clearly and is performance related to these objectives?
2 New problems – is he decisive in meeting them?
3 Authority and responsibility – are these assigned properly with adequate control?

Staff

1 Selection – has he selected a good management team?
2 Training and development – is there a training programme?
3 Does he develop subordinates by delegating responsibility with control?
4 Teamwork – is there a balanced team and does it work as one?
5 Co-operation.

(a) Does he insist on management co-operation to achieve company rather than departmental goals? Is there active co-operation or conflict?
(b) Does departmental management see these company goals and problems as ones which they must achieve?

Ability to deal with people

1 Does he create enthusiasm and *esprit de corps?*
2 Does he command confidence, respect and co-operation or does he rule by fear?
3 Is he felt to be reliable and fair?

Ability to think constructively

1 Does he think problems through and come to sound logical conclusions or does he make 'pictures'?
2 Does he show creative imagination in finding new ways to solve problems to increase profits?

Attitude to expansion
Is his management skill sufficient for the planned expansion or must this be provided for from other sources?

Personal Characteristics

Maturity and Balance
1 Is he a mature person with a businesslike attitude?
2 Does he accept criticism and suggestions or treat them as a personal insult?
3 Is he secretive or open?
4 Will he abide by group decisions?
5 Is he aware of his own shortcomings and does he practise self-criticism?
6 Does he respond well to pressure?
7 Does he give credit to subordinates or regard them as a threat to his position?
8 Is he tactful at pointing out ways for others to improve?

Consistency
Is he guided by definite principles which he always applies?

Internal Conflicts
1 Can he resolve them?
2 What effect do they have on his efficiency?
3 How do they affect his working with others?

Confidence
1 Does he have confidence in his ability to do his job and justify the bank's investment?
2 Is this matched with a sense of humility or is he an egoist who is never wrong?

Initiative
1 Self-supervision – does he make good use of time?
2 Resourceful – does he think up or originate new ideas?

Industry
Is he diligent and persistent in carrying out operations even under difficulty?

Personal Appearance
Good or bad?

Recognition of Leadership Qualities
1 Do associates consult him frequently because of his judgement and ability?
2 Is he a natural leader?

Self-Development
1 Does he have well defined objectives and a sense of purpose?
2 Can he grow with the company?

Ability to plan and organise work
1 Does he plan ahead?
2 Does he have a logical approach to various jobs?

Aggressiveness, Drive and Enthusiasm
1 Is he enthusiastic about his work?
2 Does he push despite difficulties?

Self Expression
Can he express himself clearly and logically both verbally and in writing?

Summary

1 Will this man be able to achieve the investment objectives that have been set for this company?
2 Does he understand and is he sympathetic to our method of working?
3 Will he work with us towards a common end?
4 Can we see any worsening of our relationship over a 1-2 year period?
5 Is he a man of purpose and integrity in whom we can trust?

APPENDIX 2: FINANCIAL RATIOS

Financial ratios should be used by management for checking the efficiency of their own performance against known industry standards and for providing standards for future performance. Although figures are available by industry groups,[23] companies should develop their own standards to check whether their forecasts of future sales and profits are attainable in the light of the company's existing achievements. This applies particularly to improvements in gross and net margins, return on capital, turnover of stocks and debtors, and the increased working capital required to finance an expansion in sales turnover.

The Use of Ratios

Ratios can be used for the following purposes.

The Application of Funds
These ratios show the breakdown of total assets between long-term assets, such as fixed assets (land, buildings, machinery, plant, vehicles, etc.), and working capital, such as stocks and other more liquid assets as debtors, cash and short-term investments.

The Source of Funds
A company is financed by equity capital and accumulated reserves, by short-term and long-term loans and through credit furnished by suppliers. The balance between these various sources of finance and the needs of the company must be right for the company to remain a viable concern. For this reason, the long-term requirements of the company, for funds to finance fixed assets and the 'hardcore' investment in stocks and debtors, should be financed by long-term capital (equity, reserves and long-term loans.) Expansion in stocks and debtors can then be safely financed by increased short-term facilities, which tend to be self-liquidating, if the level of activity falls. The company is then less liable to be financially embarassed in a credit squeeze than those which have financed long-term assets with short-term facilities.[24]

Liquidity
Small companies can go bankrupt because they have expanded too fast and do not have sufficient capital to finance the completion of outstanding orders. 'Overtrading' occurs when a company has insufficient working capital to finance its existing operations and depends too heavily on credit from suppliers.

Liquidity is measured by comparing the ratio of current assets (stocks, debtors, cash etc.) to current liabilities (creditors, bank overdrafts and other current liabilities). In 1968, the *current ratio* was 1.6 for quoted companies and 1.8 for small firms overall, but for fast-growing small firms the ratio fell[25] to 1.4. This figure will be affected by the profits earned by the firm, and the investment policies adopted for stocks and fixed assets. Losses or low profits can reduce the working capital (net current assets) below an acceptable level. The company is then unable to finance its future needs for product improvement and also the increase in working capital required to offset the effects of inflation.

The *quick asset ratio* measures the ratio of liquid assets (current assets less stocks) to current liabilities. It shows the firm's ability to settle short-term liabilities from debtors and cash, without having to resort to liquidating stocks and fixed assets. In the schedule (Table 3:1) the figures are as follows:

Public	companies 1.0x
Slow growing small	companies 1.4x
Fast growing small	companies 0.9x

The fast growing small companies tended to give longer credit to customers and relied more on supplier credit and borrowed funds than slow growing small firms.

The *ratio of sales to current assets* will vary for each industry. Too high a figure can indicate the firm is overtrading, while too low a figure indicates the assets are being underused.

Profitability

The principal ratio is the *return on capital employed* which shows how well assets are being used. The following formula shows that this ratio is a function of the margin on sales and the turnover of capital:

$$\frac{\text{sales}}{\text{net assets}} \times \frac{\text{profit}}{\text{sales}} = \frac{\text{profit}}{\text{net assets}}$$

Profits are defined as being pre-interest and tax, and capital employed as total assets less current liabilities but including bank overdrafts. This ratio can also be used to measure the return by product group or by location.

A similar check can also be made on the *return on net worth,* that is the net profits pre-tax earned on the share capital and reserves. When calculating the return in both cases, any dividend element in director's salaries should be excluded (i.e. any salary above the market rate for the position) as this can affect the figures. The use of the two standards allows management to measure the return on overall capital employed as well as the return on net worth, when they are considering whether to borrow money to finance a capital project. The availability of loan capital can encourage managers to consider marginal projects which reduce the overall return on capital employed. Therefore a level should be set for the overall return required regardless of the source of capital.[26]

Gearing: Loans/Net Worth
Limits must also be set on the amount of borrowings permitted. Public companies are usually permitted to borrow up to $66\frac{2}{3}$ per cent of net worth, subject to a satisfactory interest cover (see Chapter 14). Private companies are sometimes permitted to borrow up to 100 per cent of net worth.

Efficiency Ratios
These ratios show the use of the firm's assets by measuring how quickly these assets are turned over.

Sales/stock. This ratio shows how fast stocks are being turned over. Usually an average stock figure is used which is arrived at by averaging the opening and closing stocks for the financial year concerned.

Debtors/average daily sales. This ratio shows the average collection period in days for debt collection. It should be used, rather than the normal trade terms, when calculating how much additional finance is required to finance a given increase in sales.

Stocks/debtors. This ratio shows the relationship of stocks to debtors which should remain in balance, unless there is a deliberate policy to build up stocks prior to a sales campaign.

Sales/fixed assets. The level shows the efficiency in the use of fixed assets in producing sales for the company.

Production Ratios
More detailed ratios can be calculated to show the sales and profit, per man, per square foot of space, and per £1 of capital employed. In addition the total cost of sales figure can be broken down to show the percentage for manufacturing cost both fixed and variable, and for marketing, administration and research expenditure.[27]

	Manufacturing[28] Slow	Fast	All	ICFC[29] 1967-8	Quoted Co's[29] 1967
	%	%	%	%	%
Tangible fixed assets	35.0	33.3	31.5	39.0	40.4
Goodwill	0.7	1.0	2.6	0.7	2.8
Trade investments	-	-	-	1.2	3.1
Total fixed assets	35.7	34.3	34.1	40.9	46.3
Stocks and work in progress	21.6	21.0	24.9	25.3	24.4
Debtors	25.2	33.3	27.0	29.1	23.0
Cash	9.7	4.6	7.8	2.6	3.8
Investments	-	-	-	1.3	2.1
Other current assets	7.7	6.7	6.3	0.8	0.3
Total current assets	64.3	65.7	65.9	59.1	53.7
Total assets	100.0	100.0	100.0	100.0	100.0
Ordinary shares	23.6	13.1	28.2	14.4	20.9
Preference shares	2.6	1.1	1.5	3.2	2.8
Capital and revenue reserves	38.6	25.8	23.3	25.0	29.3
Owners loans	1.1	5.0	3.4	-	-
Future tax reserves	-	-	-	2.4	2.8
Net worth	65.9	45.0	56.4	45.0	55.8
Minority interests	-	-	-	0.1	2.4
Long term loans	3.8	6.5	5.1	16.0	12.5
Bank loans and overdrafts	6.6	8.5	8.6	10.5	6.2
Creditors	20.0	33.7	26.7	23.8	18.5
Other current liabilities	3.7	6.3	3.3	4.5	4.5
Total liabilities	34.1	55.0	43.6	55.0	44.2
Total assets	100.0	100.0	100.0	100.0	100.0
Quick assets	42.7	44.7	41.0	33.8	29.3
Current assets	64.3	65.7	65.9	59.1	53.7
Current liabilities	30.3	48.5	37.6	38.8	29.2
Current ratio	2.1x	1.4x	1.7x	1.5x	1.8x
Quick asset ratio	1.4x	0.9x	1.1x	0.8x	1.0x
Total debt	10.4	15.0	13.7	26.5	18.7
Debt/net worth	16.0	33.3	20.6	59.0	34.0

Figure 3:2 Financial ratios **Times covered = x**

The Schedule

The figures in the schedule (Figure 3:2) can be used as a rough guide for checking performance, for deciding how efficient the company is now and what standards should be set when preparing future budgets. It is best, however, to decide the appropriate ratios for the company and to relate these to the standards for the industry concerned, taking care that the figures are prepared on a comparative basis:

The five categories listed in the schedule are as follows:

1 Small companies – slow growing
2 Small companies – fast growing
3 All small companies
4 ICFC private companies
5 All quoted companies

The main points that should be noted from the schedule are discussed below. However it should be realised that inaccuracies can occur through differences in accounting practices between the various categories.

Fixed Assets
When trade investments and goodwill are excluded, the difference in the fixed assets percentage is not all that great between the five classifications, especially as private companies overall may not be so meticulous in revaluing their fixed assets as the ICFC companies are.

Current Assets and Liabilities
Stock levels are fairly similar for all classes, but the figure for debtors is substantially higher for the fast growing companies and for the ICFC companies. The same companies have substantially lower holdings of cash and other current assets than the other categories.

The ICFC companies and the fast-growing private companies have the same overall level of liabilities, but the former use long-term loans, while the latter rely more on creditors for finance. The current ratios and the quick asset ratios are very similar for these categories, as are the same ratios for quoted companies and for all small companies. Only the slow growing companies have much higher ratios.

Net Worth

The totals for the fast-growing and for the ICFC companies are very similar while the quoted companies and all small companies have the same levels. The slow growers conserve their assets and keep their borrowings low, and as such preserve a more favourable financial position in the short term. As small companies, especially the fast growers, tend to use their suppliers to finance their expansion, it may be more meaningful to use total assets rather than net assets when calculating the return on capital employed, as the former figure includes current liabilities.

Considerably greater use could be made of the balance sheet figures, made available in the Research Report[30], if similar figures were published for the revenue, expenses and profits of small companies. These figures would allow more overall ratios to be prepared by relating sales and profit performance to the various types of assets employed.

REFERENCES

1 Research Report No. 12, *Dynamics of Small Firms,* HMSO London 1971, pp. 23-27

2 Report of the Committee of Inquiry on Small Firms. Chairman J.E. Bolton CBE, DSC, *Cmnd.* 4811 HMSO London 1971 sections 7.4, 8.2, 8.8.

3 *ibid.*, section 8.3

4 Research Report No. 3, *Small Firms in the Manufacturing Sector,* p. 54.

5 Bolton Report, sections 8.3, 8.5 and 8.7.

6 *ibid.*, section 8.5

7 *Small Firms in the Manufacturing Sector,* pp. 55-58.

8 *ibid.* p. 56.

9 *ibid.* p. 57. One-third of small firms sell more than 25% of their output to one customer. 13.1% sell at least 50% to one customer.

10 *ibid.* p. 58

11 *The Problems of Small Business,* Monograph 17, pp. 81-136. An investigation of the concentration of economic power by the Temporary National Economic Committee. The US Government. Washington 1941. N.B. A large proportion of the sample were smaller retail business.

12 R. BROUGH *Business Failures in England and Wales.* '2nd Issue' Business Ratios. London, Dunn and Bradstreet Ltd.

13 'What Makes a Company Go to the Wall', *The Scotsman,* 20 October, 1971.

14 *The Problems of Small Business.* p. 224.

15 Research Report No. 5, *Problems of the Small Firm in Raising External Finance,* HMSO London 1971, pp. 13-16.

16 A shortfall assessment by the Inland Revenue which requires a company to distribute a proportion of its earnings unless these funds are needed for expansion if it is a close company.

17 *Problems of Small Firms in Raising External Finance.* pp. 41-44.

18 *ibid.* p. 48.

19 Research Report No. 4, *Financial Facilities for Small Firms.* HMSO London, 1971, p. 165.

20 *Problems of Small Firms in Raising External Finance,* pp. ix-xi.

21 *ibid.*, p. 34.

22 *ibid.*, p. 50.

23 Dunn & Bradstreet Ltd. can provide ratios by industry groups, and the Centre for Interfirm Comparison carries out interfirm comparison studies.

24 Research Report No. 16, *A Postal Quesionnaire Survey of Small Firms: an Analysis of Financial Data* HMSO, London, 1972, p. 7. In 1968, long term finance, expressed as a proportion of long term assets, was 1.8 for small firms and 1.6 for quoted companies.

25 Bolton Report, para. 2.17

26 ROBERT HELLER 'What Debt does to Profits', *Management Today,* July 1970, p. 101.

27 Information Note No.61 *Financial & Operating Ratios.* BIM London, 1971. *Efficiency Comparisons in Large Organisations.* BIM & The Centre For Interfirm Comparison, London 1962.

28 Bolton Report, p. 18, Table 2. XVI.

29 *ibid.* p. 13, Table 2. XIII. See also CHRISTABELLE ALLEN *Small Firm Survey,* ICFC, London 1970, and Research Report No. 17, *A Postal Questionnaire Survey of Small Firms.*

30 Research Report No. 16, *An Analysis of Financial Data.*

4

Company Profile

INITIAL MEETING

The management should aim to present, at the initial meeting between the company and the bank, a profile of the company, showing its present financial position, its potential, its future financial needs, and the terms on which the bank can invest. If all the relevant facts are readily available, little time is wasted on abortive discussions. Any information supplied would be on a confidential basis.[1]

In making any presentation, the management should bear the following points in mind:

1 Management should assume that the bank knows nothing about the company, its background, the industry, markets, products, management or customers, and should thus provide sufficient information for an outsider to make an evaluation of the company, as a potential investor.

2 The information given should enable the bank to evaluate not only the past performance of the company, but to explain how and why the company will expand from the present level of profits to the potential earnings forecast, within the stated period.

3 To outline the management's intentions for the company after the planned expansion is completed. The company can either

continue as an independent private company, or, it can, within a certain period, become a public company or merge with another group. The bank then knows whether it is required to be a long term (seven to 10+ years), a medium term (five to seven years), or a short term (three to five years) investor.

4 To outline what is required to meet this target, in finance, in management, in new products etc., so that the bank can decide if the company has or has not the ability to realise this potential.

5 To explain the present strengths and weaknesses of the company and how they will wax or wane at each stage of the growth cycle.

The management may wish to take the process in two stages. At the first meeting an initial report can be presented, giving sufficient facts for the bank to decide whether it is interested or not. Once more interest is shown, full documentation can be provided.

At the end of this chapter will be found a check list of the points that should be incorporated in any full report. In Figure 4:1 are to be found the main points, which could be presented in the initial report.

After the information has been digested, the bank, if it wishes to go further, will want one of its executives to visit the company. A presentation can then be given covering past history and present and future prospects, to illustrate the capability of the company and the markets it serves.

This is a fact finding stage, and any verification will take place later, when the reporting accountants investigate the company.

EXPLANATION OF FIGURE 4:1

In Figure 4:1 will be found a list of the main points that would be considered by a potential investor at the initial stage. Four company profiles are given. Companies A and B, as they are not overborrowed in the present financial climate, could probably obtain four to five year bank loans, and would thus have no need to part with equity. Company C represents a more likely profile of an average investment, with perhaps in addition, some of the qualities Company B has in the fields of management, products and financial control. Company D would not be a suitable company for investment, as the record is short and unstable, and as there are many unsolved problems.

The well established institutions are able and willing to handle

Company	A	B	C	D
Years from Flotation	1 -2	2-3	5-7	?
Profits Pretax (£000)	120	90	50	25
Stability				
Record and growth (last 5 years)	av. 25% p.a.	av. 20% p.a. 1 bad year	Patchy	Not proven, just beginning
Financial Condition (after investment)				
Current ratio	2.0	1.8	1.2	Negative
Overall borrowings (% net assets)	40%	50%	55%	65%
Security	Very good	Good	Over-borrowed	None
Management				
Quality and breadth	Good	Good	Accountant required	One man only
Succession	Very good second line	Some second line	Serious gaps	Nil
Entrepreneurial ability	Very good record	Good	Reasonable	Unproven
Techniques	Up to date	Needs updating	Strong improve-ment needed	Little knowledge
Integrity and co-operation	No worries	No worries	Seems OK	Questionable
Products (old and new)				
Market position and repu-tation–sound and proven	Old and new	Old only	Promising	All unproven
Up to date and competitive	Old and new	New only	Promising	All unproven
Diversification (products and markets)	Wide	Wide 1 industry	Narrow, few customers	In develop-ment, Government and sub-contract
Technical Innovation	Very good market leader	Good and recognised	Promising	Unproven
Forward Planning				
Period and content	3 years detailed	2 years detailed	1 year rough	nil
Growth Potential (3 to 5 years)				
Profits increase (average) over period	70-100%	70-90%	100-150%	No forecast
Downside – fall %	10%	30%	40%	?
– probability	15%	25%	30%	?
Sources – existing products	30%	20%	10%	No forecast
– new products	30%	40%	60%	No forecast
New – home	20%	20%	20%	No forecast
Markets – export	20%	20%	20%	No forecast
Production				
Increase over last 3 years	15%	20%	Record too short	No record
Capacity for expansion	Yes with shift working	Building ready 12 months	Sub-contract and new space in 3rd year	Mainly R & D and one off – no batch production
Scheduling	Smooth	Patchy	Rapid changes	"
Plant etc. (age and suitability)	Up to date	Some new required	Old and many gaps	Very little
Human Relations				
Communications and morale	Good	Very good	Great enthusiasm	Uncertainty on company future
Labour supply and turnover	Ok	OK	Possible labour shortage	Turnover high
Responsibilities	Well defined	Hazy, overlap	Ill defined	Non-existant
Accounting and Costing Systems				
Content and coverage	Good	Far more detail required	Very rough	Direct costs only
Completion, monthly accounts, (from month end)	15 days	25 days	Quarterly	Annual only

Figure 4:1 Company classification

companies with problems arising from growth, but not those arising from mismanagement. They do not expect their clients to be without problems, but they do expect good managements to be aware of their shortcomings, and to have a workable plan for their solution.

REASONS FOR FAILURE

Before examining the profile of a successful company, it is useful to look at some of the principal reasons why companies are not successful. They are as follows:[2]

Organisation, Management and Staff

Lack of trained management. There are several contributory factors: no training of managers; recruitment from a narrow circle; unbalanced experience, limited to one aspect – sales, production etc.; lack of general business experience and of line management; no succession.[3]

No proper definition of responsibility and authority. This leads to squabbling among managers and power politics.

No delegation. A refusal to delegate routine administration by management, which spends too much time on day to day problems, and not enough on the future of the company. In fact a lack of systematic routine administration.

Poor human relations. Bad communications between management and staff, up and down. No joint consultation, low morale and no trust in management; in fact a negative attitude on both sides.

Low pay and incentives. The company gives the minimum to employees and no more.

Selection unsatisfactory. Although job satisfaction and morale should be high in a small company, the quality of labour is too low, as the company is considered to be a bad employer.

Out-of-date management techniques. Techniques which could speed workflow and reduce costs are not considered – e.g. the use of data processing bureaux, office machines, work study, value analysis etc.

The Economic Function[4]

The industry. The industry chosen by a new entrant is often highly competitive, and the probability of success is low, for ease of entry is the principal reason rather than high potential profits, (i.e. low capital, managerial and technical requirements).
Innovation. The company often has little or nothing original to offer by way of products, process innovations or services.
Poor prospects. The owner has not made an evaluation of the potential risks and the market opportunities. Often, there is excess capacity in these industries, a poor outlook for profits, and a stream of new entries.

Marketing

Inaccurate sales forecasts. Inaccurate or non-existent sales forecasts can cause excessive investment in stock and plant, thus eating up working capital.
No product planning. Without proper market research and product planning, a firm cannot anticipate users' needs until after other firms have begun to satisfy the demand. Technological change, which can make products obsolete, is not monitored.
No marketing orientation. The company rightly fears competition as opportunities for expansion, for specialisation, and diversification are missed, and the company is, as a result, trapped in a declining market.
Faulty sales policies. Pricing is inaccurate as costs are either incomplete or not known. The sales effort is misdirected on to static or declining markets or customers.

Production

Insufficient standardisation. This leads to short runs and an overload on design and production engineering staff.
Faulty production control. This causes frequent changes and low machine utilisation and output, much waiting time, late deliveries and angry customers.
Faulty purchasing policy. The correct quantities of the right materials etc. are not available at the time required, and are not bought at the lowest price.

Bad quality control. The goods do not meet specification, and do not satisfy the customer.
Out-of-date plant and equipment. These can cause bad quality and high production costs. There is no attempt to improve production methods.
Inaccurate estimating. This is the result of bad, incomplete, inadequate or late information on costs, and therefore no proper feedback. Estimates are not based on work study standards, and prepared by trained estimators, taking all relevant factors into account, but are just rough 'guesstimates'.

Financial and Administrative Planning

Inadequate or misleading records. Very few unsuccessful firms have good records; without these, management is uninformed on the correct state of affairs. This factor has caused more trouble than any other error of management.[5]
Inaccurate costing information. Management does not have the facts to carry out a cost reduction programme.
No budget of expenses. This leads to excessive operating costs which are not offset by increased revenue.
Lack of internal controls. These are especially important on cash, expenses etc.
No tax planning. There is a crisis every time tax has to be paid.
Lack of credit control. This results in bad debts; customers' accounts are not checked before further shipments are made.
No stock control. This causes excessive, obsolete and slow moving stocks which use up the working capital of the company.
No cashflow statements. These should show expected receipts and payments.
Insufficient working capital. This is a sign of poor management.
Insufficient long term capital. Trouble ensues as decisions are taken without any idea of the financial position of the company.
Inadequate knowledge of the capital market. There is insufficient knowledge on the types of finance and the correct sources from which it should be obtained.

REASONS FOR SUCCESS

General

In any evaluation, the influence of rapid growth on the present strengths and weaknesses of a company must not be forgotten. If a company doubles or trebles in size over a three to five year period, any existing weaknesses will be accentuated, and any present strengths may be dissipated. Yet, a company must remain a viable unit, both during and after dynamic growth, which will always bring new problems to overcome.

Small companies should be evaluated, not just for their fixed assets, but also for their ability to turn their particular expertise, be it technical or market knowledge, into future profits. Innovation can create new markets, initially with a limited demand and little competition, which give the small firm the opportunity to grow as the market expands.

To exploit the potential of the company, the following qualities are needed:

Past Financial Success

There should be a record of past financial success, showing that expansion and even new products have been financed from retained earnings. Profits should show a good upward trend, with margins and sales keeping pace. The health and quality of earnings is further improved if the company has weathered a depression successfully and if earnings have expanded faster than the industry as a whole. A well managed company will have built up its assets as fast, and will have achieved a return on them which is at least as good, as others in the industry.

A careful look at the various financial ratios would show if the company was properly balanced (i.e. current ratio, sales to stocks, sales to debtors.)

Directors

To quote[6] Napoleon once again, 'In war men are nothing, one man is everything'. Although the chief executive is all important in setting the tone of the business, he needs a team to be able to achieve his objectives. There must be quality, depth and balance in all fields (i.e. research, production, marketing and finance), as one weak link can be fatal. Proper succession, especially in a 'one man' company is vitally important, as an early death with no successor available can mean a forced sale of the company at a low price. As well as technical knowledge of a company's products, the directors need a broad view of the industry and experience of the markets in which they wish to sell. The attitudes of the directors to current and future problems are of great interest in deciding their level of maturity and judgement. An intelligent attitude to competition, rather than the n.i.h. ('not invented here' – and thus no good) syndrome, shows that competitors' products are being properly assessed to find out their possible effect on the sales of the company. Those who dismiss competition can find out too late that the markets for their products no longer exist.

The directors must be profit-conscious and able to understand that technology is only important as a means of producing profits and is not an end in itself. An entrepreneurial ability is required, expecially in the chief executive, who should have shown that he can successfully anticipate market needs. Expansion comes from finding new applications for old products, and from using existing technical skills to create a new product line with new applications. The successful and profitable launching of a new product line, developed from an existing one, demonstrates that the company has skills in development, production, marketing and in financial control. A successful entrepreneur will also expand his company at a controlled rate within the resources available to him. Banks are frightened of companies which overtrade, and then ask the bank to find the cash, for if no proper security is available, additional equity might be the only possible source of new money. The bank might then be placed in a majority equity position, which would hardly make for good relations between the directors and the bank. The most serious problem a company and its shareholders can face, in a period of rapid expansion, is the failure of management to expand with the company. At a level of around 100 employees, an operating management is needed to carry out and supervise the day to day instructions from the managing director. Above this level, at about 300-500 employees, the founders of the business will need to delegate the day to day management, and concentrate on the future of the company, and on controlling its results. This needs the so called 'opportunistic manager', who is prepared to delegate and to trust his staff.[7] He will need to set standards to ensure planned performance is met, and then monitor performance by means of a reporting system, which quickly shows up any variances.

It is always difficult to predict how men will react to initial success. Some continue to grow, setting themselves higher levels of achievements, and remain flexible, aggressive and alert, whilst retaining their integrity, which is essential in a leader. Others of less ability become complacent, status conscious, suffering from 'hubris' or self love, which saps their judgement and their company's morale. The first category will always use outside advice to supplement their own skills, and are always ready to learn. The others know absolutely everything that there is to know, and are so pig headed and narrow that they cannot accept advice without injuring their self-esteem. This type of man makes a bad steward for the funds entrusted to him by the shareholders. In his own interest as a shareholder, a new chief executive is required before the company suffers a serious setback.

For this reason, all financial institutions, especially those taking a minority equity position, see the quality of management as the most important factor. It is sometimes even possible to finance from the beginning a 'start up' situation, provided that the management has an exceptional record of achievement in the field concerned. The bank may even be prepared to lend the founders some money to increase their own original equity stake, and thus make the operation more worth while for them.

Management and Staff

Management should be recruited from as wide a circle as possible to provide the right type of manager with broad experience in all relevant fields (i.e. marketing, production etc.). The company should be aware of the necessity to develop its managers to meet the problems of growth. Therefore, a management development plan, which trains managers in the new techniques of management, is required to groom them for greater responsibilities, and to help them to grow with the company. As succession is important at all levels of management, the plan will help to provide replacements for major positions in the company.

In the field of human relations, a company should be seen to have a high level of joint consultation between management and labour. The staff should be treated responsibly, given good pay, benefits and incentives, as well as opportunities to increase their skills by internal training. An enlightened personnel policy is essential for success, and especially during a period of sustained growth, which can result in very great pressures on all staff. Morale must be good for the company to survive, as not only must the existing skilled staff remain, but new staff must be attracted, and satisfied staff are the best recruiters. Where there is implicit trust between management and labour, all employees know they will benefit if the company prospers, and they are therefore prepared to work hard to meet the challenge.

Products and Markets

A good product line, reinforced by good technical know-how, provides a stable base for a company to build upon. Proprietary products give a company greater profits and a better control over their future than satellites or jobbers, which are dependent on others for the development of new customers. Companies with a 'product niche' can often adapt their products and broaden their applications to extend into new fields or into new industries. In addition, increased sales give a faster amortisation of research and development, and tooling costs. Existing customers can also be used to greater effect by broadening the product line to be able to offer them a complete range. A company should concentrate in the fields it knows, and should not dissipate its efforts, especially where the applications are unfamiliar to the sales force. A sales force must aim to produce profits from sales, and not just sales in themselves. Thus the acid test of any product must be whether it is profitable, or if it is just a prestige item.

Uniqueness

A potential investor must assess not only the capability of the company in a selected field, but also how tenable its position is, and why, whether there will be expansion in the main fields of the company's activity or not, and how efficient the company is in performing its activities. Finally, product obsolescence can be high, and product life can often be short, especially in highly technical fields; thus, uniqueness will only be maintained by a constant monitoring of the future needs of customers, backed up by a development programme.

A Clear Market Image

Customer loyalty and acceptance for the products of a small company can take two to three years to build, or longer, especially in the industrial field. A good spread of customers, especially large credit-worthy ones, can be a sign that the company is a leader in its field, and is providing a unique service. This is particularly so, when there are signs of repeat business from satisfied customers. Although satisfied customers are not on the payroll, they make the best salesmen.

It is even more impressive if the company can sell profitably in such competitive markets as the USA and Europe, as this indicates an awareness of world market conditions. Acceptance by the government as a contractor, especially in the defence or aerospace field with the appropriate quality certificate, is further evidence of customer acceptance particularly when development work has been successfully completed.

Undue dependence on the government is dangerous, however, as contracts can be delayed or cancelled for many reasons outside the contractor's control.[8] When moving into a new customer field, in which the company is unknown, it is often advisable to consider a take-over or a merger. The alternative is to face a period of two to three years, which may elapse before the products are accepted and a satisfactory volume of profitable sales is reached.

Research and Development

A small company in a technical field must have what the Americans would call a 'true time advantage' to maintain its position as a supplier of proprietary products. The alternative is to become a jobber or a satellite, working for a larger firm. Independence comes from achieving success in a technical field, then building up, improving, and gradually strengthening the position. Although past success is a sign of good management, an investor is interested in finding out whether this record will be maintained in the future.

For this reason, management must be prepared to answer the following questions:

1 What are the future trends of technology, and their effects on the company?

2 What will be the cost of keeping existing products up to date?
3 How long would it take for competitors to catch up?
4 Is there a strong patent position?
5 What is the cost of the new research and development programme?

No company can turn research and development projects into sales and profits unless there is a close and continuing attention to market needs. The cost of making wrong guesses is very high, in cost, in lost opportunities, and in lost customers. Many products have failed because they were too expensive, already in existence, not produceable, or just unsaleable. They were, in fact, brilliant solutions to non-existent problems. Over-innovation often happens when military contractors try to produce commercial products. For, in the military field, performance is all important and price is secondary. In the commercial market for industrial products, price and performance are considered together by any potential customer. A high specification and a high price can restrict very seriously the market for a product.

The potential investor will want to assess the efficiency of the management of the research department by asking the following questions:

1 Have all new products been successful, or have some proved to be abortive?
2 Have new products been launched too soon, and have they had to be modified at great cost to the company and its reputation?
3 Are the quality and quantity of the team correctly balanced for the task ahead, and do engineers and scientists stay with the company? A high staff turnover is dangerous in two ways. Firstly, the company is losing staff which may be hard to replace, and secondly, someone else is gaining their experience.
4 Are projects being completed to budget, in cost, in time, and are the product specifications being achieved?

Research departments will be judged on their record of producing profits for the company by turning their technical knowledge into competitive and saleable products.

Marketing

An efficient marketing department should aim to satisfy customers' existing needs from their original inquiry through to installation and to after sales service. Unless the sales produced are sufficiently profitable, the company will not be able to improve its market position by developing new products.

Future customer requirements should also be anticipated, and all other parts of the company should concentrate on their profitable fulfilment. However good the products, no sale will take place unless the sales management has the ability to mount a vigorous and effective sales campaign on the customers with the best sales potential. Even if the price and performance are competitive, acceptance will only follow if customers are shown how to obtain the best use from the company's products.

Distribution

The area and the customers covered by the distribution system, both at home and abroad, will indicate whether the present organisation is sufficient to meet the company's future sales targets. Although proper coverage of the market is important, the quality of the service to the customer can be an equally important factor when trying to attract a customer from a competitor's products, or when fighting to retain an existing customer. Distributors can only be expected to give this quality of service if they are trained on applications in selling, installing and servicing. Unless a company has already spent much time in visiting and servicing their distributors on a regular basis over a two to three year period, it will be unlikely to achieve a vigorous expansion in exports. Therefore any forecast expansion in export sales will be discounted, if the necessary groundwork has not been carried out.

Product Planning

The sales force should always be aware, not only of the future needs of customers, but also of the activities of competitors. Unless there is a continuous feedback from the field, both in the UK and elsewhere, the company's competitive position cannot be assessed. On this information, decisions can then be taken whether new products should be launched, old ones modified, or prices and discounts changed.

Production

Any visitor to a factory can gain a very clear image of the company by walking through the production area. The tidiness and layout of the shops and the speed with which the work is carried out all indicate the efficiency of the production management. Management must not only be able to produce to time and cost, and to specification, but should also be on the lookout for new methods and new machines to reduce costs. Therefore, techniques such as work study and value analysis should also be employed to cut costs.

Production Control

A dramatic increase in sales will place a greater load on production than on any other part of the company. Thus, the production control and scheduling systems should have already optimised production from the existing facilities. It is even more important to find out whether the systems can cope with a greatly increased output and still enable the up-to-date situation to be readily available. The system of stock control will also have to handle an increased volume of transactions, otherwise excess, obsolete and slow moving stocks will not be kept to a minimum, and the company will not achieve a balance between stocks on hand and production requirements.

Quality Control

Any defect in the quality control system may be accentuated when production increases, so an investor will be interested in the quality record that the company has established. He will want to know whether there are certain products that customers have refused to accept and which have had to be modified, and what the reject or rework rate is for the company as compared with that for the industry; for products must not only be well designed, they must also be well made and fit for the purpose supplied.

An analysis of the production function is vital, as a company with the best designers and a superb sales force backed by a good service team has little chance of success if the products are delivered late and are unreliable in service – the company only receives its money back and, it is hoped, a profit, when the customer pays his debt. This debt does not become due until the customer accepts the product as fulfilment of his order.

Financial and Administrative Control

Poor financial control is the sign of a badly managed business. Without proper figures, the management cannot know where the money is being spent, and whether jobs or products are profitable or not. If estimates cannot be reconciled with the actual costs, errors are not corrected as there is no feedback to estimating. A management that tolerates this state of affairs is unlikely to be a good custodian of the funds entrusted to it. Therefore, great value will be placed on an efficient system of budgetary control, which allows management to know where profits and losses are being made. An efficient costing system is also required, backed up by work study, which sets standards of performance for use in estimating jobs. The information should be timely, so that danger signals, such as excessive materials and labour costs, are known in time for action to be taken. The company should be aware of their profits by product, to know which products to push and which ones should be discontinued.

The time taken to prepare the monthly or quarterly accounts is also an indication of how profit conscious the management is, and how capable the accounting department will be of handling the increased pressure of work in an expansion. If a company plans to increase profits from say £50,000 to £150,000 in five years, some thought should be given to the administration required to carry this programme out. Service bureaux or simple bookkeeping machines can speed up accounting, provided action is taken in designing the systems and ordering the machines required well in advance. Without an accurate and fast accounting system, a company does not have the information it requires to plan its future and to control operations.

Planning and Growth Potential

In a recent survey, half of the small firms reported that their markets were either static or declining.[9] In the same report it was clear that exceptional growth came from new products, entry into new markets and improved market share, all primarily associated with superior management capability.[10] In an analysis of 'decayers' contraction of existing markets was given as a reason in 79 per cent of the cases, and managerial reasons in 20 per cent of the cases.[11]

Planning is vital in a small company, and the successful ones set short, medium and long term objectives for profits and assets. Any objectives are expressed in quantitative terms and are checked against the performance of competitors, or against the industry as a whole. Sales forecasts are backed up by market research reports and by careful analysis of potential sales by customer, to avoid, as far as possible, any over-optimistic forecasts.

Sales and profits will not be built up through the temporary business that government or sub-contract business brings, but through an expansion in the sales of proprietary products. A proper plan of expansion is needed to adapt the company's objectives to changes in technology and to the needs of the market. The plan must cover expansion in new fields as well as in existing ones, showing why the new fields have been chosen, and ensuring that expansion within these fields is properly controlled. Reasonable targets should be set, or the company may overtrade, and then be unable to carry out its plan.

At the end of this chapter, a check list will be found covering the various points which are likely to be raised in the course of an investigation. This is further supplemented in Chapter 6 on Forward Planning.

For the current year, once year to date figures are available, the existing order position should be assessed to find out which orders will be delivered during the current financial year. An estimate should also be made on how firm the orders on hand are, and which are likely to be delayed or cancelled.[12] After adjusting the deliveries expected for the current year, an estimate of any further orders expected, their probability, and any additional deliveries during the current year should be made. The picture should be studied for the next two years, after considering the industrial and competitive outlook, the expectations and the needs of major customers, and the trend of new orders against the same period in previous years. Any forecast of deliveries should take into consideration any possible limitations in the supply of components, raw materials, productive capacity and labour.

Finally, an estimate should be made of the trend in selling prices, and in the costs of materials, labour and overheads, to arrive at an estimate of profits throughout the period.

Financial Position and Requirements

As well as a cash-flow forecast for the future, a potential investor will be very interested in the company's use of funds over the last three to five years, to find out where the monies have come from, and how they have been used. An analysis of the past accounts will indicate the following facts:

1 The sources of funds (retained earnings, depreciation, borrowings, suppliers credit etc.), and their application (working capital, stocks and debtors, fixed assets etc.).
2 Investment in fixed assets should be analysed to see how effective this investment has been in increasing profits, or whether any estimate of future profits was made at all. This check will show the efficiency of the management in their stewardship of the funds entrusted to them.
3 Working capital should be examined to find the reasons for fluctuations, how debtors and stocks were financed, and, above all, evidence of overtrading; i.e. a current ratio which is nearly equal (1:1) or negative (1:1.5).
4 The potential investor also wishes to know if the new money required is needed to finance the existing business because inflation and competition are reducing profits, or whether it is needed to finance expansion (i.e. new products, more productive capacity etc.). In a low profit company, more money is often required to maintain the existing level of turnover, adjusted for the effects of inflation, and to bring the company's facilities up to date. Providing long-term or equity money for this type of defensive situation is not attractive to banks. If a company is not able to generate sufficient profits to finance the existing business, more and more money must be made available to finance a static, and perhaps declining, position.

To summarise, a company should be able to finance, through its own earnings, its existing business, including new products, and new machines to replace those which become outmoded, and also any increase in working capital required through inflation. New funds should only be required to finance genuine expansion in sales volume, or entries into new product or market fields.

A cash-flow statement is then needed for the next three years to find out what finance is required, when, why, and what return in profits will result. A company should allow for contingencies, as unless adequate cash is provided to exploit a competitive position, the demand can be filled by others. Allowance should also be made for any changes in policy over the future, such as longer credit to customers, additional advertising, or changes in depreciation policies and in leasing payments.[13]

Evaluation

Once the financial requirements of the company are known, a decision has to be made on how these funds should be best provided. Some can be raised by way of bank overdraft or through hire purchase, some from long term loans, and the balance from equity. The exact proportion can only be decided after the company's borrowing capacity has been calculated (see Chapter 14). The method of valuing a company is discussed in Chapters 11 and 12. The company's growth should then be estimated, after considering its market position and that of its competitors, and the outlook for its customers. The management then have to persuade an investor that they are capable of overcoming any existing problems, and those arising from growth. Only then can an estimate be made of the likelihood of the company making its forecast profits.

These strengths and weaknesses, the intangible factors such as the attitudes of management, the quality of information and the company's forecasting ability, must be considered with the present financial position, to assess the downside as well as the expansion potential. The investment will have political effects within both companies, the lender and the receiver, depending on how well the company meets its individual long-term objectives. For the private company especially, life will never be quite the same again. Either success will take the company to a public issue, or failure could result in, at best, stagnation, or, at worst, a forced sale. For this reason, both parties should be meticulous in their analysis of the future. The possibilities of failure and success must be made clear, and any weaknesses recognised and dealt with. After all reasonable measures have been taken, something has to be left to luck, but in the words[14] of Napoleon, 'secure to yourself all possible chances of success when you decide to deliver an important engagement'.

Sir Winston Churchill, in his *History of Marlborough*, gives[15] a clear idea of the depth and the compass of the investigation required on the part of management. 'All factors which are at work at the time, the numbers and the quality of the troops and their morale, their weapons, their confidence in their leaders, the character of the country, the conditions of the roads, time and the weather, and behind these the politics of the states, the special interests which each army has to guard.'

How to reconcile the special interests of the shareholders with those of any outside investor, will be the hardest and most critical decision the directors will have to take, during the negotiations.

APPENDIX 1: COMPANY INVESTIGATION

History and Capital Structure.

1 Incorporation, history, development and past trading.
2 Memorandum and articles – voting rights.
3 Share capital:
   Authorised } Voting and non-voting.
   Issued } Ordinary and preference.
4 Shareholders:
   Directors, others and who owns control?
   Who represents who?
   Who controls over 75 per cent of each class of share?
5 Loan capital – amounts, repayments and other terms.
6 Option and conversion rights – quantity, prices, dates.
7 Subsidiaries, Associated companies, Trade investments } Shareholding, cost, date acquired and from whom, and minority shareholders. Directors' and major shareholders' interests in associated companies.
8 Solicitors.

Accounts

1 Year end.
2 Auditors.
3 Audited profit and loss accounts and balance sheets – last five years.

4 Draft accounts – to cover period up to the time of investigation.
5 Work in progress and stock valuation:
  Method and consistency, e.g. cost or market.
  R & D capitalised.
  Dead and excess stock-turnover.
  Costs to complete contracts and losses brought forward.
  Finished stock (customers' orders, unallocated stock).
6 Debtors value, less bad debts reserve, and items in dispute – Aged balances.
7 Property and plant:
  Book value, valued by and date (£)
  Fire insurance value, and date (£)
  Depreciation:
    plant and equipment
    motor vehicles
    office furniture and fittings
    } Rate percentage changes S.L. or R.B.
8 Charges registered and security given.
9 Creditors – amount, aged balance, need to reduce creditors, and if so by how much.
10 Tax:
  Computations agreed up to (date)
  Surtax and shortfall clearance up to (date)
  – Any outstanding tax problems?
11 Facilities, under the following headings: Present level; Limit; Agreed period; Repayment dates; Amounts:
  Bank.
  Mortgage.
  Hire purchase.
  Factoring.
  Bills.
  Will these facilities be maintained, reduced or increased?
12 Net current assets.
13 Net asset value – less goodwill, dead and obsolete stock, contingent liabilities, warranties but including any revaluation of fixed assets.
14 Losses brought forward – type of work.
15 Net sales, gross and net profits, margins, net worth, and return on capital – last five years – reasons for fluctuations – health of earnings.

16 Ratios:
Current assets/current liabilities.
Net profits pretax/net sales.
Net profits pretax/net worth.
Net sales/stock and work in progress.
Current debt/net worth.
Total debt/net worth.

Directors, Management and Staff

1 Organisation chart – geographical, departmental.

2 Directors and management:
Names, ages, service, health.
Titles and duties.
Experience and previous jobs.
Qualifications.
Salaries, profit sharing, pensions and options.
Service agreements – copies.
Major changes and their reasons over the past five years.

3 Capability:
Top and middle management. Good and obsolescent.
Weaknesses and strengths.
Balance and depth – gaps.
Temperament (do they work together? Can we work with them?).
Integrity.
Record of profitability – in boom and depression.

4 Technical and marketing knowledge:
Customers, markets, future trends, new product potential.
Technology – monitor R & D.
Good selling record – customers and market development.
Good production record – produce to time, cost and specification.
Ability to plan, direct, and control.
Management techniques.

5 Staff:
Managerial.
Supervisory.
Sales/service.
Engineering and technical.

Production by trades: (Machine shop, assembly, drawing office).
Clerical.
Availability and training – labour turnover.
Fringe benefits – cost.

6 Employee relations:
Trade unions.
Strikes and stoppages.
Communications – good or bad.
Company spirit – do people stay with the company and give of their best?

Products

1 Existing products:
Catalogues.
Age and obsolescence – remaining life.
Market share.
Quantity sold.

2 New products and developments:
R & D programme: spending last three years.
State of development.
Technical lead.

3 Patents and trade marks:
Granted; period outstanding.
Applied for.
Countries covered.

4 Other services provided.

5 Licensing and distribution agreements (period and liability).

What proprietary products have been developed or added over the last three years and what percentage are they of the present sales? Have any development or tooling costs capitalised been amortised fully or not?

Research and Development

1 Future technical developments:
Effect on company.
Need to improve existing products.
Competition – cost to catch up.

2 R & D plan:
Co-ordinated – logical/haphazard.
Comprehensive – existing and new products.
Organisation and control – projects to time, cost and specification.
Abortive products or projects.

3 Market/product orientated:
Sales and profits from developed products.
Technical merit and innovation.
New products problems (production and test, other).

4 Staff:
Technical depth, quality and effectiveness.
Turnover.

Marketing and Distribution

1 Sales analysis (last three years):
By product – home and export.
By major customers – government sales.
Seasonal peaks and influences.
Proprietary/sub-contract.
New customers, re-orders.

2 Distribution:
Area covered – home and export.
Proportion sold by sales force and agents.
Time established in each market.

3 Customers:
List and length of association.
Industry and location.
Market image – company's reputation with industry – home and export and with government – UK and foreign.
Sales appeals – technology and special skills.
Quality.
Service and back up.

4 Competition:
Market size – outlook, growth rate, development in US and Europe.
Market shares – company and competition.
Comparative strengths and weaknesses based on users' preferences.

Will the company maintain or improve its competitive position?

5 Pricing:
  Method.
  Date revised.
  Margins (stability, fixed price contracts).
  Discounts and trade terms.

6 Service provided:
  Maintenance.
  Technical assistance.
  Fast delivery.

7 Market Development:
  Relevance of product line – company and competition.
  Single product/few customers – need to broaden base.
  Customers' future needs – large and small.
  New products – relevance and failures.
  Market survey reports.

8 Advertising and P.R.:
  Journals used – frequency and replies.
  Cost.
  P.R. activity.

9 Marketing ability:
  Aggressive.
  Thorough.

Production

1 Buildings:
  Freehold or leasehold.
  Location and adaptability.
  Modernisation required and cost.

2 Space:
  Production, storage, office, car park.
  Land for expansion.

3 Plant:
  List and age.
  Modernisation – cost.
  Idle plant.
  Layout and housekeeping.

4 Output:

Capacity
past (£) } utilisation %
present (£) } output per man.
projected (£) }
Break even point (£)
Surplus capacity – plant, space.

5 Stock control:
Method of recording receipts and issues.
Stock movement by each group (stock and work in progress).
Obsolete and excess stock.

6 Production control:
Method.
Cycle.
Economic lot size.

7 Quality:
Inspection.
Government approval – E.Q.D., A.R.B.
Rejects, rework, customer complaints.

8 Buying:
Bought in items as percentage of total manufacturing cost.
Long term agreements.
Make or buy decisions.
Cycle.

9 Production:
Methods, special techniques and skills.
Production engineering skills.
Outstanding production problems.

Financial and Administrative Control

1 Pricing and estimating:
Standards.
Feed-back period.
Price revisions.

2 Costing method:
Method – labour, materials and overheads.
Part deliveries – when are profits taken?
Efficiency and speed of systems.
Profit by product available.
Profit by cost centre available.

3 Reporting:
  Monthly P & L – when ready.
  Other reports.
4 Budgetary control:
  Efficiency.
  Capital expenditure – control and justification.
5 Reports available:
  Accountants.
  Management consultants.
6 Level of administration:
  By department (sales, production, research, finance) or by product group – good/bad.

Planning and Growth Potential (current year and next three years)

1 Year to date figures, budget/actual:
  Sales, gross margins, net and profits.
2 Existing orders outstanding:
  Customer type and financial standing – list home/export.
  Firm or cancellable.
  Delivery schedule – period.
  Weeks production.
  How closed, price, sole source, other.
  Restricted profits – ministry.
3 Estimated annual sales and net profits – next 3 years:
  General industrial situation.
  Changes expected.
  Particular industry – outlook.
  Major users – future demand and financial position (up, down or static).
  New orders trend – home and export:
    Last four months.
    Previous four months.
    Same period last year (exclude seasonal or climatic influences).
  Additional orders required to meet forecast.
  Source – where from and date must be closed by to meet forccast.
  Deliveries to be made and capacity required, and existing delivery trend.

Limitations – stock (buying availability of raw materials and components; production; labour supply).
Existing stock – raw materials, components, finished stocks.
Probability – percentage odds on making budget.
Basic assumptions.

4 Sales growth rate over period:
Company v. industry.
Reasons – new products, new markets, greater market share, home or export.
Outstanding problems.
Technical, production, quality or acceptability.
Why should company increase sales or increase market share?

5 Competition:
Trend, past and future – better/worse.
Over supply or not?
Advantages – company and competition.
Acceptance of new products.
Imports and export trend in company's markets.
Will company maintain or improve competitive position or not – give reasons?

6 Costs – next three years, for industry and company:
Labour costs: % increase.
Material costs: % increase.
Overhead costs: % increase.
Fixed costs: % increase.
Additional overheads required.
Total costs: % increase.
Costs offset by better buying, productivity improvements, new plant or processes.

7 Margins:
Prices – elastic or inelastic, better, worse, same.
Can company charge enough to cover increased costs, including new product costs?
Margins, up, down, same.

8 Contingency plan, if sales don't materialise.

9 Evaluation:
How likely is the forecast to be achieved (%)?
Does the company have a good position, with satisfied customers, and is it able to produce profitably?
Is the increased rate of new sales forecast too high?

Does it involve entry into a new field, where the company is unknown, does not know the customers, or the industry requirements?
Has company met past budgets? Give details.

Financial Requirements (Next three years)

1 Debtors:
   Level.
   Terms – number of weeks – now, future and for industry.
   Age.
   Bad debts.
2 Stocks:
   Turnover – number of weeks – now, future and for industry.
   Obsolete stocks.
   Normal profit on work in progress.
3 Creditors:
   Level.
   Number of weeks – now, future and for industry.
   Must reduce or not.
4 Repayments:
   Bank.
   Other loans.
   Bills of exchange.
5 Other liabilities:
   Dividends.
   Profit sharing.
   Redundancy.
   Re-negotiation of Government contracts.
6 Capital expenditure:
   Machinery etc. – for new products, for modernisation, of both factory and plant.
   Past and present trend.
   Research and development.
7 Amount of capital required:
   Working capital.
   Long-term capital.

Cash Flow (Next three years)

1 Current asset ratio.

2 Amount working capital and capital expenditure required.
3 Sources:
 Overdraft: amount/limit/security.
 Cash flow.
 Other borrowings – block discounting, hire purchase, factoring.
4 Borrowing ability:
 Interest cover.
 Cash flow: ability to repay loans.
5 Inflow, savings possible.
 Lower work in progress and stocks, lower debtors.
 Administration lower.
 Greater utilisation – increased output per man.
 Sale of surplus plant and capacity.
 Make or buy decisions.
6 Outflow, losses:
 Obsolete stock and finished goods.
 Work in progress, losses brought forward.
 Redundancy.
 Additional capital expenditure.
 Creditors – reduction in level required.
7 Net requirements.
8 Borrowing ability – after investment.

Company Evaluation

1 Unsolved problems (past and future):
 Dangers, one-product company.
 Strengths and weaknesses – skills required.
 Ability and money to put them right.
2 Financial position and future requirements.
3 Growth potential:
 Growth over next three years.
 Competition – will company maintain/improve position?
4 Management – good/bad, succession, record of profitability.
5 Technology – good/bad – gaps.
6 Systems and administration – major changes required.
7 How long to improve profitability and put problems right?
8 Profitability:
 Good record.
 What are we buying, and why?

Company Valuation

1 Assets or earnings basis.
2 If on assets – if asset value is doubtful will a part of the price be paid initially and the balance when the asset value is established?
3 If on earnings:
   On existing or future projected earnings.
   If on future earnings – will the full purchase price be paid only when these profits are achieved plus back interest or will part of the purchase price be repaid if profits are not achieved?
   Is any incentive void if profits fall more than *X*% below levels of earnings laid down?

Company Value Now and in Future (Next three years)

1 On earnings:
   Multiple.
   Revised lowest possible earnings.
   Company takeover value now.
   At present and in future.
   Capital gain over three years.
2 On assets:
   Asset cover.
   Cash flow – times.
3 Similar companies:
   F.T. Actuaries index for section.
   Price earnings ratios for similar companies and asset cover.
   Discount required for variations in size and for being a private company etc.
   Compare percentage annual growth and profitability for industry, for these companies and for the company.
4 Equity option:
   Percentage; value, period and dividends.
   Value at flotation date.
5 Debenture:
   Amount.
   Repayment dates.
   Term.
   Interest rate.
   Security.

Cover – assets and interest.

6 Directors' salaries:

Service agreements.

7 Dividends:

Existing shareholders.

Bank.

Conclusion

Why does the company represent a good investment?

1 Management depth:

Gaps and succession.

Is expansion within the management's ability or is it too ambitious?

2 Technical or cost advantages.

3 Administrative level – improvements.

4 Production – new facilities required.

5 Financial strength.

6 Marketing.

7 Past performance (last five years) v. forecast growth (next three years).

References

1 All the reputable institutions require their employees to sign a secrecy declaration to preserve their customers' secrets. However, it is nevertheless advisable to consult the company solicitor on suitable wording for conditions under which information is made available; e.g. that information can only be used for the purpose for which it is supplied, and that it cannot be disclosed to third parties without the written permission of the company.

2 *Spanners in the Works*, The Institute of Works Managers. London 1963
Problems of Small Business, The Manager, BIM London 1963
D. INSULL, *Thrusters and Sleepers.* Allen and Unwin Ltd., London 1965
Bolton Report, sections 10.5 and 10.6

3 In 23.5% of a sample quoted, the reason for the takeover was given as succession (*Dynamics of Small Firms,* p. 19).

4 J. MARTINDELL, *The Appraisal of Management,* Harper Bros, New York, 1962, p. 11. *Small Firms in the Manufacturing Sector,* p. 60.

5 *ibid.* p. 61.

6 J.C. HEROLD, *The Art of War – The Mind of Napoleon,* Columbia University Press, New York, 1955, p. 289.

7 *Small Firms in the Manufacturing Sector*, p. 50.

8 Contracts can be cancelled or delayed through political reasons – i.e. changes in policy, or through failure of another supplier, or because the money allocated is wanted more urgently on another project which is already overspent.

9 *Dynamics of Small Firms*, p. 20.

10 *ibid.* p. 31.

11 *ibid.* p. 32.

12 In the computer industry a customer can place a blanket order for *x* number of machines over a two year period to obtain maximum discounts. There is no obligation to take up all or even any machines. When the order is not taken up in full, the period is often extended to say three years, rather than invoice the customer at a higher price.

13 A.R. ENGLISH, *Valuation of Shares in Unquoted Companies,* ICFC, London, pp. 3-6. Particular emphasis is placed on the effect of leasing agreements on profits, as the major part of the rent is paid in the primary period. In the secondary period, the rent is nominal. Thus, past profits may have been depressed by high primary charges and in the future the rents will be much lower. On the other hand, a firm, which is about to replace leased equipment, will probably face greatly increased rental charges in the future.

14 MONTGOMERY OF ALAMEIN, *A History of Warfare,* Collins, London 1968, p. 364.

15 *ibid.* p. 296.

5

Preparation by the Company for Investment

In one of the research reports commissioned by the Bolton Commitee, three very interesting comments are made:

'We also found considerable disquiet at the quality of advice in these matters that firms received from their professional advisers. There may be what we might call an "advice gap".'[1]

'A complaint which was voiced by almost all finance companies visited was that, frequently, the accounts of small firms are hopelessly out of date, not properly audited and produced with the Inland Revenue rather than a potential lender in mind. In such circumstances, a finance house has no option but to place the least favourable interpretation upon the information that is in fact provided.'[2]

The report also saw a need for 'the education of managers of small firms in techniques for evaluating their development proposals and the presentation of these to financial institutions; and in such matters as keeping up to date financial records and making cash flow projections without which potential lenders are discouraged.'[3]

Any company approaching a bank for finance obtains a far more favourable reception if they put forward a complete case. The bank can then make a quick evaluation of the proposal. Proposals which drag on tend to be dropped, as the bank and the company's management become more and more disenchanted with each other.

A company which submits a proposal giving the full facts regarding the past, the present and its financial needs for the future, will be received with interest. More important, should it be a borderline case for acceptance, good presentation may swing the decision in favour of the company.

ADVISERS

The client should have good advisers to support him when he approaches a bank for equity finance. Many of the bank's staff will be solicitors or accountants. In addition, for new issues or mergers, the bank will use the services of solicitors or accountants who specialise in corporate finance.

A small company should use professional advisers who are 'au fait' with current company law and practice, and who have experience on issues and mergers. Large firms know public company standards and the requirements of banks for any investigation required; they are thus in a position to handle the bank's advisers on equal terms.

ACCOUNTANT'S REPORT

It is preferable to approach the bank with a completed report, prepared by a leading firm of accountants, rather than wait for an investigation by accountants appointed by the bank. The report will enable the management to correct any deficiencies which come to light, before approaching the bank. The accountants will then confirm that these actions have been carried out.

If the company's auditors are well known in the City, an independent investigation may not be necessary. Normally, their audit and report would be accepted. If any investigation was required, it would be confined to checking the validity of their audit.

Before such an investigation takes place, certain basic information must be made available by the company.

Property

An up-to-date valuation should be prepared by a suitable valuer who is used to dealing with industrial property. This report should cover all properties owned by the company, both freehold and leasehold. Each property should be valued on a 'going concern' basis. The details required are as follows: location, date acquired, age, extent, details of extensions and alterations, planning consents outstanding, infringements, possible compulsory purchase orders, space for extensions, and value after any extensions or any redevelopment. For leasehold properties, the terms of the lease are required.

Existing Financial Facilities

Bank managers and others providing financial facilities should be informed that the company is considering the possibility of raising long-term capital. Banks or other financial institutions should be asked to confirm in writing: the facilities available, the present level, the interest rate, repayment dates etc. This information is needed for: bank overdrafts, hire-purchase facilities, export finance, and any other source of finance. Any of these financial institutions may then request to be considered as a possible source of long-term capital.

Auditors

The company's auditors will need to be informed that they are to prepare a report, or that they must co-operate with the investigating accountants.

Before the investigation can begin, the following documents are required:

1 Audited accounts (trading, profit and loss accounts, and the balance sheets for the last five years for the company, its subsidiaries and any associated companies).
2 Interim accounts covering the period between the date of the last accounts and the current date, if this represents a period of more than six months.
3 Monthly management accounts covering the period between the last accounts and the present.
4 Details of tax computations agreed with the Inland Revenue for

the period, and the written down tax value of the plant etc.

5 Clearance that no short fall assessment is due under Section 77 of the Finance Act 1965, and that surtax clearance has been obtained since incorporation.

6 Details of possible estate duty liabilities on the company on the death of a controlling shareholder.

Company Secretary/Solicitor

The investigating accountants will wish to see the following documents and records for every company to be investigated:

1 The certificate of incorporation.
2 A copy of the memorandum and articles.
3 Copies of any mortgages, debentures, or other charges registered.
4 Statutory books and books of accounts (*Note:* all returns due should be made as the investigating accountants will have examined the official file at Companies House, to see if the details recorded are correct and up to date.)
5 Deeds of freehold properties and leasehold agreements.
6 Bank certificates authorising the signing of cheques etc.
7 A brief history of the company prior to, and since, incorporation.
8 An organisation chart of the company (directors, management and departments).
9 Contingent liabilities – any documents or correspondence covering:
   (*a*) Hire purchase or block discounting agreements
   (*b*) Bills payable
   (*c*) Leasing agreements
   (*d*) Factoring agreements
   (*e*) Correspondence on any legal liabilities or disputes with suppliers, debtors or others.
10 Insurance policies outstanding.
11 Pension scheme – trust deed.
12 Details of long term agreements with suppliers or customers (including rental, licensing, distribution and service agreements).
13 Catalogues of: products and price lists; patents and trade marks.
14 Operating information – sales analysis for period: by product and by major customers; for home or export; orders outstanding

by product or customer.

15 Forward budgets for sales, net profits and cash flow where available.

The investigating accountants need to be instructed on the scope and content of the report required. In the Appendix to this chapter will be found an abridged list of the contents suggested for such a report on a manufacturing company. In the case of a retail, merchanting or rental company, some of the requirements would be different. Each case would be judged on its merits by considering the critical factors for that industry.

Scope

The companies to be investigated must be defined. The investigation should cover any subsidiaries, either wholly or partially owned, and any associated companies in which the directors or shareholders of the main company have an interest, in order to find out whether profits are being siphoned off to these associates. The period should be defined (e.g. five financial years, ending 31st December, from 1967 to 1971, and also for the period covering five months from 1st January 1972 to 30th May 1972).

Purpose and Content

This is to verify that the accounts show a true and fair picture of the business over this period (profits, losses, assets, liabilities and contingent liabilities).

The investigating accountants will prepare revised trading, profit and loss accounts, and balance sheets covering the period, incorporating any adjustments they think are required. These adjustments will be reconciled with the last audited balance sheet. Distortions in the trading and profit and loss accounts could occur through:

1 Insufficient depreciation.
2 Items charged in incorrect periods.
3 Changes in the basis of accounting.
4 Insufficient reserves for bad debts or warranty repairs.
5 Obsolete stock.
6 Expected losses on contracts.

7 Additional potential liabilities for taxation.[4]

On the net asset side, debtors, creditors or work in progress could be valued incorrectly:

1 Charges not registered.
2 Fixed assets over- or under-valued.

Any company avoiding payment of tax by making wage or salary payments from petty cash, committing purchase tax frauds, or charging capital improvements to plant and buildings as expense items, is open to heavy penalties for tax evasion. On the other hand, the company may not be claiming, or being allowed the capital allowances or grants to which they are entitled.

THE AUDIT

In many private companies, the audit is only important to verify taxable profits as the shareholders and management are often the same people. However, when there are outside shareholders, it is even more important that the audit is of the highest professional standard.

The investigating accountants should be asked to suggest any improvements that could be made to the systems used for costing, cash control, the recording of stores receipts and issues, and financial management. They should also be asked verbally if the last audit was up to public company standards, and how far it was necessary for them to carry out their own checks, if those of the present auditors were unsatisfactory.

The auditors are appointed by the shareholders in general meeting, and not by the directors. They have a statutory duty[5] to certify to the shareholders that the accounts give a true and fair view of the state of affairs, profit or loss of the company, and that the accounts are prepared in accordance with the Act.[6] The bank must have complete trust and confidence in any auditor appointed; they require an auditor to be independent, and able to resist pressures from management. He must be able to carry out an audit to public company standards, and to have sufficient skills to be able to assist the company to improve its accounting and costing procedures should this be necessary. These requirements may be satisfactorily met by the existing firm, or by appointing a new firm, either as sole, or as joint auditor.

CONCLUSION

Once the report is prepared, the directors should examine it, and where possible carry out the recommendations. The reporting accountants should then confirm in writing which of their recommendations have been carried out, and why others are not being adopted at the present time.

The report will give the company a firm foundation upon which to build up a projection for the future. The information also will be useful later on, should the company wish to make a public issue.

The next stage is the preparation of the long-term plan to outline the company's expansion over a period and the finances required to carry out this programme.

APPENDIX 1: INVESTIGATION BY REPORTING ACCOUNTANTS

Scope

To cover the years from – to – and to include the company and its subsidiaries and associated companies.

General Information

1 Incorporation – formed by and date.
2 Nature of business.
3 History of business, including period before incorporation.
4 Directors, past and present.
5 Premises initially and at present, giving periods of occupancy.
6 Registered office.
7 Company secretary.
8 Solicitors.
9 Auditors – changes.

Directors – Executive and Non Executive, and Company Secretary

1 Names, ages, functions, nationality, date of appointment in period.
2 Emoluments – salary, pensions, fringe benefits, expenses, stock options, profit sharing.

3 Service agreements – period and notice for termination.
4 Transactions between directors and the company – any assets, which have been or are likely to be acquired from the directors by the company, or rented to the company by them, or to any subsidiaries.
5 Management succession – any gaps, changes, in salary or position envisaged, promotions, retirements, – organisation chart – is succession assured or not?
6 Board meetings frequency.

Managers and Senior Executives

Names, ages, service, qualifications, salary and service agreements.

Other Employees

1 List employees by departments, male/female, weekly/monthly. Approximate rates.
2 Staff recruiting – adequate labour supply – working conditions – wage rates – competitive.
3 Staff relations and unions – forthcoming wage demands – effect of equal pay.
4 Fringe benefits.

Pension Scheme and Life Assurance

1 Insurance company and date started.
2 Eligibility – age and service.
3 Cost per annum – employer and employee.
4 Benefits – life assurance, *X* times year's salary. Retirement – after *X* years at *Y*% of final salary.
5 Is cover adequate, or not? If not, cost to make cover adequate.
6 Is scheme solvent?

Products

1 Describe products – age and possible replacement date – catalogues.
2 Annual sales by product or product group – analysed by discount given for home and export markets.

3 VAT – are products subject to VAT?
4 Other services provided – maintenance.
5 Packing, delivery and returnable containers – how charged?
6 Patents and trade marks – details, expiry dates and countries.
7 Licensing agreements/distribution agreements – products sold or made under licence; covering products licensed from or licensed to other companies – expiry dates and countries – minimum royalty or sales levels.

Customers

1 Annual sales to principal customers by product – home and export (at net prices over period) – government or fixed price sales; limited margins.
2 Selling organisation and selling methods – home and overseas – sales by sales force – sales by distributors.
3 Pricing – method used and frequency of revision – discounts and credit terms (company and industry – home and export) – government regulations – special customer agreements, (details).
4 Advertising and sales promotion – annual spending last five years.
5 Warranty and service – liability for service at plant or in field – service organisation (home and overseas) – warranty costs to date and in future – equipment reliability (problems of dispute or equipment acceptance).
6 Trend of sales – reasons for fluctuations – trend is up, down or static.

Competitors

1 List competitors both home and overseas – price and other advantages – nature of competition.
2 Limitations on competition – tariffs or special agreements.
3 Company's relative standing in the field.
4 Market analysis carried out.

Gross Profits

1 Define gross profits – e.g. after direct labour and materials,

factory overheads of $x\%$ and a handling charge of $x\%$ on materials.

2 List gross profits and margin by year – by major product groups – by home and export.

3 Reasons for fluctuations in margins – e.g. price or discount changes, fixed price contracts, losses on contracts – material and labour costs (changes in wage and material rates or in labour efficiency) – overheads (changes in overhead rates or in overhead structure and costs).

Net Profits

1 List net profits pretax or losses by year and show margin on sales.

2 Define net profits before tax; after all expenses of working and management including:
   (*a*) Directors' remuneration.
   (*b*) Depreciation.
   (*c*) Interest paid and received.
   (*d*) Rents payable and receivable.
   (*e*) Private venture R and D.
   (*f*) Add any special receipts for know-how or royalties.
   (*g*) Full provision for expected losses.
   (*h*) Adjust for any provisions not required.

3 Explain any significant fluctuations.

4 Are profits and expenses in their correct years?

Research and Development

1 Projects and spending over the last three years – by projects – by percentage of sales.

2 Proprietary products developed – proportion of sales now.

3 Private venture R and D written off in year or capitalised – if capitalised how amortised – details.

4 Have projects been overspent or kept within budget?

5 Customer R and D, are these projects – clearly defined – budgetary estimates or fixed price – covered fully by an order.

6 Number of staff and qualifications.

Depreciation

1 What rates of depreciation are being charged in the accounts for the following classes of equipment:
   (*a*) Plant and equipment (%).
   (*b*) Office equipment (%).
   (*c*) Motor vehicles (%).
   (*d*) Electrical and heating (%).
   } straight line or reducing balance
2 Are these rates adequate, or is a higher rate required to allow for compensation?
3 Have there been any changes in the period or are any envisaged?
4 What are the corresponding taxation rates?
5 What proportion of depreciation is not allowable for tax?
6 What assets are not depreciated or amortised?

Directors' and Senior Management's Emoluments

1 What amounts including directors' fees were included in the accounts over the period?
2 Do these amounts include all bonus payments, fringe benefits, pensions etc.?
3 Directors' expenses, analyse and ensure that they were properly documented – unusual items.

Dividends

1 List dividends paid each year since incorporation.
2 Dividends paid since last accounts.

Fixed Assets – Land and Buildings

1 List properties by location, age, area – if freehold or leasehold, any land for expansion, the terms of the lease (rent and unexpired term) and state of repair, adaptability.
2 Check the title of the properties and evidence of ownership.
3 Date acquired, how, why, and from whom, cost and present market value, and when revalued.
4 Current fire insurance valuation.
5 Details of extensions and alterations.

Trade and Other Investments – Shareholdings in Subsidiaries

1 Give details, when acquired, why, from whom, cost, present value, equity holding and other shareholders.
2 Details of other investments.

Plant, Equipment etc.

1 Give the book value of the following, general description, age, state of repair, etc.:
   (*a*) Plant and machinery.
   (*b*) Office furniture and equipment.
   (*c*) Motor vehicles.
   (*d*) Electrical and heating equipment.
2 Value – give book, market and fire insurance values – date of any revaluations.
3 Is there a plant asset register – is it complete and does it record main additions in the period?
4 Evidence of ownership.
5 Surplus or standby equipment.

Stock and Work in Progress (see ICA Standard)

1 What has been the method of valuation over the period?
2 Is the method used cost or market, whichever is lower?
3 Has it been consistent?
4 What is the book value for the following items: materials and components; work in progress and finished stock.
5 Has proper provision been made for excess, slow moving, and obsolete, faulty or redundant stocks?
6 Are material, component, and sub-assembly stocks balanced or excessive in view of current requirements?
7 Are demonstrators and prototypes included?
8 Will a normal profit be made on finished stock and work in progress?
9 Are costs to complete known on all jobs, and should any provision be made for expected losses?
10 Does the valuation include an internal profit?
11 How often is a physical inventory taken?
12 Examine stock sheets at the balance sheet dates.

13 What proportion of stock and work in progress is for customers and what proportion are shelf items?

Partly Completed Contracts

1 How are profits taken on partly completed contracts?
2 When part shipments are made, are profits taken on or before completion?
3 Is allowance made for any losses which can occur before final acceptance?
4 Are costs to complete estimated at the year end?
5 Are progress payments in line with work carried out and are there any overpayments?

Trade and Other Debtors

1 Book value of debtors and list of items aged by invoice date.
2 Examine for disputed and overdue items, bad debts, special credit terms, or agreed postponement of payment because of equipment faults.
3 Is the provision for bad debts sufficient?
4 Is the system of credit control satisfactory, judging by the bad-debt experience over the period?
5 List loans to employees and directors – value and repayment.

Tools, Dies, Moulds, Patterns etc.

1 Check basis for charging customers and writing off these items.
2 Does the company retain part value of special tools for customers?

Trade and Other Creditors

1 Book value of trade and sundry creditors and list items by invoice date and check against statements to discover any items in dispute giving reasons.
2 What claims are outstanding?
3 How far is payment in arrears and what effect has this had in losing discounts?
4 Special purchase contracts – what liabilities exist for forward

purchases and are there liabilities for cancellation charges, under buying agreements, or for royalty payments under licence agreements?

5 List purchases from principal suppliers over the period.
6 Is the company single sourced on any major item?
7 Have proper accruals been made for holidays, and sales commissions on shipments made?
8 Has any provision been made for warranties on equipment installed?

Hire Purchase and Leasing Agreements

1 List all agreements showing contract date, amount and date of final payment.
2 Is there any sign of a major change of policy in the period to switch over to leasing or to hire purchasing equipment; what were the reasons, and does this policy change make the results in the period not strictly comparable?
3 Will costs increase over the future, as new equipment must be leased or acquired, or will costs decrease, as the primary leasing period for expensive equipment is nearly at an end?

Contingent Liabilities

1 What capital contingent liabilities exist?
2 List any bills payable by amounts and dates due.
3 List any special contracts – forward sales or purchases.
4 List any other liabilities – legal actions, guarantees, claims etc.
5 Government contracts or completed work – is there any liability for renegotiation of prices on any work already invoiced?

Share Capital and Borrowing Powers

1 The authorised and issued share capital – any changes since incorporation in share capital (new shares issued, capitalisation issues, changes in par values, new classes of shares).
2 List any options or conversion rights outstanding.
3 Outline the extent of any special rights outstanding, as to dividends, voting, repayment of capital, transferability etc.
4 List all shareholders, giving details of interests of directors and

their families or trusts controlled by directors.

5 Who controls the company?

6 Disposal of shares – give dates of disposal, numbers sold, who sold to whom, at what price, and the basis for valuation.

7 Are there any agreements to dispose of shares between parties?

8 Is there any death duties insurance outstanding for the older principal shareholders?

9 Capital and revenue reserves – list reserves by classification and origin.

10 Borrowing limits – what limits are permitted by the articles, and what are total borrowings?

11 List any debentures, mortgages, and other fixed interest borrowings outstanding – amounts, interest rates, security, redemption etc.

12 Bank overdraft facilities – give details as follows: bank and branch, present level, limit, security, and repayment date.

13 Is the bank looking for a reduction or is it prepared to continue or increase the facility?

14 Has the company a good reputation with the bank?

15 List other charges registered, fixed and floating.

16 List hire purchase, factoring and leasing agreements.

17 List directors' loan accounts, amounts outstanding and dates due.

Taxation

1 Taxation computations for the period – examine correspondence with the Inland Revenue for income tax, corporation tax, and capital gains tax to see what items are in dispute.

2 Are there any losses or capital allowances carried forward?

3 Is the control over PAYE, purchase tax and VAT adequate, and are payments up to date?

4 Are there any capital items charged to revenue, e.g. repairs or alterations or replacements to plant or buildings?

5 Has clearance been obtained since incorporation, for surtax or shortfall assessments up to the date of the last balance sheet?

6 Estate duty liability – is there any liability under sections 46 and 55 of the Finance Act 1940, which the company has incurred on the death of a controlling shareholder, within seven years of his death?

7 List and compare the taxation values of fixed assets at the date of the last balance sheet with the book values.

Systems

1 What books are kept, who keeps them, and are they up to date?
2 Is the minute book up to date?
3 The accounting system
   (*a*) Are costs kept by job or product?
   (*b*) Are overheads allocated to jobs?
   (*c*) As shipments or partial shipments are made are these costs eliminated from work in progress?
   (*d*) Are cost, financial, and management accounting systems adequate?
   (*e*) Does the overhead rate include all fixed and variable expenses?
4 Are monthly accounts prepared and compared with budgets, and how soon is action taken over any variances?
5 Is control over cash and expenses adequate?
6 Stores records – is the recording of issues and receipts carried out correctly? Check records for correctness of recording entries.
7 Does the pricing system take into account all the applicable costs, and is any action taken over faulty estimating?
8 Production control – is the system adequate for the company's needs?
9 Are forward budgets prepared for sales, expenses, profits and cash flow, and how accurate have these been in the past?
10 Insurance cover – the type of cover, the company, premium, term and expiry. Is the cover adequate?
11 How efficient has the audit been over the period?
12 Has the company ever carried out cost-reduction exercises?

Summary

1 Prepare revised balance sheets and profit and loss accounts for the period incorporating the various points which came to light during the investigation.
2 Explain the trend of profits over the period, bearing in mind the effects of any changes in the methods of accounting, methods of financing, price changes, increases in costs not compensated by increased revenue etc.
3 Prepare schedules showing the employment of assets by major product groups and the earnings these assets generated.

4 Prepare a source and application of funds schedule, showing how earnings were employed and whether this investment produced additional profits.
5 Was the company able to earn sufficient profits to up-date its products and plant over the period?
6 Outline any special factors relating to the industry which should be known when evaluating the value of the company.
7 List the principal ratios over the period:
   (*a*) Current assets to current liabilities
   (*b*) Net profits to net sales
   (*c*) Net profits to tangible net worth
   (*d*) Net sales to inventory
   (*e*) Current debt to tangible net worth
   (*f*) Total debt to tangible net worth
   (*g*) Debtors to sales
   (*h*) Debtors to inventory

Since the Date of the last Accounts

1 Examine sales, gross profits and net profits for the period and compare with the same period last year and prepare a statement on the current position and prospects.
2 List any major changes in prices for products, services, materials or labour.
3 List the value of orders on hand, compared with the same period last year and how firm these orders are, who are the customers, and how solvent they are (*Note:* especially distributors). Give the following details: amounts, products, customers, price, any profit restrictions, estimated profitability if sole source and cancellation terms.
4 New products – details of developments.
5 Reconcile the cash balances at the date of the last balance sheet with that at present, showing major changes – capital expenditure, special items, dividends, work in progress and any additional liabilities.
6 Compare actual performance against budget for sales, expenses, profit and cash.
7 From the information available on results to date and orders on hand, does it appear likely that the budgets will be achieved?

REFERENCES

1 Research Report No. 4. *Financial Facilities for Small Firms,* HMSO, London 1971, p. 69.

2 *ibid.* p. 165.

3 *ibid.* p. 74, 6a.

4 During one investigation, it is said that the reporting accountants were told that management burnt two stock sheets and that this enabled them to pay their tax promptly.

5 Companies Act 1948 – Section 152 (1).

6 *ibid.* – eighth schedule.

6

Forward Planning

CREDIBILITY

The Bank

One of the research reports examining the origins of the growth and decay of small companies found that exceptional growth came through new products, entry into new markets and improved market share, all primarily associated with superior management capability. The main reason for decay was the contraction of the existing market resulting in falling turnover and profitability. The managements of these firms had failed to launch new products, break into new markets, or improve profits through greater efficiency.

Growth, which had come about through superior management ability, had usually taken place as a result of a decision taken in the past, and was not necessarily attributable to the ability of the present management.[1]

A banker invests to make a capital profit and not to maintain an uneconomic business. He is therefore anxious to maximise his success rate and to do so within a period of between three to five years.[2] He knows the dangers that can beset small companies, which are dependent on the sales of a few products, and subject to violent changes in demand, quite outside their control. He deals daily in international markets and understands how changes in the external environment can adversely affect the competitive position of countries and their local industries. He has seen how publicly quoted companies have made short term profits, by not meeting future market needs in providing new products at competitive prices.

A banker will want to know how any expansion will be achieved, why earnings will increase, and how this will be carried out in the face of international competition from large companies. He will question the management to see whether they have the facts to prove to him that these new markets are genuine growth markets. The company must be able to demonstrate that it has the capability to exploit these opportunities.

Risk

The more comprehensive and detailed the plan, the greater the likelihood that all the problems and factors, both external and internal, which the company may face now and in the future have been considered. In the corporate plan, the objectives and strategy of the company will be laid down and also assumptions made on market growth and on competition. Any expansion in profits from the sale of new products may be heavily discounted because of their high mortality rate, both in development, in production and in customer acceptance. The plan must also show that the organisation structure is suitable for the increased level of operations and that there are sufficient people with the correct skills and experience to carry out the plan. In addition, the reporting system proposed must enable management to control the enlarged organisation. A banker can only have confidence that future forecasts are likely to be met if he knows that the correct actions are being taken today, which will bring profits in three to five years time. Management can only take such decisions if they have up-to-date information on the company, its markets, and the general economic environment, and also the future trends in these fields. Thus, the existence of a comprehensive plan will enable the bank to decide quickly whether they wish to invest or not.

Forecasts

A company budget will be prepared from the plan showing over the next two years, the sales, operating costs and net profits expected, together with a projected balance sheet and cash flow statement for the period. If the forecast is for a longer period, it should be subject to a regular annual review. In preparing these statements, the company should take care that the various financial ratios (i.e. the return on capital employed, stock turnover etc.) are reasonable and attainable (see Appendix to Chapter 3). In assessing these forecasts, the following facts will be considered:

1. How do these forecasts relate to past performance?
2. Do the forecasts for new products and new markets look attainable or over-optimistic, both for the level of sales and for the time-scale expected?
3. How well has the company met previous forecasts?
4. Is the level of increase in sales and profits well above, well below, or in line with the expected expansion for the industry?
5. If the company is forecasting a greater market share, at whose expense will this be gained and how will their competitors react?
6. What probability of success is placed on achieving the forecast (i.e. 60/40, 50/50) by the marketing director?
7. Is the forecast based on an expected increase in sales overall, or on forecast sales to individual customers, and what is the probability of achieving these sales? (*N.B.* Beware of bulk orders placed by distributors.)
8. Is there any specific customer forecast, divided into sales to existing and to new customers, and has double counting been eliminated?[3]

The bank may wish to verify these forecasts by checking their probability with some of the company's large potential customers.

COMPANY SUCCESS

Characteristics

For small companies, there is a high degree of correlation between exceptional growth and entry into new product fields, new markets and improved market share, which are all signs of superior management capability. A decline in a company's fortunes comes from a contraction of markets, and greater competition followed by falling profits.[4]

While the giant corporation is concentrating its talents and cash on the large markets, on the edge of these markets are areas in which the small company can operate profitably. Its leverage is higher than the large corporation, in that good management in the right small business can produce much faster growth in profits than it can in a far larger business.[5]

The characteristics that a banker would expect from a small company would be as follows:[6]

1 Growing sales and profits from new products and markets, serving growth industries.
2 Stability of earnings even in a depression.
3 A product niche with established products in a market, where the company was recognised as a market leader, preferably with some unique products with a 'true time advantage'. The company must have demonstrated its ability to improve profits by cost reduction.
4 High employee morale – with worthwhile goals.
5 Energetic management, which is well rewarded, is sound, and has depth.
6 Ability to develop new products.

Management

In a marketing sense only, successful small company managements may wish to sail close to the wind, to be able to take advantage of any small changes in demand. They must, therefore, have an intimate knowledge of wind, weather and tides in the markets they serve. They must be ever watchful for both opportunity and danger which could sink their frail craft. Because of the high correlation between growth and entry into new markets and new products, the management of a successful small company should be 'opportunistic entrepreneurs' with the following qualities:[7]

1 Risk takers and innovators, concentrating their efforts after carefully identifying their objectives.
2 Know what they are doing, and why; where their strengths and weaknesses are, both today and tomorrow, and have the ability to weigh alternatives and decide on the best way.
3 Know how to survive against large companies, by being adaptable, spotting high growth and profit areas.

4 Be able to enter and leave markets quickly, and use their assets to best advantage.

5 Have a deep market knowledge, and be successful in picking areas where they can compete within their capabilities on quality, short runs, specials, lower prices and technical assistance. In fact, in areas where they can make a high contribution, but are not attempting to compete on volume production or mass distribution. Small firms can compete by offering either an overall service, or by designing new products, carefully tailored to meet market needs at a reasonable cost.

ENVIRONMENT[8]

Effects

No airline pilot, even an inexperienced one, would ever concentrate on the performance of his engines and ignore the weather outside. He knows he has no control over the environment, so he must be aware of storms, fog, ice and wind so that he can take these forces into account in setting his course. He may even decide to alter course to avoid them, or even change his destination. But he will never ignore their existence. In the same way, external business conditions are quite out of the control of the business man. These forces can expand or reduce the size of the company, its markets, or alter its composition or character. The only correct assumption about the environment is that it is unlikely to remain the same and that the future cannot be predicted from the past.

Some of the reasons for the increase in the importance of the environment to companies are listed below:

1 An increase in the rate of change, through new technology, new patterns in demand etc. – rising consumer affluence leading to new demands for different products.

2 Greater complexity of industrial products.

3 Shrinking profit margins, and falling sales, excess capacity and rising costs through inflationary wage demands.

4 Shorter product life, and as competition increases – falling selling prices.

5 Greater competition through large companies competing internationally, and profiting from the dismantling of trade barriers; e.g. EEC.

6 The expansion and contraction of markets, as demand changes, so that growth markets are short-lived.

Monitoring

Corporate growth, by and large, proves to be the result of integrated company strategies which capitalise on the opportunities found in future environmental change.[9] Management should therefore sense change, and either avert danger or profit from opportunity, by implementing the correct strategies to achieve these aims. To increase profits over a period, a company should anticipate and identify these trends, both their upturns and downturns, in sufficient time to develop the correct products to fill the anticipated demand.

Companies will only be able to increase profits in the future, by knowing about the factors which are likely to influence market growth, sales, profits, competition, products and customers, now and in the future.

'We should devote a considerable part of our time, efforts, and our money, to making what we do now obsolete: if it can be done and we do not do it, someone else will and our markets will disappear overnight.'[10]

Political

The company can be affected in any of its major markets anywhere in the world by changes in governments or by major policy changes. For instance, any change in government policy on procurement, or any assault on the monopoly position of large companies, giving greater opportunities to small companies to compete in these fields.

On the other hand, industrial relations laws, consumer protection laws, EEC regulations or anti-pollution laws will bring problems to small companies.

Economic

The economic conditions in each country in which the company sells its products should be monitored as the following factors can affect demand:[11]

National Expenditure
The trends of Government spending, consumer demand, industrial investment, and the future expectations in these fields; the health of the earnings of the major customers of the company.

Credit Policy
The influence of government policy on the availability of money for investment may cause companies to change their future expectations of demand and thus their investment policy.

The Balance of Payments
Changes in exchange rates can affect the competitiveness of the company's and competitors' products in home or export markets; e.g. the recent changes in parity between sterling and the US dollar made American goods more competitive in both the UK and in Europe. Devaluation can also affect the value of contracts already negotiated, if they are in foreign currency, as well as the future business prospects in the country concerned.

International Trading
Import quotas, tariffs, special arrangements for developing countries to market their products in the UK (e.g. textiles), and Communist Block trading agreements can all affect market size.

Price Indices
Prices of raw materials, components and labour can change the competitive position.

Taxation
Changes in company taxation, VAT, investment incentives, free depreciation and changes in close company legislation can alter predictions already made on cash flow, and on the pay back of investment projects.

Technological

The management must be aware of the potential developments in the industry or from outside, which could affect demand for the products of the company. They must know the effect of this change in demand on the present products and also on any future products proposed. Technological change may reduce a company's sales, by reducing the demand for customer's products, through the arrival of a new competitor; for example, the effect of electronics on the adding and calculator market, especially from Japanese products. On the other hand, better, cheaper or more reliable components may open up new fields by reducing the price of a product so that it can compete with the product already serving the market.

Social

Changes in population, in births, marriages or in the age structure, any new requirements for leisure and education, shorter working hours, or improved communications, can alter the demand for products in either direction.

The Market

To be able to forecast demand and sales, a company must have information on:

1. The types of users, their expected purchases, both by quantity and time, and their location.
2. The needs of users, now and in the future, as to price, performance, quality, delivery, service etc.
3. The economic position of the industry or market, over-capacity, price cutting, new industry standards set by large users – as in the computer industry, changes in the structure of the industry as suppliers become competitors or customers fill their own demands. In the latter case, this could result from the takeover of a competitor by an existing customer.
4. How to distribute the goods, how much to make or to buy, what profit return to set, and over what period should new development and plant be depreciated.

It is characteristic of engineers to be very keen on research and development which they understand, but market research, which can show what the company should design, is often felt by them to be a suitable subject for economies. Research in both fields is required to ensure that products will meet future customers' needs. No experienced engineer would expect a development project which involved mechanical and electronic engineering skills to succeed unless engineers with both these skills were working on the project.

THE PLANNING PROCESS

Ideally, the chief executive of any company should spend at least one-third of his time[12] assessing the future position of the company, by monitoring the objectives decided upon, and the company's expectations, and the reliability of the targets set. He can aim to ensure overall that the resources of the company are employed to the best advantage, remembering always that the environment is always changing, and that any plan needs to be updated at regular intervals or whenever major events occur which invalidate the assumptions on which it is based.

The planning process goes through the following stages before the final plan is produced.

Preliminary Objectives
The company sets the objectives in profits and sales that it expects to achieve within a definite period.

External Opportunities and Threats
The company must gather facts, analyse data and predict trends in the fields and markets which the company supplies now. It must assess markets with high profit potential which are within the capacity of the company to find the best products and opportunities for long term growth. Assumptions must also be made about the factors affecting the company, those favouring its success and those threatening its chances. In each field, the rewards must be balanced against the risks taken.

The Position Audit
This should find out what the strengths and weaknesses of the company are, what are its capabilities, and how the prospects of the company are influenced by external conditions.

The Company Objectives
The company objectives are confirmed. Sub-objectives are set for sales and profits after selecting the new fields which the company will enter to achieve its aims.

The Corporate Strategy and Plan

The overall plan and sub-plans for each sector of the company are drawn up.

Implementation

The action to be taken to put the plan into effect is decided upon, together with the resources required. The time-scale to achieve the objectives set, down to departmental level, is also agreed.

Control

The method of measuring performance against the forecast is critical. In addition, certain assumptions have been made about the market, its growth rate and customer needs, which must be correct if the plan is to succeed. Other assumptions have been made about the resources available to carry out the plan. The control system must identify potential problems early on, so that any risk to the company through changing conditions can be reduced, especially those changing forecasts of profits or sales. Despite changing conditions, the original objectives may still be able to be achieved, but in a different time scale. However, in other cases the plan may have to be redrafted with new objectives.

BASIC OBJECTIVES[13]

The primary objective for all parties is to achieve a public issue or takeover in four to six years. To go public, earnings pre-tax must rise to at least £150,000 in this period.[14] An objective should also be set for the return on capital employed, which should be calculated before interest and tax on the net worth of the company and its loan, overdraft and debenture monies. As well as setting the final profit figure for the end of the period, standards should be set for each year.

Method

Once the primary objective is agreed upon, the board must decide upon the means whereby this objective will be achieved. The expansion will take place by increasing sales, profits and the return on capital employed. Definite objectives should be set for each of these, both for the annual increase and for the final level at the end of the period of the plan.

The various objectives to be fixed are as follows:

Sales

To maintain the existing growth rate in sales of *y* per cent per annum (or to specify individual growth rates for each year); for the three years ending 197*x*, to reach an absolute level of sales in this year of £*s*.

Profit on Sales

To reach an annual level of pre-tax profits of £*p* by 197*x* by the following means:

> increasing the margin on sales from the existing level of *y*% to *z*% at the end of the period; or
> maintaining the margin at the existing figure and increasing overall profits at the same rate as the increase in sales.

As margins tend to contract with inflation and as competition increases, some assumption should be made about the possibility of reducing costs or increasing productivity over the period to remain profitable in a price war; for example, the company will, by increasing productivity and by value analysis, reduce costs by *x*% per annum in each of the three years of the plan. An assumption on price levels should also be made, as well as assumptions on the annual rate of cost inflation.

Working Capital turnover

Standards should also be set for increasing the turnover of assets in stock and work in progress, and debtors by greater efficiency.

Indebtedness (see Chapter 14)

The company must operate within certain accepted levels, which will restrict its ability to borrow. These can vary from industry to industry, but overall they are:

1 *Interest cover* (pre-interest and tax) four to five times.
2 *Secured borrowings level* $66\frac{2}{3}$ per cent of net assets, i.e. 40 per cent loan, 60 per cent share capital and reserves, which can be increased to a 50/50 ratio in certain circumstances.

3 *Overall borrowings:* a ratio of from one to one-and-a-half times share capital and reserves, depending on the size and financial condition of the company.
4 *Current ratio* (i.e. the ratio of current assets over current liabilities: the extent to which the company is being financed by its creditors). This ratio in the Bolton Report was 1.4 for fast growing companies and 1.6 for the slow growers.[15]

The company's financial needs must be restricted to the funds generated by retained earnings (profits after tax and dividends plus depreciation), and to any funds it can borrow.

Dividend Policy

While considering the financial needs of the company, management should decide whether dividends are to be paid during this period or whether the company is to concentrate on financing growth from internal resources. Here advice should be taken from the company's tax advisers on the possibility of a shortfall assessment by the Inland Revenue during this period.

Markets

The company may wish to set objectives for entering new markets, for launching new products or for breaking into new customer fields, at home or abroad. Especially if the company depends too heavily on one customer.

1 A level may also be set for the share of a certain market that the company wishes to achieve by the end of a certain period.
2 The company may wish to exploit an existing product or technical advantage or to develop such a position in a related field, e.g. to build up technical expertise in a certain market. It may wish to increase product reliability or to give improved maintenance cover. Any objective should be expressed quantitatively, e.g. to achieve a mean time between failure of x hours or to ensure that maintenance calls can be dealt with in x hours.

Employment

To maintain at least current levels of employment and to maintain a high level of morale by training and developing existing staff where possible, to fill management and supervisory positions.

Other objectives that can be set could include acquisition policy, overseas distribution, advertising, sales promotion, public relations, personnel policies. All such policies must be related to the existing situation and any new objectives set, after considering the present situation and possible external factors.

POSITION AUDIT

The Past

Assuming that the company has either had prepared an accountant's report, or has up to date accounts available, it has the facts to evaluate past performance. With this information, the present position can be assessed and the future predicted. The gap, if any, between the objectives set and what can be achieved with the present product line organisation and facilities is known. It is vital to know the following facts:

1 *Net assets* – showing up to date valuations.
2 *Net profits* – over the last five years, broken down by product and any reasons for fluctuation in profits, margins or sales.
3 *The return on capital* – what return on invested capital has been achieved and whether any products have been unsuccessful and why.
4 *Forecasts* – has the company achieved its past forecasts of sales and profits?
5 *Existing strengths and weaknesses* – in each major field of activity, marketing, production, research and development, and finance, for example, to assess profit by product; a company has to know which products sell themselves and which ones require effort to sell.

The Present[16]

The task now is to project the future earnings of the company for its existing products and for those in development. Any external factors which will influence demand or profits need to be considered. This activity should be carried out for each product group sold by the company. The following points should be studied:

The Market

What has been the past expansion and what future expansion is expected over the period?

Sales and Market Share

What is the present market share of the company, and what is projected and when? Is the increase in sales too great to be achieved both from a marketing and production viewpoint? Is the company increasing sales above, below or in line with the market increase?

Prices and Margins

What are the economic conditions in the industry? Is the product near to the end of its life and, if so, how much will prices have to be cut each year? *N.B.* A determined attempt to obtain a larger share of a declining market could cause severe price cutting. This study may reveal that certain lines may have to be phased out, as their margins are too small to justify their existence.

Costs

The trend of costs must be studied, taking into account inflation, wage settlements and material costs, but also taking into account any cost reduction possible. In certain cases a product may be redesigned, given a new identity, and sold with an increased margin. An estimate should be made of any increases in overhead costs, which could arise from increased activity, such as an expanded sales force, or from increased production facilities.

Cash Generation

Retained earnings and depreciation are shown for each year, as inflow. The outflows are capital expenditure and increased working capital for stocks and work in progress, less any increase in creditors. The amounts required in each year for any increase in net working capital can be calculated by examining the ratios of stocks and debtors and creditors for the company in the past, to sales turnover. These ratios may have to be revised if the company has to hold higher stocks to give faster delivery, if longer credit terms have to be given to customers, or if creditors are paid more quickly, to increase purchase discounts. The figure can be taken as about 20 per cent (a fifth) of increased sales, but should be calculated for each industry.[17]

Average Assets
The starting and finishing figures for fixed assets at the beginning and end of each year are divided by two to arrive at the average figure.

Other Ratios
Gross profits and net profits are shown as a percentage of sales for each year. The return on capital employed is calculated for each year on the average assets.

The Gap
Finally the gap between the profits required and those forecast is shown. This is the gap that the company must fill to achieve its objective.

STRATEGIC PLAN

Purpose

The purpose of the strategic plan is to find out if the company needs to move from its present position to achieve the objectives set within the time-scale allowed and, if not, when and how it should change direction. From the study of the present position, the company will be aware of the following facts:

1 The profits forecast for the existing products and those under development for the period, allowing for any cost reduction possible, and any changes in prices.
2 The likely effect of the external environment on the prospects of the company. What dangers it should plan to avoid, and what opportunities are available to be exploited.
3 The present position of the company, its strengths and weaknesses.

The objective is to direct the activities of all sectors of the company to achieve the aims set. All the resources and talents of the company should be employed to give the best return possible. The correct resources must be committed at the right time, in the correct quantity and must be properly used. The plan will show what action should be taken, when, and with what results, to achieve the objectives. Actions on possible acquisitions, new product developments and licensing have to be taken now to yield profits in the future, before the return from existing products has begun to fall.[18]

Filling the Gap

The company is aware of the gap between profits from its present and its new products and the profit objective set. The best possibilities should now be selected to enable the objectives to be reached, or else the objectives should be revised. Whether a gap exists or not, the company will also wish to find answers to the following problems:

1. *Technical or market gaps* – either new product or market opportunities or threats which the company must meet, either to its key products or in its principal markets, at present or in the future.
2. *Growth rate* – whether the company is growing as fast as the market and its competitors, or not.
3. *Balance* – whether the company is dependent on one industry, one product, or even one principal customer.
4. *Excess resources* – the surplus resources which the company must employ or else dispose of, because certain products are being phased out.
5. *Other limitations* – what other limitations exist, which are holding the company back?

The various alternatives possible have to be assessed, and the ones most likely to yield profit over the long term should be chosen. Consideration should be given to the degree of risk involved, by projecting the effects on the company should any of the assumptions on markets, prices, and the timing of the receipt of orders prove to be incorrect.

Company Development Plan

At this stage the company has decided the objectives that are to be achieved, and what new activities are required to meet the profit forecasts. The company then has to produce the following plans to implement the necessary actions.

Diversification Plan

This plan will outline how the company proposes to diversify into new fields and new markets, whether this will be achieved by acquisition or not and, if so, what standards must be set for any acquisitions and what companies are to be considered. The objective can be met perhaps by licensing a product, or by forming a joint company with, for example, an American company to exploit the potential market in Europe. On the other hand, the company may decide to undertake its own research and development in this field. In all cases, the effect on the company's competitive position over the long and the short term, will indicate the action to take to optimise the potential growth prospects.

Market and Product Development Plan

This plan covers the activities of the company in its existing product and market fields. A decision may be taken to expand sales by increasing sales to existing customers by adapting existing or developing new products, to fill present or future needs; a comprehensive plan of the developments proposed is required. Assessments should be made of the probability of meeting the technical, cost and time objectives laid down, as well as the sales targets. In addition, the manpower and facilities available have to be allocated, and an overall budget prepared.

Operating Plans

Detailed organisation is needed in each sphere of the operations of the company, to ensure that programmes are initiated and facilities, money and staff are allocated to meet the schedules. In all cases, budgets must be prepared, which can be monitored to see how the company is progressing against target.

Marketing

The assumptions on the market must be stated:

1 Competition
2 The sales expected
3 Actual and potential customers
4 Pricing and discount policies

5 Distribution methods
6 Sales promotion
7 Advertising and public relations budgets
8 Salesmen's compensation
9 Any methods to improve selling effectiveness

Production

The work load, production methods, new facilities, cost reduction plans, testing and quality control, and cost targets should be included in the plan.

Management

The organisation, management and staff required, should be explained, what staff are available, how the gaps will be filled, and when organisational changes will be made.

Financial and Administrative

This plan will consist of budgets and cash flow statements for the whole plan, draft balance sheets, operating statements, plans for better use of existing resources, how the finance will be provided, and any improvements required in the reporting system to monitor the plan.

CONTROL

Throughout the life of the plan, there will be certain variables and sub-objectives which must be achieved within a certain time if the objectives are to be met. These critical points must be monitored regularly to find out current performance. Any new information on the environment, which alters the existing assumptions, could result in a revision of the plan. Project plans on the progress of research and development projects, revised sales forecasts, actual performance against budget are all vital information. Finally, the plan must be revised when it no longer represents the best way in which the company can use its resources to the greatest advantage (see Figure 6.1).

	Past Years			*Current*	*Future Years*		
	-3	*-2*	*-1*	*Year*	*+1*	*+2*	*+3*
Operations							
Market (£)							
Increase (%)							
Market share							
Sales by product †							
Increase (%)							
Price levels							
Direct costs							
Gross profit							
Net profit							
Tax							
Earnings							
Dividends							
Retained earnings							
Cash Flow							
Retained earnings							
Depreciation							
Other							
Total inflow							
Capital expenditure							
Extra working capital							
Other							
Total outflow							
Net inflow +							
Net outflow –							
Average Assets							
Fixed assets							
Net working capital							
Net assets							
Statistics							
Gross profit/sales (%)							
Net profit/sales (%)							
Net profit/net assets (%)							
Dividend cover							
The Gap							
Sales increase required (%)							
Gross profit increase req'd (%)							
Net profit increase req'd (%)							

Figure 6.1 Sales Forecast* (£000)

* See also D.R.C. HALFORD Business Planning Chapters 13 and 14, for detailed account of how a forecast is prepared and amended until the forecast sales and profits equal the objectives set.

† The schedule on sales should be backed up by a forecast of sales by customer – existing and projected – showing the probability of a sale, when the order and the delivery are expected, and past sales, by customer.

An institution's decision whether or not to invest in a private company will be greatly influenced by the quality and depth of the management's forward planning and its credibility with regard to the company's existing performance.

No one likes entrusting their money to someone who has only a hazy idea of where he is going and therefore little understanding of the problems he may meet in the future. A fatal crash or forced landing may be their only reward.

APPENDIX 1:

POSITION AUDIT FOR NEW AND EXISTING PRODUCTS[19]

Markets

Size, structure, trends.

Existing Total Markets

Sales and profits for the last three years, including substitutes and products with similar uses and applications:

By country.
By industry group.
By product group.

1 Fluctuation in demand: over past three years has demand fluctuated for home and overseas markets and if so why?
2 Market type: is the market expanding, contracting, static, or is a new market being developed?
3 Demand type: is demand seasonal, one time, or is there a replacement market?
4 Price stability: how stable have prices been? Give reasons for any fluctuations.

Environmental

1 Political:
   (a) Government changes and their effects on demand.
   (b) Current government policies and future trends – e.g. monopoly and small business legislation.

(c) Attitude towards industry.

2 Economic:

(a) Population trends.

(b) GNP – boom/recession – health of earnings in main customers; Credit squeeze/relaxation; Capital investment trend.

(c) Balance of payments, the effect of fluctuation in exchange rates or any devaluation on the demand for competitive and company products in principal markets.

(d) International trading practices, tariffs, EEC, import quotas, undeveloped countries' imports.

(e) Price indices – effect on costs of inflation – rate per annum; for raw materials and components; finished goods; cost of living.

3 Technological: Home and overseas:

(a) Effect on existing and proposed lines and on demand for these products.

(b) Suppliers – effect on the market and on the products available of cheaper components or materials.

(c) Competition – competitive developments and their effects.

(d) Substitutes – external to the industry and their effects.

4 Social effects:

(a) A shorter working week – costs – increased leisure.

(b) Changes in the age structure of the population.

(c) Educational policy changes.

Technical Standards

1 Market leader: who sets the standards, the largest user or largest producer?

2 New production techniques: will there be resistance to new products or techniques?

3 Specific requirements: specific future product requirements resulting from changing industry standards – interface requirements. Time scale and advantage of these new standards over existing products.

User Needs

Price performance.

1 Price trends: possibility of reduction in prices over the period.

2 Specifications/price: essential and desirable characteristics.
3 Design, styling, quality and reliability: standard and performance required.
4 Delivery and stocking requirements: required for equipment, spares and supplies.
5 Service/maintenance and after sales service requirements: on maximum response time for answering service calls.
6 Credit: customers requirements and industry standards.
7 Economic criteria: pay back etc.

Customers and End Users

1 Customers and end users: trends in requirements and practices.
2 Past sales by Company } by customer. by industry.
3 Existing customers: future expected demand.
4 Other customers: future expected demand.
5 Customers' preferences: why have customers changed from company and from competitors?
6 Large users: which ones are likely to supply their own needs.
7 Profitability: customers and end users (i.e. their purchasing power).

Competition

1 Product lines: relevance and life cycle of competitors' and company's product line.
2 Financial position: profitability, overtrading and over capacity.
3 Prices and terms: company's and competitors.
4 Market shares: home and export – company and competitors – last three years.
5 Sales appeals: reputation, strengths, weaknesses – company and competition; distribution, service, quality, price, discount, delivery, key selling points and reputation with customers (complaints).
6 Technology: state of developments, patents, licences etc. company and competition.
7 Costs: high or low cost producers – company and competition.

Potential Market

1 Demand potential:
   (*a*) Next three to five years – maximum/minimum.
   (*b*) By country.
   (*c*) By industry and customer.
   (*d*) Pattern of demand.
2 New products and applications required:
   (*a*) Volume and timing.
   (*b*) Potential life cycle.
3 Price levels:
   (*a*) Expected by users.
   (*b*) Expected by suppliers.
4 Market leader: reaction to an attempt to reduce his market share by a new entrant.
5 Sales organisation: required for sales, distribution, service, by geographical regions.
6 Sales promotion and advertising: efforts required.
7 Customers' acceptance of change: factors preventing or assisting customers from changing suppliers – e.g. long term agreements.

Company Marketing

1 Company's business:
   (*a*) What customer needs do we satisfy?
   (*b*) Do we satisfy all needs in a field or only a few?
   (*c*) What will customers need in three to five years time? How will our products match up (life cycles)?
2 Products:
   (*a*) What new products should we introduce and when?
   (*b*) Will these new products strengthen our new product line by making it more complete, or will they compete with existing products?
   (*c*) Which existing products need to be phased out and when?
3 Market image:
   (*a*) Will our image be strengthened?
   (*b*) Will our reputation help to sell it or not?
   (*c*) Is it a move into a new technology, or into an expanding growth market?
   (*d*) What features will influence success or failure?

4 Existing customers:
  (*a*) Can existing customers use it?
  (*b*) Market share expected
  (*c*) Potential customers
  (*d*) Freedom to change – long term contracts with discounts
5 New customers and new markets:
  (*a*) How long will it take the products to become accepted by new and existing customers in established markets and in new markets?
  (*b*) How long before volume orders will be placed, (i.e. when product has been incorporated into an existing or new design)

Distribution

1 Distributors:
  (*a*) Will our new products strengthen our position with our distributors?
  (*b*) Are our distributors as credit worthy, as well trained, as aggressive and as well equipped as our competitors?
2 Salesmen:
  (*a*) What is the ability, quality, aggressiveness and level of training of our salesmen as against competition? (Use of selling time)
  (*b*) How effective is our sales effort – at home and abroad?
  (*c*) Is the compensation of our salesmen and distributors as good as our competitors?
  (*d*) Level of training required.
  (*e*) Can our organisation cope with the expected demands for service and technical assistance?
3 Sales promotion, advertising and P.R.:
  (*a*) How effective are we compared with our competitors?
  (*b*) What are our plans for the future?
4 Launch timing:
  (*a*) Design.
  (*b*) Evaluation.
  (*c*) Product testing.
  (*d*) Field trials.
  (*e*) Production.
  (*f*) Evaluation and acceptance.
  (*g*) Volume orders!

Research and Development

1 Manpower and expertise: the availability of suitable manpower and skills to solve problems – must company learn or acquire those skills?
2 Technical position: patents – company and competition – technical lead.
3 Development or licence: decide which.
4 Development: technical and cost feasibility, expenditure required.
5 Testing and evaluation: requirements to be met and how these differ from existing standards.
6 Manuals: preparation work on manuals for operating and maintaining the equipment.

Production

1 Techniques: can existing techniques be used, or must new ones be learned?
2 Productive capacity:
   (*a*) Existing space utilisation.
   (*b*) Additional space required.
   (*c*) Utilisation and output over the last three years and over next three years.
   (*d*) Quantity and type of additional plant and equipment required for volume including the new products:
      replacements.
      test equipment.
      special facilities.
      mechanical handling.
   (*e*) Quality and performance; standards and inspection required.
   (*f*) Cost reduction plans and expected increases in productivity.
   (*g*) Tooling requirements.
   (*h*) Cost feasibility – low or high cost producer.

Buying

1 Components and materials: types and quantities required.

2 Suppliers: number, past delivery and quality performance (avoid single source).
3 Prices: next three years.
4 Make or buy decisions.

Labour

1 Existing labour force: age and capability by category.
2 Labour supply: available by category.
3 Labour force required over period: quantity, type, skills.
4 Labour relations: communication – strikes and reasons.
5 Pay and conditions: compare – settlements.
6 Labour turnover: reasons.

Management

1 Existing management:
  (*a*) Age, experience and ability to grow.
  (*b*) Capability versus competition.
  (*c*) Turnover last three years.
2 Succession:
  (*a*) Development and promotion plans.
  (*b*) Existence of No. 2's.
  (*c*) New management required.
3 Turnover: Last three years.
4 Management view of company: future prospects.

Organisation

1 Organisation chart.
2 Job descriptions.
3 Communications.
4 Operating decisions: day to day assignment of operating decisions.
5 Planning and budgeting.
6 Reporting: information required and frequency.

Budgets

1 Direct costs: labour and materials for the various production

quantities required for each product – possibility of cost reduction.

2 Production overheads:
   (*a*) Management and works administration.
   (*b*) Amortisation of tooling and R & D Costs.

3 Management and Administrative overheads: salaries.

4 Selling and distribution:
   (*a*) Salaries.
   (*b*) Distribution.
   (*c*) Advertising.

5 Overall operations budgets:
   (*a*) Effects of varying production levels.
   (*b*) Breakeven charts.

6 Cash flow: Cash flow for the projected inflow and capital outflow.

7 Profit:
   (*a*) DCF return – will project earn sufficient cash to repay capital cost in the initial safe period to provide a satisfactory return?
   (*b*) Probability of reaching sales volume by time expected – possible delays?
   (*c*) How vulnerable to a price cut especially if a high breakeven point or if a high boughtout content?

REFERENCES

1 Research Report No. 12. *Dynamics of Small Firms,* HMSO, London 1971, pp. 31-32.

2 *Financial Facilities for Small Firms.* 1 success, 1 failure, 3 plodders is mentioned as the normal success rate, p. 139.

3 A company can supply products to several customers, all bidding for the same contract. When statistics are being collected from customers on forecast sales, allowance should be made for this.

4 *Dynamics of Small Firms,* pp. 30-31.

5 'The New Entrepreneur', *Management Today,* January 1971, p. 10.

6 *Planning in Business,* Stanford Research Institute, California, 1963, p. 2.

7 E.F.L. BRECH, *What is your Business*? BIM, London, 1969, p. 5.

8 See also: *Environment Change and Corporate Strategy,* Stanford Research Institute, California, 1960.
D.R.C. HALFORD, *Business Planning,* Pan Piper, London 1971.
H.F.R. PERRIN, *Focus the Future,* Management Publications Ltd, London 1971.

9 *Environment Change and Corporate Strategy,* Stanford Research Institute, California, 1960, p.2.

10 D.R.C. HALFORD, *Business Planning,* p.140.

11 See *Overseas Investment – A Guide to Planning for UK Manufacturers,* BIM, London, 1968.

12 For small companies, the chief executive may find that the only time he has available for thinking about the business is outside the office – e.g. in the bath, or on the golf course.

13 H.F.R. PERRIN, *Focus the Future,* pp.23-27.

14 Some merchant banks require pre-tax profits of £200-£250,000 before they will sponsor an issue.

15 Bolton Report, p.18.

16 D.R.C. HALFORD, *Business Planning,* Chapters 13/14.

17 *Business Ratios,* Dunn and Bradstreet, Issue 3, p.44.
Note: By industry, ratios of sales/net current assets for quoted companies are shown by industry and vary from 3 to 5 times, but in certain cases rise to much higher figures for distributors.

18 *Dynamics of Small Firms,* p.28. The particular managerial capability or luck in choosing a growth market will generally have taken place in the fairly remote past and may not stem from the capability of the present management.

19 See also: *Overseas Investment* – A Guide to Planning for UK Manufacturers; H.F.R. PERRIN, *Focus the Future; Policy Formation for the Smaller Company,* BIM, London, 1969.

7

Initial Negotiations

INTRODUCTION

After the initial investigation and evaluation have shown a bank that a company is likely to be a profitable investment, the parties must negotiate the terms on which an investment is to be made. In any initial write up given to the bank, the company should indicate the broad investment terms that it is prepared to accept.

Whether or not these terms will be acceptable to the bank will depend on the existing position of the company and the potential future value to an investor. Both parties must negotiate these basic terms until either agreement is reached, or the whole project is abandoned. Only after settlement of the basic terms can the drafting of the various agreements start.

LETTER OF OFFER

Once the initial negotiations have taken place, a bank, if it has decided it is interested in making an investment, will make the company an offer.

A letter of offer is written to the company, outlining the basic terms on which the bank is prepared to invest. This offer is subject to the following conditions:

1 To a satisfactory report by the investigating accountants, confirming that the financial position of the company is not materially worse than has already been disclosed to the bank. (*Note.* If the company has already submitted a satisfactory accountant's report, one important and time-consuming step has been eliminated.)
2 To the completion of a formal agreement, to the necessary amendment of the memorandum and articles, and to the directors giving the usual warranties on tax, estate duty and the proper conduct of the affairs of the company.
3 To acceptance taking place within the time limit laid down. The bank may ask for a second copy of the letter to be signed and returned as acceptance of the terms. However, it is certainly open to the company to accept certain conditions, and to suggest amendments to others. No return letter should be sent to the bank before consulting the company's solicitors and auditors.

The points normally covered by a letter of offer, are to be found in a check list at the end of this chapter. In subsequent chapters, equity participation and loan facilities are discussed, and also the covenants required by the company and the directors.

AGREEMENTS

The following documents are required to be completed before an investment is made by a bank.

Shareholder's Agreement

This document defines the rights and duties of each party, protecting the bank's position as a minority shareholder (see Chapter 9). It also defines the method by which the bank will take an equity stake in the company.

Debenture Trust Deed

This deed secures the debenture, lays down the terms of the loan, and defines the relationship of the debenture with any other secured loans, such as a bank overdraft. It also lays down the limit for secured and overall borrowings. In many respects, the terms of this deed are very similar to those found in a trust deed for a publicly quoted debenture.

Warranties, Covenants, Indemnities and Undertakings

Both the documents above contain the following types of clauses:

Warranties
These warrant the correctness of the accounts and other information given to the bank, on which a decision to invest was made.

Undertakings
These are concerned with the future conduct of the company, which could adversely affect the value of the bank's equity, or the asset or earnings backing.

Covenants
These relate to the appointment of the bank as the company's financial adviser, on each party's obligations at the time of a public issue, and on the appointment of auditors.

Indemnities
The directors and their personal representatives (i.e. executors) indemnify the bank against any additional claims for tax, for damages, and for legal costs for remedying any breach of any undertaking, covenant or warranty, given in the agreements. The guarantee is 'joint and several', so that the bank can proceed against one, all, or some of the directors, whose liability is unlimited. Hence, very careful consideration must be given before these warranties, indemnities and undertakings are given, but especially to those which relate to future performance, and thus restrict the freedom of the company in the future.

Memorandum and Articles

Amendments to the memorandum and articles are required before any changes can be made in the capital structure of the company. (i.e. any increases of the authorised and/or issued share capital, the right to appoint special directors, special dividend rights etc.).

Service Agreements

The directors will be required to sign service agreements, laying down their salaries, pension rights, other fringe benefits and any profit-sharing arrangements. There may also be a clause requiring the directors not to compete with the company on certain conditions, should they leave their employment with the company.

Board Meetings, and Extraordinary General Meetings

Agendas, resolutions and minutes have to be prepared before holding the necessary meetings, to approve any changes in borrowing powers, the raising of a debenture, increasing the company's share capital, and for allotting any shares to the bank.

WORKING RELATIONSHIPS

Although these agreements are necessary, the investment will only be successful, if both parties build up a good working relationship with one another. Both sides must want to make the operation a joint success, by contributing their special skills, whilst respecting one another's rights and opinions. As one company lawyer said: 'The test of a good investment is whether or not the agreement is left unconsulted in the filing cabinet, as the parties consider the needs of the company to be more important than their individual rights.' For this to happen, the company must not only be successful, but there must also be mutual trust between the directors and the bank.

In the next chapter, the sections of the shareholder's agreement, relating to equity capital, are examined, and in the following chapters the company's bargaining position and the valuation of the equity are considered.

CHECKLIST: LETTER OF OFFER

Stating terms on which a bank is prepared to invest.

Conditions

Accountant's report. Subject to a satisfactory accountant's report,

showing that the financial position of the company is not materially worse than has already been disclosed.
Formal agreement. Subject to the completion of a formal agreement, to the amendment of the memorandum and articles, and to the directors giving warranties on tax etc.
Time limit. Subject to acceptance of the terms before a certain date by signing and returning a copy of the letter.

Capital Structure

To avoid any confusion, the following points are stated as basic assumptions:
Share capital. The authorised and issued share capital is confirmed by restating the number of shares in each class, authorised and issued, and their par value.
Options etc. The existence of any options or conversion rights outstanding, either into share or loan capital, and if none a nil return.
Loan capital. Details of any loans by the bank, directors' loans or other loans.
Subsidiaries. The names of any subsidiaries should be listed, together with their share capital, issued and authorised.
Other companies. Other companies to be acquired.
Future capital structure. Authorised and issued.

Debenture

Principal amount. £xx,xxx now made available. £xx,xxx to be provided between *(date)* and *(date)* provided that net profits, as defined, for the year ending *(date)* reach £xx,xxx.
Interest rate. *X%* payable half yearly in arrears.
Security. A first floating charge on the company's assets, undertaking and goodwill, ranking *pari passu* with the bank overdraft. The bank overdraft being limited to £xx,xxx. Directors' loans as unsecured loans, to rank after the secured loans, to bear interest at *X%*, and to be repaid on (*date*). *N.B.* After the repayment of the debenture, subject to any limitations imposed by the bank.
Repayment

1 The period of the loans xx years.
2 Repayment to start on *(date)* and end on *(date)* by means of

X equal installments of £xx,xxx.

3 Right to early repayment by the company.

Borrowing restrictions. To be imposed on secured and overall borrowings.

Equity

Type of share. Ordinary, preferred ordinary or preference.
How acquired. Purchase, subscription, option or conversion.
Option or Conversion Rights. Period *X* years from *(date).*
Number of shares. Or equity per cent and limit in equity per cent of increased equity.

Valuation

1 Price or formula based on net profits, or on asset value, between *(date)* and *(date).*
2 Multiple options, if any.

Dividends

1 Bank.
2 Other shareholders.
3 Overall limit or cover.

Public Issue

At the time of a public issue:
Issuing house. Bank to act as issuing house.
Conversion. Any special shares held by the bank to be converted into ordinary shares.
Shares for public issue. The proportion of shares to be made available on a public issue by the existing shareholders and the bank, e.g. pro rata or 50-50.

Board of Directors

Directors to retire. Mr. O and Mr. P to resign with £x,xxx compensation each.
Directors' remuneration.

1 Salary and pension Mr. Q £x,xxx.
2 Salary and pension Mr. R £x,xxx.
3 Commission, if any.
4 Overall limit on directors' emoluments.

Service agreements. Mr. Q and Mr. R to enter into service agreements for *X* years.
Insurance. Mr. Q's life to be insured for £xx,xxx, while the debenture is outstanding.
Bank nominee director. The right to appoint and remove director. Remuneration to be paid by the company.
Other interests of directors. Any arrangements to be made on properties used by the company, on interests in subsidiaries or in associated companies.

Costs

The company to pay the bank's legal, accounting and investigation costs.

8

Shareholder's Agreement 1: Equity Capital

INTRODUCTION

This chapter covers the principal clauses in the shareholder's agreement, which is signed by all parties, relating to the acquisition of an equity interest by a bank.

CLASS OF SHARES AND DIVIDEND RIGHTS

The bank can purchase or subscribe for new shares of a class which is already authorised in the memorandum of association, e.g. ordinary or preference shares. Alternatively, a special class of share can be created and the memorandum and articles changed accordingly.[1] A preferred ordinary share can be issued with a fixed cumulative dividend, payable half yearly. The dividend policy must depend upon the financial position of the company, and upon the needs of all the shareholders, as follows:

The Bank
The bank will want a return on its money and may wish to restrict dividends where there are debentures outstanding.

The Directors
They will prefer to receive earned, rather than unearned income, so would be happy to agree to restrict dividends or to declare none; provided that their salaries fully reflect the current market rate for their jobs, with an extra incentive for achievement. From the point of view of the company, paying directors' salaries, assuming they are fully allowable for tax, is preferable to paying dividends which are paid out of taxed profits.

The Shareholders
They will not object to the policy outlined above, if the directors are also the principal shareholders. However, where there are outside shareholders, who are not employed by the company, but who have been receiving dividends, any restriction on dividends could represent a severe hardship.

DIVIDEND POLICY

The dividend policy must be decided after considering the existing financial position of the company and its future financial needs. Outside shareholders of a company with pretax profits of £100,000 would be unlikely to agree to a severe restriction or total limitation on the payment of dividends; whereas shareholders in a company with pretax profits of £40,000 would be more likely to be building up their capital, and already forgoing dividends, prior to the bank's investment. The possibilities are as follows: either,

1 A fixed cumulative preferred dividend is paid to the bank. A similar dividend is paid to the ordinary shareholders and then all dividends declared subsequently are shared equally among all the ordinary shareholders; or
2 After the preferred ordinary dividend is paid, all further dividends are shared equally; or
3 All ordinary shareholders are treated the same.

Except when dividends are requried to be paid under a shortfall distribution direction,[2] an overall limit can be placed on the payment of dividends, unless the bank agrees to waive this limit. This can be expressed as follows:

1 Except for the cumulative preferred dividend, no dividends are to be payable if net profits after tax, as defined, are below £*X*.
2 Any dividends paid after the preferred ordinary dividend must be covered *X* times by net profits after tax, as defined.

In the case of new shares, these normally rank in full for any dividends declared in the financial year in which the shares were issued, but not for any dividends relating to earlier periods. However, should conversion take place after the half year, then the dividend can be reduced in proportion to the period. *Note:* in the case of conversion rights, it is wise to ensure that one does not pay both interest and dividends on the loan monies converted into equity. e.g. Monies converted in month four of a financial year should not receive interest for four months as well as an annual dividend. If shares are held for less than a year, then the dividends payable should be strictly proportional to the period for which the shares were held.

ACQUIRING AN EQUITY HOLDING

The bank can acquire an equity share interest in various different ways:

1 By purchasing existing shares.
2 By subscribing for new shares.
3 By obtaining an option to subscribe for shares at a certain price within a certain period.
4 By means of conversion rights, attached to a debenture or loan stock.

Note: Any shares issued must be free of all liens, charges or encumbrances, and have all rights attached to them as laid down in the agreement.

PURCHASING EXISTING SHARES

If existing shares are to be purchased from some of the present shareholders, share transfers signed by the shareholders have to be lodged with the company. The directors then have to register the shares in the name of the new shareholder.

The dividend rights must be defined showing whether these shares are *ex* or *cum* any dividend that has been declared, or when they become entitled to any dividends declared subsequently.

SUBSCRIBING FOR NEW SHARES

The company must issue an allotment letter for any new shares to be subscribed by the bank, showing the class and number of shares, the subscription price and the entitlement. Before this can be done, a resolution will have to be passed, increasing the issued (and possibly the authorised) share capital of the company, at an extraordinary general meeting.[3] The directors will also have to authorise the issue of the allotment letter. When payment is received by the company, a share certificate is issued in the name of the bank and the necessary returns are filed with the Registrar of Companies.

Assuming that the bank is to subscribe for 25 per cent of the issued share capital, as increased by the new subscription, the present share capital must be increased by $33\frac{1}{3}$ per cent to enable the necessary shares to be available for allotment.

Example

Present issued ordinary share capital	75 shares
Increase ordinary share capital by $33\frac{1}{3}$ per cent	25 shares
New issued = ordinary share capital	100 shares

Shareholders – original	75 shares	75 per cent
– bank	25 shares	25 per cent

Formula

$$\frac{\text{new subscription as percentage of final equity}}{\text{existing equity as percentage of final equity}} = \text{Increase required in existing share capital.}$$

$$\frac{25}{75} \times 100 = 33\tfrac{1}{3} \text{ per cent}$$

OPTIONS TO SUBSCRIBE

The bank can be given the right to subscribe for shares as follows:

Class of share

X% preferred ordinary shares of £1.

of the allotment letter. When payment is received by the company, a
issued share capital, as increased by the new subscription, the present

Period

To be exercised either wholly or in part within *X* months of the issue of the annual audited accounts for the *X* consecutive years beginning (*date*). The company is restricted from altering the date of the end of the financial year. The option can be exercised immediately, if a public issue or takeover is about to take place, or if the issue of the accounts is unreasonably delayed. *Note:* A three to five year option period is normal, either starting immediately, or from a date laid down in the agreement.

Option Price

The price at which the option is to be exercised, is either fixed, or depends upon a formula.[4] If the formula depends on pre-tax net profits achieved, a multiple (six to eight) will be stated, which is to be applied to either the pre-tax net profits achieved in the last financial year, or to average pre-tax net profits over a period (for example, the last three years). The formula is as follows, and can be based on net profits or net assets. In all cases, the issued share capital is the number of shares issued *before* the option is exercised:

(*a*) *Net Profits*

$$\text{price per share} = \frac{\text{actual or average net profits x multiple}}{\text{issued share capital (pre-option)}}$$

(*b*) *Net Assets*

$$\text{price per share} = \frac{\text{net assets or average net assets}}{\text{issued share capital (pre-option)}}$$

Note: Both net assets and net profits would be closely defined.

Number of shares

There are two possible methods:

1. The actual number of shares is fixed, with the price per share being fixed or variable.
2. The value of the amount payable is stated, the number of the shares subscribed depends on whether the price is fixed or variable (fractions are normally excluded).

Where the number of shares subscribed is variable, it is advisable to fix an upper limit. For example, the option is exercisable into not more than 30 per cent of the total ordinary equity issued, preferred and ordinary, after full exercise of the option. Otherwise, if profits fell, the bank could acquire control. The bank may also ask for a lower limit, (for example, 15 per cent), in case profits rose faster than anticipated. As already explained, if percentages of equity are used, it must be made clear whether these percentages relate to the share capital, before or after, the exercise of the option. The share capital must also be clearly defined (preference and ordinary, or ordinary only).

Multiple Options

It is possible to negotiate multiple options, which give the bank the right to exercise its option at various stages of development. This arrangement can be used as a compromise solution where there is a dispute about the multiple, the level of profits or the starting date for exercising the option.

For example, *first option.* Into 25 per cent of the issued share capital, prior to exercising the option, at a fixed price of £x per share. This fixed price option gives the bank the right to subscribe early on before the loan monies have increased profits substantially. In this case, the share price would be based on the company's existing market value at the date of the agreement, using either an earnings, or an asset valuation.

Second option. Into 20 per cent of the issued equity, before exercise of the second option. A factor would be applied to net profits for the year, prior to the exercise of the option (or to an average level of net profits), to arrive at a value for the company. A delay could be imposed upon the exercise of the second option to allow the company time to build up profits.

Example

		Issued Share Capital			Option
	Equity (%)	Prior	New Shares	Final	Period (yrs)*
First Option	25	80	20	100	1 – 3
Second Option	20	100	20	120	3 – 5
Final	$33\frac{1}{3}$	80	40	120	

* from the signing of the agreement

Unissued Shares
Sufficient unissued shares must be kept by the company to satisfy the option. (Hence the reason for the upper limit of the shareholding in order to define this figure.)

CONVERSION RIGHTS

These rights are attached either to loan stocks or to debentures, to allow all or part of the loan to be converted into equity on terms similar to those contained in an option agreement. Part of the loan is therefore applied to subscribing for the new shares, and the balance is repaid on maturity. Very nearly the same effect can be obtained if the proceeds of any subscription for shares in an option agreement must go first towards repaying any loan outstanding.

PROTECTION OF CONVERSION RIGHTS AND OPTIONS TO SUBSCRIBE

During the time that options to subscribe or conversion rights are outstanding, the following restrictions must apply to the company and its subsidiaries, otherwise the original rights granted could be watered down and their value reduced. The following clauses are referred to as 'anti-dilution' restrictions:

1 Unless any conversion rights or options are adjusted accordingly, the company will not make any reduction of capital involving repayment of capital, or reduction of uncalled liability, nor will it make any capital distribution.
2 The creation or issue of any new class of equity capital shall be prohibited.
3 No capitalisation of profits or reserves shall be effected except in shares of the appropriate class, and in the case of such an issue the conversion or option rights shall be appropriately adjusted.
4 If any offer or right is given to the shareholders to subscribe or purchase shares, the option or conversion rights outstanding (i.e. the subscription price or the number of shares) will be adjusted appropriately so that the rights or options are not diluted by such an offer.
5 No repayment of any convertible loan or debenture stock will

be made until after the conversion period has expired.

6 Convertible loan stock holders can be given the right to convert within a defined period after a voluntary liquidation, in order to participate equally with other shareholders in the assets available for distribution.

These restrictions have been adapted from those laid down by the Stock Exchange for publicly quoted options and convertible loan stocks.[5]

DEFINITION OF NET PROFITS

Net profits for the calculation of any option price or conversion terms, are defined as follows:

1 Excluding non-trading profits or losses, but including receipts for 'know how'.
2 Excluding profits and losses of a capital nature.
3 After deduction of all private research and development expenditure.
4 After charging all expenses of working and management, including directors and former directors emoluments, proper depreciation and amortisation, and interest.
5 After proper provision for losses on contracts, past or present, and for bad and doubtful debts. *Note*: Past contracts relate to Government contracts, where progress payments can be re-negotiated, if the costs or overhead rates are revised after the job has been completed.
6 After deduction of tax.
7 After making such adjustments, as the auditors shall think appropriate.

MEMORANDUM AND ARTICLES

Any changes required in the memorandum and articles of association, to enable the agreement to be implemented, will have to be agreed and a draft initialled by both parties.

These changes will be carried out during or before completion by holding an extraordinary general meeting. The type of amendments are as follows:

Share capital. Any alteration of the authorised issued share capital, any reorganisation of the share capital, any capitalisation of reserves, the creation of a holding company, conversion of director's loans into equity, or the creation of a new class of share for the bank, e.g. preferred ordinary shares.
Borrowing limits. Any variation in borrowing limits required.
Dividends. The dividend rights must be laid down for all classes of share.
Special director. The right of the bank to appoint a special director will be recorded, together with their right to change this director as required, and to appoint an alternative.
Size of the board. The maximum size of the board may have to be changed, either to make a place for the bank director, or because no new directors are to be appointed above a certain number.
Quorum. In certain cases, the bank may want the quorum at a board meeting to include the special bank director, unless a notice and the agenda for the meeting was circulated *X* days before the date of the meeting. This clause would only be applicable, where the financial management of the company was considered to be very unsophisticated.

PUBLIC QUOTATION

The following agreements are made between the parties:

(1) The bank will act as an issuing house for a public issue on terms generally available from a reputable issuing house.
(2) The timing of the public issue will be the decision of the company, after consultation with the bank. If the bank refuses to act in any public issue, the company should have the right to use another issuing house, and the bank should co-operate fully and take all the necessary steps to make the issue a success as if it were acting as the issuing house. It will also agree to release the company from the agreement. *Note:* this prevents the bank from blocking any public issue, in order to gain control of the company by subscribing more equity. Normally, the bank would be the first to recommend a public issue, to release its funds for investment elsewhere. Therefore, this situation is unlikely to occur.
(3) Prior to any public issue, the bank's preferred ordinary shares will be converted into ordinary shares, with no compensation, except

for the payment of any dividends outstanding.
(4) If the shares are offered to the public by means of an 'Offer for sale', 35 per cent of the issued share capital must be made available to the market. Each shareholder, therefore, makes this proportion of shares available from his holding. On this basis however, if the bank acquires more than 20 per cent of the total ordinary shares issued, then the existing shareholders will not retain control. The percentage acquired by the bank can safely be increased to 30 per cent if the bank agrees to make available *half* the requirements for a public issue from its shareholding. This factor should always be considered when any discussion is taking place on the bank's equity entitlement.

Example

1 *Each give up 35 per cent of their equity holding*

	Public %	*Bank* %	*Family* %	*Total* %
Before issue		20	80	=100
After issue	+35	–7	–28	
	35	13	52	=100

2 *50-50 Split*

Before issue		32	68	=100
After issue	+35	–17.5	–17.5	
	35	14.5	50.5	=100

It may be advisable to agree some level of profits at which a public issue will be made; e.g. over £150,000 pre-tax, in the unlikely event that the bank wishes to block a public issue.
(5) If an offer is made for all the shares, the parties will consult together. Again, the bank should *not* be able to block any takeover which is in the interests of all the shareholders, provided the offer is made available to all the shareholders.
(6) No party can make a transfer, either directly or indirectly, to a third party (i.e. a non-shareholder) without the other's approval.[6] The bank may ask for similar rights to transfer its holding between the companies within the group. There is no objection to this provided that control of these companies does not pass from the bank.

The bank must undertake to keep the shares in a company controlled by the bank, or else it has, in effect, transferred these shares to a third party, which could be one of the company's competitors.

CHECKLIST: CONTENTS OF A SHAREHOLDER'S AGREEMENT

Parties
Recitals. Share capital, subsidiaries, directors and shareholders.
Agreement conditional upon – new shares being created – new articles being adopted – completion of service agreement – bank's right to costs.
Option – class of share – number of shares – price per share – option period (normal, and on takeover or public issue) – dividend rights (all shares) – unissued shares.
Warranties. Past performance.
Indemnities. Tax and damages.
Future warranties
Bank as financial adviser – information – special director – monthly reports and board meetings.
Auditors
Public quotation
Definitions
Period of agreement
Transferability.
Notices
Schedule 1. Shareholders.
Schedule 2. Properties.
Schedule 3. Patents.

REFERENCES

1 Companies Act, 1948, Section 61(i)(a).
2 Finance Act, 1965, Section 77.
3 Companies Act, 1948, Section 61(i)(a).
4 Companies Act, 1948, Section 57: No shares can be issued at a discount, i.e. below par value, without approval of the court.
5 *Admission of Securities to Quotation,* Stock Exchange 1969, p.10. Options; p.91 – Conversion rights.
6 The original shareholders must have the right to transfer their shares within their immediate family to avoid death duties, or on death.

9

Shareholder's Agreement 2: Covenants, Warranties and Indemnities

INTRODUCTION

The purpose of the shareholder's agreement is to record clearly the undertakings given by the parties, and their obligations to one another. The bank decides to invest as a result of information given to them by the company, and in this agreement, therefore, the directors warrant that this information is true, as they would do in a prospectus for a public issue.[1] In both cases, the directors are personally liable. The warranties are designed to force directors to disclose any irregularities, or to suffer the consequences.

Any conditions, therefore, which are inconsistent with these warranties must be disclosed. Disclosure should be made by letter from the company's solicitor to the solicitor for the bank, after careful consultation between the directors, the auditors, and the company solicitor. One important reason why these undertakings are required is the relatively weak position of a minority shareholder under existing UK Company Law.

MINORITY SHAREHOLDERS' RIGHTS

A minority shareholder has certain rights, if he feels he is being oppressed,[2] that is, if the company is not being operated for the benefit of all the shareholders. Aggrieved shareholders can also call for an investigation by the Department of Trade and Industry, if they hold more than 10 per cent of the shares issued.[3]

Such operations are however costly and take time, and the results are uncertain. In the absence of specific minority rights, banks require certain limitations on the powers of the company to change the *status quo* without their approval, which could be speedily enforced in the courts if necessary. These limitations cover any acts which could reduce the value of the investment of the bank, and are thus written into the agreement. The company, on the other hand, must ensure that these restrictions are not such that they can be used to further the interest of the bank, at the expense of the company and the other shareholders.

By examining the type of limitations required, both in the shareholder's agreement and in the debenture trust deed, the directors will be aware of their existence, and will have discussed the implications with their advisers.

A bank will always ask for all possible safeguards, and finally settle for only the protection it requires in a certain situation. The level of limitations required depends on the financial position of the company, the level of risk for the bank, and the character, capability and reputation of the management.

The shareholder's agreement, apart from the option conditions, contains the following clauses:

PARTIES

The bank (purchaser), the company (the company), the directors and the principal shareholders (the vendors).

RECITALS

1 That the authorised and issued share capital is as follows: e.g. £100,000 in ordinary shares of £1.00 of which 75,000 ordinary shares are issued and fully paid.

2 That the directors represent that the company has no

subsidiaries or trade investments, and that there are no associated companies, in which the directors or any shareholders have any share interest.

3 That the directors are the only directors of the company, and that the shareholders are as listed in the attached schedule.

WARRANTIES

These warranties are given by the company, the directors and the major shareholders, both jointly and severally, in respect of the company and its subsidiaries. Most of these warranties underline the importance of careful groundwork in the company secretarial field, such as filing proper returns with the Registrar of Companies, valuing the fixed assets of the company, and disclosing any factor which could reduce this value; for example, possible compulsory purchase orders, or breaches in the covenants of a lease that might result in a lease being forfeit.

Most of these covenants, relating to books, accounts and tax are reasonable, as any accounts showing a true and fair position of the financial position of the company should meet these requirements. The same applies to special contracts, or litigation resulting in onerous commitments. The clauses are as follows:

1 Legal requirements

(*a*) That the legal requirements of the Companies Acts have been met on the incorporation of the company, for all issues of shares and debentures, and that all documents, required to be filed with the Registrar of Companies, have been filed.

(*b*) That the company has committed no breach of the Exchange Control Act 1947.

(*c*) That all documents on which stamp duty is payable, have been stamped.

(*d*) That the company has power to execute this agreement, without contravening the law or the memorandum and articles of the company.

2 Accounts

(*a*) That the accounts for the last *x* years, ending (date), have been prepared on a recognised and consistent basis, and comply with the requirements of the Companies Acts.

(*b*) That they represent a true and fair picture, and that they set forth the assets, liabilities, reserves and provisions of the company, correctly at each date.

(*c*) That, at the date of the last audit, the net asset value was not less than that shown in the balance sheet.

(*d*) That full disclosure and provision in the accounts have been made for all liabilities, known and anticipated, present and contingent, including taxation up to the date of the last accounts. That all encumbrances, onerous commitments in existence or under negotiation, and all guarantees have been disclosed.

(*e*) That book debts will realise the full nominal amount, less any reserves for bad or doubtful debts. *Note.* All items in dispute and equipment not accepted by customers as well as overdue accounts must be disclosed.

(*f*) That stock and work in progress and finished stock have been valued on a recognised and consistent basis, over the last *X* years, and that these valuations have been used in the accounts. That all old, obsolete and redundant stock has been written down, so that its present book value, at the date of the last audit, does not exceed the lower, of either cost or net realisable value (see ICA recommendation).

(*g*) That all research and development has been treated as an operating expense, and written off against revenue, unless it is covered fully by an order from a third party.

(*h*) That the taxation returns have always been prepared on a true and proper basis, and that all proper returns have been made. That the reserves in the balance sheet cover all tax due at any time, up to the date of the last audit, including capital gains tax, corporation tax, added value tax, or any other tax or duty payable.

(*i*) That there is no dispute with the Inland Revenue, and that the company has taken no action which could result in a return of investment grants.

(*j*) That clearance from surtax and against a shortfall distribution assessment, under Section 77 of the Finance Act 1965, have been obtained from incorporation up to the date of the last audit.

3 **Taxation**

That at this date, there are no anticipated liabilities for taxation, except as disclosed.

4 **Dividends**

That since the date of the last accounts, no dividends have been declared or paid. *Note.* The purchase price was related to the net assets as shown in the last accounts, and any undisclosed dividends paid will have to be deducted from the agreed value of the company.

5 **Books and Records**

That these record accurately all transactions entered into by the company, or to which it has been a party, that these have been prepared in accordance with generally accepted accounting practices and standards, and will be in future maintained in the same manner, and kept fully up to date.

6 **Fixed Assets**

(*a*) That the schedule attached records accurately all properties owned by the company.
(*b*) That the company has good and marketable title to its freehold and leasehold properties, and to all fixed assets, included in the accounts.
(*c*) That these assets are free from all mortgages, charges, debentures, encumbrances, hire and hire purchase agreements, bills of sale, or payment on deferred terms.
(*d*) That their use does not contravene any law or bye-law, and that all covenants have been and are being observed.
(*e*) That no notices affecting the assets have been served, or are likely to be served by any local authority or by any other person.
(*f*) That the insurance policies give prudent cover, and cover all customary risks, and are in force and not voidable.

7 **Personnel**

(*a*) That there are no service agreements that cannot be terminated with less than *X* months notice without compensation.

(*b*) That there is no obligation to pay or contribute to any pension or retirement benefits for any past employee or their dependents.

8 **Patents and Licence Agreements**

(*a*) That the company holds undertakings from all employees to assign any patent or invention to the company. *Note*: This is only good business practice.

(*b*) That the company has not entered into any agreements or licences covering trade marks, patents, inventions, processes, 'know how', or other industrial property.
Note: Either industrial property is being sold or acquired, and in the latter case, normally, obligations are being entered into. Such transactions must be disclosed.

9 **Litigation**

That there is no litigation or arbitration pending or threatened, except for trade debtors, as already disclosed, and that there are no unsatisfied judgements or orders against the company.

10 **Contracts**

That there are no onerous and long term contracts, not in the ordinary course of business, which involve special obligation of a material nature.

11 **Share and Loan Capital**

That no issues of share or loan capital will be made, and that no part of the share or loan capital of the company is or will be under option.

12 **Priority Creditors**

That the company will pay promptly all debts and liabilities, which in a winding up would be paid in priority to other debts. *Note*: Of particular importance where there is a debenture outstanding.

13 **Recitals**

That the recitals and statements in this agreement are true and correct.

14 **Since the date of the last accounts**

That the company has carried on business in the ordinary course, and that the financial position of the company is not affected by losses, unusual circumstances or other changes.

15 **Disclosure**

That all information, which is material for the purchase of shares, and which could affect the value of the shares, has been disclosed in writing. That the directors will disclose in writing after this date, and before completion, any matters not consistent with these warranties, and any changes in the financial position or prospects of the company since this date. *Note*: The last two clauses are designed to force the directors to disclose any material event which could alter the valuation by the bank, and which is based on information given by the company. The directors, as already stated, are personally liable if they fail to disclose such events between the signature of the agreement and completion.

INDEMNITIES

These indemnities are given jointly and severally by the directors, and are binding on them or their personal representatives, now and in the future, as follows:

1 Tax assessed now and in the future, for the company or for any subsidiary, not disclosed in the balance sheet at the date of the last audit, and not disclosed in writing to the bank.

2 Any loss or damage incurred by the bank:

(*a*) Through the directors not fulfilling any part of the agreement, either directly or indirectly, i.e. breaches of warranties, covenants or undertakings etc.

(*b*) From any claims made by third parties.

(*c*) In respect of the shares held by the directors at the time of the agreement.

Any reduction in assets, caused by such a claim, and all costs and expenses incurred by the company in settling such a claim.

3 Any claims for surtax on any person, now or previously, as a shareholder or participator under:
- (*a*) Section 245, Income Tax Act, 1952
- (*b*) Section 78, Finance Act, 1965
- (*c*) Sections 296 and 300, Income Tax and Corporation Tax Act, 1970

4 Estate duty payable by the company under:
- (*a*) Part IV, Income Tax Act, 1940
- (*b*) On the death of a person, who prior to the agreement was a member (shareholder) of the company, or any subsidiary or who made transfers of property to the company before the date of the agreement.

5 Any recovery of tax from the company, or cancellation of any tax advantage under:
- (*a*) Sections 21-28, Finance Act, 1960
- (*b*) Section 32, Finance Act, 1969
- (*c*) Sections 460-488, Income Tax and Corporation Tax Act, 1970 resulting from transactions prior to this date.

6 Any claims for tax assessed, now and in the future:
- (*a*) On a shortfall in distribution, Section 77, Finance Act 1965, Section 289, Income Tax and Corporation Tax Act, 1970.
- (*b*) Section 83, Finance Act, 1965.
- (*c*) Capital dividends paid in 1965-1966.
- (*d*) Sections 278-279, and 286-288, Income Tax and Corporation Tax Act, 1970.
- (*e*) Income tax payable on distribution under Schedule F.
- (*f*) Sections 21-28, Finance Act, 1960. Sections 75-77, Finance Act, 1965. Concerning loans to participators, or in consideration for restrictive covenants.

7 Part IV and Schedule 16, Finance Act, 1968.

As tax matters are constantly changing, this list must only be taken as an indication of some of the indemnities required. An up-to-date list should be obtained from the legal and tax advisers to the company.[4]

The directors and shareholders would be advised to decide how any liabilities which may become payable should be divided.

Normally, any liability would be shared in direct proportion to the shares held in the company. An agreement should be drawn up between all the vendors, clearly laying down their share of any liability.

REFERENCES

1 Companies Act 1948, Section 43 – Civil Liability for Misstatements in a Prospectus.
2 Companies Act 1948, Section 210 – Oppression.
3 Companies Act 1948, Section 164 – Department of Trade and Industry investigation.
4 A list of indemnities required from public companies is given in *Simon's Taxes* vol. D., 3rd edition, Butterworths, 1970, section D2-508, p. 312.

10

Shareholder's Agreement 3: Further Undertakings

INTRODUCTION

The company and the directors, jointly and severally, undertake with the bank, that neither the company nor any subsidiary will carry out in the future any of the actions listed below, without the previous written consent of the bank.

These warranties can broadly be divided into three sections: equity, assets and earnings, each of which could have an adverse effect on the value of the investment by the bank.

EQUITY

Equity items affecting the bank's share of the earnings available:

Equity. Making any issue of shares, options, alteration of rights, reduction in share capital, repayment of the share premium accounts, or the capital redemption reserve, or any capital reorganisation, or entering in a scheme of arrangement with its creditors (see Chapter 8).

Memorandum and articles. Making any changes, except as required by this agreement, and convening any meeting with a view to making any such alterations.

Business. The company will remain in the same line of business, and carry on the business in the ordinary course.
Financil year end. The company will make no change of date of the year end from (*date*). *Note*: This could affect any existing option or conversion agreements.

ASSETS

The following actions could affect the asset position of the company, and thus the asset cover for any debenture. The company will not:
Subsidiaries. Make any issues of share capital except to the holding company. Make any disposal of any share capital in a subsidiary, or create any mortgage or charge except in favour of the company, or assign any debt, owed to it by a subsidiary.
Guarantees. Guarantee the obligation of third parties, or give credit except for normal trade credit.
Loans. Except for inter-company loans, make any loans to other persons or companies, except for reasonable loans to employees.
Borrowing and charges. Borrow any monies, or create any mortgages or charges, on the whole or part of the assets of the company.
Disposals. Sell or dispose of any substantial part of the assets of the company, business or undertaking, except to subsidiaries, or in the ordinary course of business. This ensures that the assets will remain under the control of the company and will not be depleted by the unlawful act of any person.
Acquisitions. Make any acquisition of shares or assets in any other business.
Insurance. The company will undertake to keep the company's stock, equipment and property insured to the full replacement value. *Note*: Avoid giving any undertaking to place all insurance business through the bank.
Agreements. Enter into any agreements or licences, on products or patents, 'know how', or any other long-term contracts or liability of a material nature, involving long term obligations.

EARNINGS

The company will not:

Directors. Increase the total remuneration, including fees, over the totals in the service agreements attached to this agreement. Appoint

any new directors, or negotiate any new service agreements. Make any payments to past directors or their dependants, other than the payment to the special bank nominee director.
Distributions. Make any payment or distribution of profit or return of capital to the shareholders, except for dividends on the cumulative preferred shares, except for any shortfall distribution required by the 1965 Act. *Note:* this clause must reflect the dividend policy agreed.
Salaries. Make any alteration in the terms of employment of those persons earning more than £*x,xxx* per annum, including the negotiating of any new service agreements. *Note:* The bank may wish to vet any press release by the company dealing with the financial position of the company or mentioning the name of the bank.

ACCOUNTS

The following policies will be adopted in the preparation of all accounts of the company or the subsidiaries:
Research and development expenditure. That this item will be treated as an ordinary expense, and written off against revenue, unless the work is carried out for a third party.
Partly completed contracts. That profits on fixed price contracts will not be taken, unless delivery of items is made in whole or in part, and accepted by the customer.
Cost of delivered items. That all costs for delivered items, on which profits have been taken, will be excluded from work in progress.
Losses on contracts. That full provision will be made in work in progress for the total expected loss on any contract.
Taxation. That appropriate reserves for all taxation will be made (capital gains, income tax, corporation tax etc.)
Depreciation and amortisation. That proper and realistic depreciation and amortisation policies will be adopted.
Stock valuation. That the book value of all stock will be cost or net realisable value, whichever is the lower, and that all out of date, redundant and excess stocks will be written down to salvage value.
Debtors. That reserves against bad and doubtful debts will be set up, which are sufficient to cover all bad debts.

FINANCIAL ADVISER

1 The bank is appointed financial adviser to the company and its

subsidiaries, and in conjunction with the auditors will advise on the form of accounts, accounting and other records to be adopted by the company and its subsidiaries.

2 The bank will have the right to appoint a director, an alternate director, and to change them at will.

3 The company will pay this director a fee and expenses. If any dispute occurs, the fee will be fixed by the bank.

4 Monthly board meetings will be held to consider the monthly financial statements to be supplied to the bank, and also a report from the managing director.

REPORTS TO THE BANK

The directors will jointly and severally undertake to keep the bank closely informed on the business of the company, and its subsidiaries, by providing the following:

1 Annual trading and cash budgets for three years ahead, to be submitted three months before the start of the new financial year.

2 Audited profit and loss accounts within four months of the year end.

3 Monthly financial statements within three weeks of the month end.

4 Notices of all general meetings and resolutions, 30 days before a meeting, and copies of all circulars to shareholders or debenture holders.

AUDITORS

The appointment of the auditor is to be agreed by both parties. In the absence of agreement, each side will nominate an auditor to act jointly for both the company and any subsidiaries.

COMPLETION

1 New memorandum and articles of association, as initialled by both parties, must be adopted.

2 Board changes must take place as required by the bank. Every director resigning, must acknowledge that he has no claim

against the company (or that his claim is limited as follows – Mr O. *£x,xxx,* Mr P. *£xx,xxx*).

3 Service agreements must be entered into by Mr Q. and Mr R., according to the draft initialled by Mr Q. and Mr R. for the vendors, and by Mr A. for the purchasers.
4 If existing shares are being purchased from other shareholders, rather than the bank subscribing new shares, the company and the directors must register the transfer to make the bank the holder of the shares.
5 The various indemnities and warranties must be signed.
6 The company must obtain from all employees, undertakings to assign all inventions and patents to the company (if applicable).

Completion will take place before (*date*) (or at a later date to be agreed by both parties), at the office of X.

The bank can break off negotiations and rescind the agreement with no liability to either party, except that the bank is entitled to recover out of pocket expenses for its own investigation and for legal and accounting fees from the company, for the following reasons:

1 If completion does not take place as agreed.
2 If the above conditions are not carried out.
3 If there is a breach of warranties.
4 If new matters become known, which are material for the value of the shares, and which are inconsistent with the warranties given.

MISCELLANEOUS PROVISIONS

Personal Representatives
The agreement will bind the directors' personal representatives.

The Period
The period of the agreement to be as follows:

1 Warranties and indemnities relating to past performance – these should be able to be cleared within two to three years of signing the agreement.
2 Restrictive undertakings on future behaviour can exist as follows:

(*a*) During the option period, and while the bank holds *X*% of the equity; or
(*b*) After a period of eight to ten years, or when the debenture is repaid, whichever is the shorter; or
(*c*) Just prior to a public issue.

Transfer
The agreement is not transferable, except by agreement of the other parties.

Costs
The company to pay the investigation costs of the bank, stamp duties, legal fees and disbursements. *Note.* The company can negotiate a limit to these expenses.

Notices
How notices under the agreement are to be given.

11

The Bargaining Position of the Company and the Capital Structure

THE BARGAINING POSITION OF THE COMPANY

The purpose of all the preparatory work outlined in the previous chapters is to enable the directors to assess the financial requirements of the company and its bargaining position.

Before discussing this in detail, there are two fundamental points which require an answer:

Shareholder Support

1 Do the directors know and represent the views and requirements of all the shareholders?

2 Have the directors consulted their solicitors to find out the types of resolutions and the majorities required to pass the necessary amendments to the memorandum and articles? The action required may vary from company to company depending upon the provisions in the memorandum and articles.

3 If they are dependent on the votes of outside shareholders to pass these amendments, do they know these shareholders' views

and reactions to their negotiating aims?

4 Are the directors clear as to how far they can go in any negotiations with a bank, and on what points they need to consult their outside shareholders? If this action is not taken, the outside shareholders could frustrate any deal made between the directors and the bank.

Need to Complete

How strong is the present financial position of the company? Does it have to complete the transaction within a certain time in order to stay in business?

If the deal must be completed within a certain time, the company has no freedom to manoeuvre and must accept the best terms it can obtain. The banks will find this type of company much less attractive since well managed companies seldom get into such situations.

On the other hand, if the finance is for new projects, and the commitment has not been made without funds to back it, the company *need not* complete. It is naturally in a far stronger bargaining position, and more attractive as an investment.

THE PRESENT POSITION

The directors will have a clear idea of the position of the company, as follows:[1]

Past record – Performance – trend of earnings.
Present financial position – Accountants report – net assets.
Management – Capability and maturity.
Future prospects and growth – Considering future developments in the company and in the industry.
Present market position and reputation – With customers, suppliers, and competition.
Customer spread – Home and abroad.
Products – Up to date and meet market requirements – Good quality and service – Competitively priced.
Problems – Any unsolved problems.
Present market value – If 100% of the company is acquired by a competitor.

THE INVESTMENT RISK OF THE BANK

The risk to be taken by the bank can be assessed by considering the following factors:

Capital – Capital required v. capital gain.
Level of risk – Downside potential (i.e. possible fall in earnings) – anticipated growth v. past performance – capital and interest cover for the loan – capital and dividend cover for the bank's shareholding.
Period of risk – The risk depends on the period of time before a public issue, based on the present size and expected growth; for example, present pre-tax profits of £100,000 expected to grow to £150,000 in two years, and then go public.

All of these factors affect the terms of investment offered by the bank, and the number of limitations that the bank will wish to impose in the agreement on the future performance of the company.

THE NEED FOR CLEAR COMPANY OBJECTIVES

The directors must always start any negotiations with a financial institution with a clear idea of:

1 The objectives they must achieve (e.g. amount of loan monies).
2 What investment terms they are prepared to offer (e.g. equity per cent).
3 What restrictions on the future activities of the company they are prepared to accept (e.g. borrowing limits).

All of these terms must be approved by the shareholders, with the necessary majorities. The terms must also be treated as a 'package deal' as many are interrelated. For instance, whether a family retains control, after a public issue, depends on the equity holding of the bank, and the shares each party makes available on a public issue (see Chapter 8).

The overall objective is to obtain the finance required for the lowest equity stake possible, and with as few restrictions as possible on the future freedom of operation of the company. The various matters that must be considered are as follows:

1 The capital structure of the group.
2 The company valuation.
3 The equity stake by the bank and the other shareholders.
4 The board, and the organisation of the company.
5 Debentures.
6 Restrictions imposed.

THE CAPITAL STRUCTURE OF THE GROUP

The first step is to decide upon the composition of the group, to give it a good earnings and net asset base for borrowing.

The Composition of the Group

Answers to the following questions are required:

Share Capital
What is the authorised and issued share capital for the main company?

Options
Are there any options or conversion rights outstanding, either into debentures, loan stock, preference or ordinary shares, or into any other form of equity?

Minority Interests
1 What subsidiaries, if any, exist, and are they wholly owned? If not, what percentage of the equity is held, and should the minority interests (i.e. outside shareholders' shares) be acquired by the company?
2 Can the subsidiary become a member of the charging group[2] to secure any debenture, or must it be acquired?
3 If shareholders own shares in the main company and also in one of the subsidiaries, is there a conflict of interest, which can only be solved by acquiring all the shares of these companies?

Associated Companies and Trade Investments
The bank may be suspicious if there are long term arrangements between the company and associated companies (or subsidiaries), especially if shares of the subsidiaries are owned by the directors and existing shareholders of the main company.

The directors should consider whether any such company should be acquired, by issuing shares in the main company to their shareholders. The valuation used must be an 'arms length' transaction, and should have the backing of the auditors and solicitors for the company to show that the valuation is fair and reasonable to all parties.

Properties
Certain of the properties of the group may be owned by existing shareholders who have granted leases to the group. Provided any such transfer does not involve the payment of substantial capital gains tax by the present owners, the asset base of the group is improved, if these properties are acquired at a fair market price by means of an issue of shares. The properties and other assets should be revalued, but only the net amount of the increased value, after deducting any capital gains tax liability, should be added to the value of fixed assets. At the same time, the depreciation rates should be reconsidered, in case they too need revision.[3] Surplus properties and assets should be sold to release liquid assets for reinvestment.

Directors' loans
Such loans should either be converted into equity, to broaden the equity base of the company, or converted into unsecured loans, with fixed interest rates and maturity dates occurring after the repayment of any debenture or secured loan.

Capitalisation Issues

If the company has substantial capital and revenue reserves, arising from revaluation of the properties and from retained earnings, these can be distributed *pro rata* to existing shareholders by means of a capitalisation issue.

The issue of shares to the existing shareholders is known under a variety of names, all meaning the same thing: capitalisation issues, scrip issues, free issues, bonus issues. In all cases, there is no change in the net assets of the company, because this issue is a bookkeeping entry, transferring sums from capital or revenue reserves to issued share capital.

Each shareholder receives his entitlement in proportion to his existing shareholding.

Example

The issue of five bonus ordinary shares for every two ordinary shares held on (date).

(a) *Shareholder: Ordinary shares held*	*Market price and value*		*Asset value per share*	*Total*
2 shares held	@ £1.75 =	£3.50	£1.40	= £2.80
5 bonus shares	nil		–	–
7 shares	@ £0.50	£3.50	£0.40	£2.80

N.B. After this capitalisation issue, earnings and assets per share are reduced by two-sevenths of the previous figure (e.g. asset value from £1.40 to £1.00).

(b) *Company*		*Issued ordinary share capital*	*Revenue Reserves*	*Total equity capital*
Before issue	1,000 shares of £1	£1,000	£4,500	£5,500
New shares	+ 2,500	+ £2,500	–£2,500	–
After issue	3,500	£3,500	£2,000	£5,500

It is good practice, from time to time, to transfer amounts from reserves to issued share capital to keep both amounts in balance.[4] However, sufficient revenue reserves should be left to pay any dividends required if the company makes a loss.[5] Although any reserves belong to the existing shareholders, they do not have to be distributed prior to any investment by the bank. Since the valuation is agreed for the company, and therefore is not affected by an increase in the number of shares issued. This change only reduces the price per share proportionately.

The Share Premium Account

When new shares are issued, the balance of the subscription price, above par, is credited to the share premium account as follows:

A share of £1 nominal value, issued at £1.50, increases the issued share capital by £1 and the share premium account by 50p. The same remarks made above, on the distribution of capital and revenue reserves, also apply to the share premium account. Although the share premium is paid in recognition of the present value of the company and therefore belongs to the existing shareholders, any distribution has no effect on the total value of the company.

EXTRAORDINARY GENERAL MEETINGS

General

Meetings must be called to approve any changes proposed, in the group capital structure, giving the correct notice for each type of resolution.

If these resolutions are approved by the majorities required, the appropriate returns must be filed with the Registrar of Companies. The type of amendments required will be as follows:

Increase of Share Capital

The 1948 Companies Act gives the company power to increase the share capital by an ordinary resolution,[6] (i.e. one passed by over half the votes of those present and voting), provided that the company is so authorised by the articles.[7] If this power does not exist, the articles (and in certain cases the memorandum) will have to be amended by a special resolution requiring a 75 per cent majority.[8] Unless the articles so provide, once unissued shares exist, the directors have power to issue any shares remaining unissued.

Classes of Shares

Preference shares may be issued, if a company is so authorised by the articles.[9]

The articles can give a company the right to issue shares preferred, deferred or with other special rights, as regards dividends, voting, and return of capital, by means of an ordinary resolution in general meeting.[10] However, if the issue prejudices any special rights already conferred, the articles normally provide that a special class meeting, of the class of share affected, must be held to approve such action.[11] An extraordinary resolution, requiring a 75 per cent majority, is required to be passed before such special rights are amended. Even if this resolution is passed, shareholders representing not less than 15 per cent of the issued share capital of that class may apply to the court, which has power to disallow or confirm the variation.[12] If the memorandum lays down specific shareholders' rights, it may be necessary to amend the memorandum and the articles.[13]

Borrowing Powers

The articles normally include provision for the directors to borrow, mortgage or charge the undertaking of the company, also the property and uncalled capital, and to issue debentures.[14]

In Table A of the Companies Act, 1948, the borrowing limit is set at the nominal amount of the issued share capital, excluding temporary loans from the company's bankers in the ordinary course of business. The company in general meeting can approve a resolution to borrow in excess of the limit provided for in the articles by means of an ordinary resolution.

Other Amendments

Other provisions, such as the power to appoint a special director, will require an amendment to the articles, needing a special resolution which must be passed by a 75 per cent majority.

In Table A, an ordinary resolution is required to change the number of directors that can be appointed to the board.[15]

A bank may also require a restriction on the issue of the shares, except to existing shareholders on a *pro rata* basis. The directors may also wish to give existing shareholders the right to transfer shares to their family and dependants, either on their death, or while they are still alive.

REFERENCES

1 See also A.R. ENGLISH, *Valuation of Shares in Unquoted Companies,* ICFC, pp. 3-6.

2 Chapter 14, Debentures and Loans. The charging group is composed of the company and its subsidiaries, which guarantee the debenture stock, and create a floating charge on their assets, as collateral security for the debenture.

3 *Admission of Securities to Quotation,* Stock Exchange, p.14, Section 13 (ii) (b).

4 For public companies, increasing the number of shares tends to widen

the market. Also a higher issued share capital tends to improve the credit image of the company.

5 Dividends can only be paid out of current or retained earnings, and not out of capital or capital reserves, as this is a reduction of share capital, requiring court sanction. Companies Act 1948, Sections 66-68.

6 Companies Act, 1948, Section 61(i) (a).

7 Companies Act, 1948, Article 44 Table A.

8 Companies Act, 1948, Section 23.

9 Companies Act, 1948, Section 58, Article 3 of Table A.

10 Companies Act, 1948, Article 2, Table A.

11 Companies Act, 1948, Article 4, Table A.

12 Companies Act, 1948, Section 72.

13 Companies Act, 1948, Section 23: A special resolution is required to be passed by 75 per cent majority.

14 Companies Act, 1948, Table A, Article 79.

15 Companies Act, 1948, Table A, Article 94.

12

Company Valuation

METHOD OF VALUATION

General

A company is valued either on its earnings or net assets, or on a mixture of both methods. Therefore, the capitalisation of reserves does not increase the value of the company to a purchaser. However, acquisitions of properties or companies, or a revaluation of assets, will increase the assets of the company and possibly the earnings, and will therefore enhance the company value.

Net Profits

The valuation is arrived at by the following formula:

net profits x factor = company value

Net profits can be either for the last year, the forthcoming year, or an average of the last three years. Either pre-tax or post-tax net profits can be used, but the post-tax factor, (price earnings ratio) is greater than the pre-tax factor by the level of corporation tax.

This tax is taken[1] at 40 per cent so that a pre-tax factor of 6 times is the same as a price earnings ratio of 10 times.

For example

Pre-tax net profits	*Post-tax net profits*
500 x 6 = 3,000	After 40% corporation tax 300 x 10 = 3,000

Apart from this consideration, the size of the factor depends on the size of the company, financial standing, and expected growth.

Net Assets

In the case of a new company, a very small company with no earnings record, or a company being acquired solely for its assets, an asset valuation should be used as follows:[2]

Net assets at *(date)*	£150,000
Less goodwill	£5,000
Less tax equalisation reserve	£5,000
	£10,000
	£140,000
Increased value fixed assets	£ 20,000
	£160,000
Less preference share capital (cost at redemption)	£ 10,000
Net assets attributable to ordinary shareholders	£150,000
Ordinary share capital:	
100,000 shares of £1.00 =	£100,000
Net asset value per share	£1.50

The Value after a New Subscription

The value of a company, after a new subscription of shares, is the existing company value plus the value of the new subscription. This is precisely what happens in a rights issue, when shareholders are given the right to subscribe in cash for new shares as follows:

Example

Rights issue of one new ordinary £1.00 share at £2.00 for every three shares now held.

Shareholder	*Shares held*	*Market price*
	3 existing shares	@ £4.00 = £12.00
	1 new share – fully paid	@ £2.00 = £ 2.00
	4 shares	@ £3.50 = £14.00

Company:	*Issued share capital (£000s)*		*Company value (£000s)*
Before issue	1,200 shares @ £4.00	=	£4,800
New shares	400 shares @ £2.00	=	£800
After issue	1,600 shares @ £3.50	=	£5,600

The company market value is increased by the amount of subscription. However, in the case of this rights issue (one for three), earnings must rise by $33\frac{1}{3}$ per cent to compensate for the increase in equity. Only then will earnings per share return to the pre-rights issue level, and only after this will the earnings per share rise.

Subscription by the Bank

The same applies when a bank subscribes new shares, as earnings per share are diluted. Earnings per share will rise to the previous level when the increase in earnings balances out the increase in issued share capital.

Example

Company value (£000s)	=	*Net profits pre-tax (£000s)*	*x Factor*
£320		£80	x 4

Issued share capital (£000s)			*Price*		*Company value (£000s)*
Before issue	40 shares	@	£8.00	=	£320
New shares	20 shares	@	£8.00	=	£160
	60		£8.00	=	£480

The issued share capital and the company value have increased by 50 per cent and the factor (or multiple) has also increased by 50 per cent from four to six (£80 x 6 = £480). Net profits pre-tax must, therefore, increase by 50 per cent to £120 (£120 x 4 = £480) to restore the factor to the previous level.

MARKET PRICE VALUATION

Investment Valuation

The method of valuation to be discussed is for investment only, and not for estate duty purposes.[3]

In addition, there can be variations in the value per share depending on the size of the holding as follows:[4]

1 A holding of under 10 per cent is unable to block a pre-emption bid under Section 209 of the Companies Act 1948.
2 A holding of over 25 per cent is able to block a special resolution.
3 One over 51 per cent gives the purchaser control of the company.
4 The value of the shares can be affected by the rights of other shareholders; i.e. restrictions on transfers, special class rights, rights to appoint directors, rights of transmission on death.

However, this chapter covers the valuation of a minority holding of between 25-35 per cent with suitable protection of minority rights, as this is the normal holding for a bank.

An Imaginary Portfolio

English[5] recommends that an imaginary portfolio is constructed taking similar shares in a similar industry and comparing price earnings ratios,[6] dividend yields, dividend cover, assets per share, past trends of earnings, and future expectations. The shares can be compared with the price earnings ratios and dividend yields for the *Financial Times* Actuaries Index for the relevant industry group.

MARKET DISCOUNTS

Before constructing this portfolio, it is worth while examining the various discounts and premiums which exist in the market place, depending on the relative attraction of different shares as investments. These discounts are:

1 Market spread

2 Discount for the absence of a quotation
3 Size discount

Market Spread

This spread can be seen clearly by examining the different price earnings ratios in a sector of the market, quoted in the *Financial Times.*

For example on 11th March 1972.

	Price earnings ratios			
	Companies		*Financial Times*	
	high	*low*	*Actuaries Index*	
Drapery and stores	50.4	5.4	Stores	24.97
Engineering and metal	58.4	5.5	Heavy	20.55
			General	16.31

This illustrates the spread which can exist, and is represented by investors' expectations and forecasts of the various companies' future earnings.

Discount for the Absence of a Quotation

The level[7] of net profits pre-tax, at which the company can obtain a London quotation for its shares, is around £150,000. However, as the company is unknown to investors and as it may not have a long and impressive record of earnings, the shares are usually offered to the public at a discount. In addition, as 35 per cent of the equity must normally be offered to the market to avoid close company status, this can represent a substantial number of shares, which can only be offered at a discount.

In one of the Bolton Committee Research Reports,[8] the results of a study are quoted as follows: 'Merrett and Newbould found an average market discount of 17.7 per cent on a sample of 24 offers of sale, and 26.8 per cent on a sample of 19 placings. There was a tendency for market discount to vary inversely with size, though the sample was too small for any strong conclusions to be drawn.'[9]

Elsewhere discounts of 20-33⅓ per cent are quoted for valuing companies with no quotation, and restrictions on the transfer of shares. An example is given of an unquoted company with net profits pre-tax of £592,000 and here a discount of 15 per cent is considered reasonable.[10]

Example: Levex

An offer for sales was made by this company to the public on 9th March, and the prospectus and comment appeared in the *Financial Times* on 6th March 1972. The company has had a short but successful record in the jersey knitted fabrics field. However, the *Financial Times* noted that there was spare capacity in the industry, the major US market had gone sour, following the US surcharge on imports, and the dollar devaluation. Margins therefore, were likely to be depressed, especially as American stock was likely to flood onto the UK market. Specialist expertise was now needed, and sizeable retail outlets. One large customer had an equity investment in Levex, and Levex had an equity stake in this company. Levex also had strong ties with other large users, and was stated in the prospectus to be a low cost operation.[11]

The comparison with similar shares was as shown[12] in Figure 12:1.

	Prices 6.3.73	Dividend cover	Dividend yield	Price earnings ratio	Year end	Earnings (£1,000s) pre-tax	Earnings (£1,000s) after tax
Nova (20p)	190p	2.4	x 4.5%	9.3	31.3.71	684	417
Fairfax (10p)	100p	2.2	x 4.7%	9.7	30.6.71	513	307
Textured Jersey (10p)	86p	3.2	x 3.8%	12.2	30.4.71	352	211
Levex (20p) (issue price)	53p	1.88	x 4.72%	11.28	31.8.72	235	141*
		1.16	x 4.72%	18.27	29.8.71	145	87

Figure 12:1 Comparison of Levex with Similar Shares * Forecast

Levex's price was based on a forecast to August 1972, but in the first four months of the current financial year, it had achieved net profits pre-tax of £99,366, just under 70 per cent of the previous year's figure. The *Financial Times* felt that the price was asking for a lot 'in comparison with the historic price earnings ratios of the other companies'. The *Investors' Chronicle* felt that the company might have a difficult debut. However, the size of the issue was small and could be easily supported in the market. On the balance, this paper's opinion was that the shares would go to a premium, and the issue could prove to be a medium high flier.[13]

The issue was well oversubscribed, and the price on 16th March 1972 was 65½p, representing a price earnings ratio of 13.9 on forecast earnings. Investors, therefore, felt that the Company's future prospects justified this premium. (See Figure 12:2.)

Prices			Company	Price Earnings Ratio			Dividend Yield		
6.3.72	16.3.72	10.1.73		6.3.72	16.3.72	10.1.73	6.3.72	16.3.72	10.1.73
190p	178p	184p	Nova Jersey	9.3	8.6	9.2	4.5	5.1	4.6
100p	93p	75p	Fairfax Jersey	9.7	9.1	8.4	4.7	4.8	6.3
86p	90p	84p	Textured Jersey	12.2	13.0	11.9	3.8	3.6	3.9
53p	65½p	71p	Levex (forecast)	11.28	13.9	10.3	4.72	3.8	3.6
Financial Times Actuaries Textiles Index				16.75	17.12	14.49	4.52	4.42	4.12

Figure 12:2 Comparison at Later Date

Over this period, the price of Fairfax had fallen as had the index, those of Nova and Textured Jersey had dropped marginally, while the price of Levex had risen.

After excluding profits from companies acquired during the year ended 31st August 1972, net profit pre-tax for Levex exceeded the prospectus forecast of £235,000 by £6,000.

The *Investors' Chronicle* commented that Levex had reduced its dependence on exports by building strong links with retail and fashion chains. It also felt that the historic PE ratio of 10.3 at 71p, hardly did justice to current prospects or to the sort of growth rate this energetic management was obviously aiming for.[14]

Size Discount

A further discount is applied to those shares with a short record of earnings, which are well below the level of earnings required for a public issue. In one of the research reports commissioned by the Bolton Committee, the following points emerge:

(*a*) Net profits[15] of £25,000-£50,000.
(*b*) Price earnings ratios of six to nine for conversion within two years.[16]
(*c*) One example was given of a price earnings ratio of six for a firm

with net profits pre-tax of £50,000, post tax £27,000 – valuing the company at £162,000.

It is possible to construct a table showing the discounts, which would apply based on a market price earnings ratio of, for example, 12.5 (see Figure 12:3).

	Category	Pre-tax net profits (£000s)	Discount %	Price earnings ratio 40% Corp. tax	Pre-tax multi-plier	Assumed loan cover
	Already public	£150-200	-	12.5	7.5	Good
1	Ready for public issue	£150-200	24-20	9.5-10.0	5.7-6.0	Good
2	Very large	£100-149	28-24	9.0- 9.5	5.4-5.7	Good
3	Large	£ 75- 99	32-28	8.5- 9.0	5.1-5.4	Good
4	Medium	£ 50- 74	40-32	7.5- 8.5	4.5-5.1	Reasonable
5	Small	£ 25- 49	48-40	6.5- 7.5	3.9-4.5	Equity finance
6	Embryo	£ 10- 24		asset value or par		
7	New companies	£ 0- 9				
	Loss makers					

Figure 12:3 Discounts

Naturally any valuation must consider the past earnings record of the company and the future expectations, and this table can only be taken as a very rough guide.[17] Shares of companies of size 6, new companies and lossmakers should be valued or issued at par value. Any loans made to companies of size 5 and under are unlikely to be covered properly, both for assets and interest. In this case, these loans are really equity monies, as their security is very uncertain. It is for this reason that some institutions are not prepared to lend to companies with pre-tax net profits below £50,000.

REFERENCES

1 Financial Times Prices and Financial Times Actuaries Indices use Corporation Tax at 40%.
2 A.R. ENGLISH, *Valuation of Shares in Unquoted Companies.* ICFC, pp. 8-10.
3 *ibid.* pp. 11-12.
4 *ibid.* pp. 2-3.
5 *ibid.* p. 7.
6 A price earnings ratio is a method of valuing a company by applying a factor to the earnings of the company. Individual shares can be valued by applying a factor to the earnings per share or by dividing the share price by the earnings per share to arrive at the price earnings ratio.
7 Bolton Report, p. 174. *Note:* some merchant banks will not handle quotations for companies with net profits pre-tax of under £200,000-£250,000.
8 *Financial Facilities for Small Firms,* p. 38.
9 A.J. MERRETT and G.D. NEWBOULD, *Comparative Efficiency of Methods of Issue,* The Manchester School, January 1966.
10 A.R. ENGLISH, *Valuation of Shares in Unquoted Companies,* ICFC, p. 10.
11 *Financial Times,* Prospectus and Comment, 6 March 1972.
12 *Financial Times,* Prices, 6 March 1972.
13 *Investors' Chronicle,* 3 March 1972.
14 *Investors' Chronicle,* 12 January 1973, page 179. See also *Financial Times,* 9 January 1972.
15 *Financial Facilities for Small Firms,* pp. 138, 143.
16 *ibid.* p. 139.
17 *ibid.* p. 138.
18 The level of price earnings ratios will depend on the current level of the stock market. In addition there could easily be a spread of about 20% on the downside and about 10% on the upper limit, depending on future growth prospects, type of industry, past record (i.e. size four becomes 6.0 to 9.4).

13

The Equity Holding of the Bank, Service Agreements and other Matters for Negotiations

THE EQUITY HOLDING OF THE BANK

General

From Figure 12:3 showing the level of size discounts, it is clear that the value of a company increases, as the earnings grow, in two ways.

(*a*) As the earnings increase, the base to which the price earnings ratio is applied, increases in size.
(*b*) As the earnings of the company begin to show an upward trend, its record becomes more established, its size increases, and thus it justifies a higher price earnings ratio.

In the case of companies of sizes one and two, it is likely that any investment will be made by purchasing existing equity or by subscribing new ordinary shares. Any loans to these companies are likely to be able to be justified on normal commercial public company terms. However, the majority of investments will be made in companies of sizes three, four and possibly five, and in this case, the terms are likely to be as follows:

Type of share Preference or preferred ordinary.
Convertible Debenture[1] 50 per cent convertible into equity.
Interest Rate 11 per cent.
Conversion In three to five years.
Equity Percentage 25 to 35 per cent.
Price Earnings Ratio six to nine.
Period A bank will expect to be able to realise the investment in three to five years by means of a public issue or takeover, but five to seven years is a more likely period.
Capital Gain To compensate it for the inevitable losers, a bank will aim to achieve a capital gain of 200-400 per cent on the original cost price in about five years.

Equity Holding

A bank is negotiating not about the size of its equity stake and the other terms, but about a potential capital gain. For an adjustment in each constituent can affect the capital gain as follows:

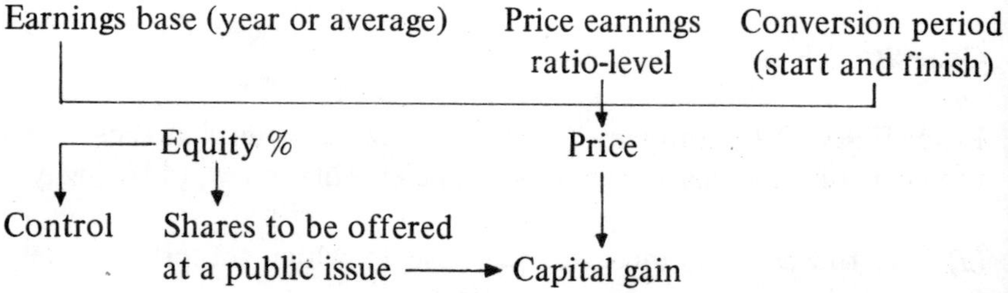

Note: if the issue is successful, the offer price may well be exceeded within a short period, giving a higher potential capital gain to those still holding shares. *Thus, these terms must be treated as a package.*

Control
If the directors wish to retain control after a public issue, they should be aware that retaining control will depend upon:

1 Fixing an upper limit to the equity holding of the bank.
2 The proportions of the equity that can be made available without losing control at the time of a public issue are,[2] if pro rata, not more than 20 per cent, if 50-50, not more than 30 per cent.

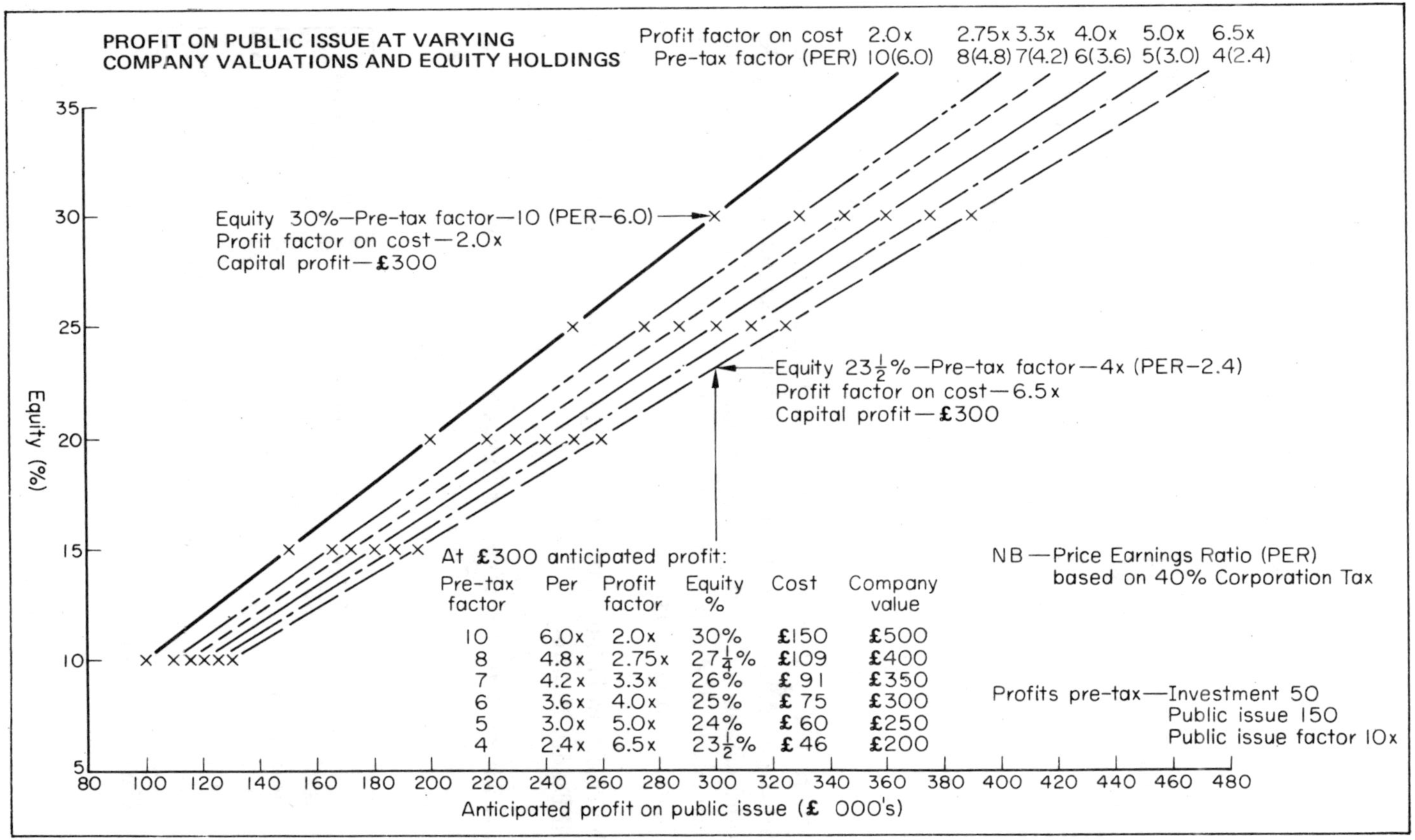

13:1 Profit on public issue at varying company valuations and equity holdings

Therefore, to start with, the bank should be offered a low equity and this figure increased, provided the bank makes shares available at a public issue on a 50-50 basis.

Price

From Figure 13:1, it can be seen that a stable capital gain can be maintained for a bank by lowering the purchase price and the equity percentage. For instance, a profit of £300,000 on original cost can be made, assuming the public issue terms are achieved by using:

Purchase p.e.r.	*Equity (%)*	*Profit factor on cost*
6.0	30	2.0 x
4.8	27¼	2.75 x
4.2	26	3.3 x
3.6	25	4.0 x
3.0	24	5.0 x
2.4	23½	6.5 x

If there is any possibility of a death-duties valuation on shares in a private company on the death of a majority shareholder, a low price would establish an 'arms-length' valuation. This basis can be used for a valuation if death occurs within three years, and thus an assets valuation can be avoided.[3]

The Profit on Public Issue at Varying Company Valuations and Equity Holdings

It is assumed that investment takes place when net profits pre-tax are £50,000, and that flotation occurs when net profits pre-tax have reached £150,000 at a price earnings ratio of 6.0.

	Valuation for investment (All amounts £000s)						**Valuation for public issue**
Pre-tax profits	50	50	50	50	50	50	150
P.E.R.	2.4x	3.0x	3.6x	4.2x	4.8x	6.0x	6x
Pre-tax factor	4.0x	5.0x	6.0x	7.0x	8.0x	10.0x	10x
Company value	200	250	300	350	400	500	1500

Figure 13:2 Company Valuation

THE BOARD OF DIRECTORS

Board Changes

Inactive directors will have to retire, and their compensation should be fixed. The functions to be performed by each director should be clearly defined. The bank will also require the nominee director to be paid by the company. This salary should be agreed during the negotiation.

Directors Salaries and Benefits

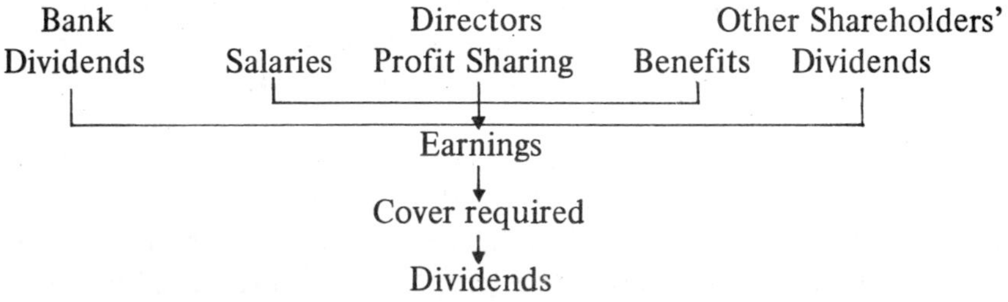

The directors' salaries should reflect current market rates. It may be more beneficial to pay the directors a commission on profits, if they are the only outside shareholders, rather than pay a dividend on their shares. In this case, the commission should be based on the increase in earnings per share, adjusted for any new issues of shares or for any acquisitions. An overall limit is usually fixed for directors' emoluments expressed as a percentage of net profits as defined.

Service Agreement

A check list will be found at the end of this chapter, listing the likely contents of a service agreement. A service agreement should be approved by a resolution of the board, and the director concerned should normally not vote on his own agreement.[4,5] The critical items are as follows:

1 Job description, duties and period of agreement.
2 Salary, expenses and pension rights; transferability on leaving the company, cost of living increases and any profit sharing. (*Note:* the basis of calculation must be defined.)[6]

3 Other fringe benefits – cars, holidays, sick pay.
4 Equity holdings and options – the rights available to the director, and his rights on leaving the company.
5 Restrictions, if any, on other directorships in family companies.
6 Patents and inventions – the assignment of any patents etc. to the company, while employed. If the company wishes to extend this right to new patents developed within *X* years after leaving the company, this could affect the performance of the director in any subsequent job.
7 Restrictive covenants[7] – the company may seek to bind the director from competing, directly or indirectly, with the company's business as now carried on, for *X* years after he ceases to be employed. He may also be prevented from being an investor in any competing company which is not publicly quoted.

As all such covenants are *prima facie* in restraint of trade, they can be declared to be void by the courts if they are considered unreasonable, and not in the public interest. The onus of proof is therefore on the company, and it must not attempt to take away a man's livelihood, nor must it attempt to stifle legitimate competition.

A director can reasonably ask that this limitation be imposed only if he leaves on his own account, rather than if he is dismissed or if his contract is not renewed. On the bank's side, a restriction of this nature is reasonable, as otherwise a research director could spend money in developing a product, and then leave and start his own company. The parties must consult their lawyers to find out what is reasonable in the light of current statute and case law.[8] A clause restricting a director from disclosing confidential information is often found in service agreements.

DIVIDEND POLICY

The dividend policy must reflect the level of company profits, and the future financial requirements. In the case of companies of sizes 1 and 2, there is no case for giving the bank special priority for dividends. In the case of companies below size 2, a preferred ordinary dividend will probably be required. Here the interests of other shareholders must be considered. These shareholders should receive a similar dividend to the preferred ordinary shareholders, and then all shareholders should participate equally in any further dividends declared.

The only restriction on dividends in the case of companies of sizes 1 to 3 should be a requirement that no further dividends be declared unless they are covered X times by earnings. The cover figure must be fixed after considering the future financial needs of the company and the priority percentages for loan interest and dividends (see 'Priority Percentages' in Chapter 14).

Companies below size 3 (i.e. net profits pre-tax below £75,000) are likely to want to restrict dividends to build up their cash flow, especially if the directors are also the majority shareholders.

DEBENTURES AND LOANS

The method of negotiating loans is covered in subsequent chapters (see Chapters 14 and 15). If the debenture is convertible, the company should negotiate for conversion of half the debenture into equity. In fixing the interest rate, the parties should consider the interest and capital cover for the debenture. If the cover is good, the only disadvantage of a private company debenture to a bank over a quoted debenture is the non marketability; but this must be offset against potential capital profit from the investment.

BANK RESTRICTIONS

The type of restrictions which are likely to be required have been outlined in Chapters 9 and 10. The golden rule in such negotiations is not to cavil at clauses which a public company would have to accept, on such matters as share options, debentures, indemnities etc.[9] (For instance, on the initial quotation of a company, the Stock Exchange may require continuing indemnities on tax and estate duty from the directors.)

As far as possible, any restrictions should be in the form of limits and not vetoes; e.g. borrowing limits rather than an overall restriction on hire purchase and other borrowings. Therefore, the main field of negotiation is in the further undertakings likely to be required by a bank (see Chapter 10).

PERSONAL GUARANTEES

A bank may ask for personal guarantees from the executive directors, either as security for the debenture, or for the bank overdraft.

Naturally, the extent to which this can be resisted depends upon the future potential of the company, either as an investment or as a customer of the bank. In the case of companies below sizes 4 or 5, such a request could be reasonable, provided that the limits and the conditions under which the bank will agree to release the guarantee are fixed; e.g. if profits pre-tax reach £*X* (see Chapter 12). Otherwise a bank may never agree to give up the additional security. Directors' guarantees should also lapse automatically on leaving the company as otherwise directors may be sued by a bank long after they have left a company. The protection given is illusory if the director has all his assets in the company and is not a man of substance in his own right. A bank holding such a guarantee must decide if it is prepared to sell up the director's house and furniture over his head as security for the loan, and then assess the likely effect of this action on local opinion and on the bank's image.

It may be because the bank is fearful of the risk it has taken, and is not sure that it has evaluated the situation correctly. The directors should quote Mr J.P. Morgan, who once stated during a Congressional Inquiry that commercial credit did not depend upon possessing money or property but on character. Money could not buy it because a man he did not trust could not get money from him for all the bonds in Christendom. But men without any financial backing whom he trusted could borrow any amount because he believed in them.[10]

CHECKLIST: SERVICE AGREEMENTS

1 *The Parties*

(*a*) The company } Names and addresses
(*b*) Mr Q

2 *Term*

(*a*) Start
(*b*) Finish
(*c*) Normally a fixed term is stated and thereafter *x* months notice can be given to terminate the agreement.

3 *Duties*

(*a*) Define duties, job and location
(*b*) Responsible to whom?

(*c*) Required to give his whole time and attention to the company
(*d*) He must use his best endeavours to serve the company diligently and to comply with company policy
(*e*) What outside activities are allowed? For example, directorships of family firms

4 *Confidential information*
That company information classified as *confidential* will be kept secure, both during and after his employment with the company.

5 *Inventions and Patents*
To be revealed by the director and assigned to the company as its exclusive property while he is employed. Thereafter, any provisions for giving the company first refusal for any patents or inventions developed within *x* years of leaving the company.

6 *Emoluments*
(*a*) Salary and any increments and dates
(*b*) Commission or profit sharing base, when earned and paid
(*c*) Equity holdings and options – rights available and rights on leaving for whatever reason.
(*d*) Pension rights and transferability for him and his family
(*e*) Paid holidays – frequency and duration.
(*f*) Expenses
(*g*) Cars
(*h*) Other benefits
(*i*) Sick leave – *X* months at £*X*; *Y* months at £*Y*.

7 *Right of Company to Terminate*
(*a*) If the director becomes bankrupt
(*b*) If the director commits a criminal offence (excluding perhaps motoring offences)
(*c*) If the director is unable to carry out his duties for *X* months because of illness or incapacity. The company will have the right to terminate after *X* days or *Y* continuous months of incapacity in any period of 12 months.
(*d*) For dishonesty or grave misconduct
(*e*) For any breach of this agreement – i.e. failure to obey reasonable directions of the board.

8 *Restrictive Covenants and Non-competition*
(*a*) The period of the restriction after leaving the company
(*b*) The field of activity
(*c*) The geographical area
(*d*) The extent of the restriction

9 *Documents*
All documents to be returned to the company on departure

10 *Disputes*
To be settled by arbitration by the Institute of Directors or the CBI acting as arbitrators.

11 *Notice*

Note: Either party has a right to damages for any breach of the Service Agreement. Skilled legal advice must be sought in this event.

REFERENCES

1 *Financial Facilities for Small Firms,* p. 39
2 See Chapter 8. Shareholders Agreement 1, Equity Capital, Public Quotation, Assuming that 35% of the equity is offered to the market.
3 See A.R. ENGLISH, *Valuation of Shares in Unquoted Companies,* ICFC, p. 12.
4 *Notes on Specimen Form of Director's Service Agreement,* The Institute of Directors. The Institute also publishes a specimen form of service agreement.
5 See also JOHN HAMWAY, 'The Vital Points to Watch', *The Director,* March 1970, pp. 398-400.
6 A. READ, *The Company Director, His Functions, Powers and Duties,* Insitute of Directors, p.124.
7 *ibid.*, p. 141.
8 T.M. ALDRIDGE, Oyez Practice Notes, No.52, *Service Agreements,* 2nd edition Oyez Publications, London, 1969, pp. 65 and 83.
9 *Admission of Securities to Quotation,* Stock Exchange.
10 R.L. ALLEN, *The Great Pierpoint Morgan,* Harper & Bros, New York, 1948, pp. 225-226.
EDWIN P. HOYT JR., *The House of Morgan,* Frederick Muller, London, 1968, pp. 319-20.

14

Debentures and Loans

INTRODUCTION

Part of the monies provided to finance a company will be in the form of equity, and the rest by means of a debenture, or a loan.

When a company has sufficient assets and earnings, it can charge these as security for the payment of interest and the final repayment of the loan.

The company then has a loan at a fixed rate of interest for a definite period. The overdraft facilities can then be used for financing fluctuations in working capital requirements. As the overdraft is not being used as permanent capital, the company is less vulnerable to restrictions on bank lending in a credit squeeze.

Any loan, whether secured or not, involves the company in accepting some restrictions on future activities which could reduce the security available for the loan. These restrictions are more onerous in the case of private companies than they are for public companies. For private companies, the terms, including the interest rate, will vary according to the capital and interest cover for the loan. The conditions likely to appear in a debenture trust deed are examined below.

In Chapter 15 an account is given on how the company should arrive at its borrowing capability, and what points should be guarded against in any negotiations with financial institutions.

TRUST DEED

Parties

The company, its subsidiaries, the directors and the bank.

Recitals

The company and its directors have to state that the facts are as follows:

1 Existing charges outstanding.
2 The directors are not acting 'ultra vires', and that they have resolved to borrow these sums.

Principal

There may be an initial loan. An additional sum may be available at a later date provided that net profits exceed the level defined. (For example, initial loan £75,000. If net profits are not less than £100,000 in 1971, another £50,000 can be borrowed in 1972 by giving 30 days notice. The initial £75,000 could only be drawn during the period 1971-1972.) If initially, the full amount is not required, the loan should be available in 'tranches' of £25,000.

Interest Rate

The fixed interest rate for the period of the loan is stated. The interest is payable six monthly in arrears on fixed dates.

Purpose

For financing working capital, stocks, plant and machinery in its existing line of business.

Repayment

The principal monies and any interest due become payable:

1 If the security is enforceable.

2 On maturity, a ten year debenture would be repayable, either, at the end of the ten year period, or in equal annual instalments over the last x years on a fixed date in each year. For example, five equal instalments over the last five years.

3 If the interest rates fall over the loan period, the company may be able to borrow at more favourable rates; therefore, the right for early repayment by the company should be negotiated. In the case of a ten year debenture, the company should be able to repay the loan after five years.

Security

The security for the loan can be as follows:

1 A mortgage debenture, secured on the freehold and leasehold properties including all fixtures, but excluding plant and machinery. (This is called a fixed charge.)

2 A floating charge on the undertaking, property and assets of the group, both present and future, including uncalled capital.

3 A combination of 1 and 2 above – a fixed and floating charge.

Priority

Debentures of any class secured by a fixed or floating charge can rank first, second or *pari passu* with any other charges, e.g.

mortgage debenture – first fixed charge
debenture – first floating charge
second debenture – second floating charge
bank overdraft – second floating charge, *pari passu* with the second debenture.

The position of the bank overdraft must be defined in relation to the debenture. According to the company's financial position, the bank will decide if it is prepared to accept an overdraft ranking *pari passu* with a debenture, both secured by a first floating charge. The amount of the debenture will have already been fixed, and the debenture holders will require that there is an upper limit on the bank overdraft; all amounts above this limit being secured by a second charge. On liquidation, a fixed charge has a prior claim over all creditors in respect of the assets charged. A floating charge has a prior claim over all creditors except for priority creditors (rent, rates, wages and tax etc.).[1]

Charging Subsidiaries

Subsidiaries become charging subsidiaries by giving a floating charge over their assets as security for the debenture. To do so, they give joint and several guarantees to the parent company and execute collateral charges. However, where a subsidiary is not wholly owned, minority shareholders may have to give their approval before the assets can be charged. Approval is required from the minority shareholders if the subsidiary has a public quotation. Where the assets of a parent company and subsidiaries are charged as security for a debenture, they are collectively referred to as the charging group. This collateral charge subsists until the principal monies and any interest outstanding are repaid.

Where there are charging subsidiaries, it is normal to have an overall bank overdraft for the group, with facilities being made available to subsidiaries and the individual debit and credit balances being offset against one another.

Non-resident subsidiaries, whose assets are not under the control of the courts in the UK, are usually excluded from the charging group. If a subsidiary is not in the charging group, the debenture holder's security is restricted to the value of the holding company's shareholding in the subsidiary. Thus, in the case of a non-charging subsidiary, the debenture holders rank after all creditors, and after any preference shareholders, if the holding company only holds ordinary shares. For this reason some groups make a policy that all the group properties are owned by the holding company. New subsidiaries are usually required to become charging subsidiaries when they are acquired.

Immediate Repayment

The debenture security becomes enforceable immediately against the charging group, if in the case of the company or any of its subsidiaries, any of the following occur:

1* A notice is issued or an order made for a winding up, or if a receiver is appointed, except if this is in favour of another charging subsidiary.

2* A judgement is made against the company for an amount over £500, or if an execution or a distress warrant is levied, and payment is not made within two to four days.

* Normal clause in a public company debenture

3* Any stoppage of payment or any threat to cease to carry on its business.[2]

4* Any change occurs in the nature of its business, or if any other mortgage or charge ranking equal, or in priority to, the existing debenture is created, including allowing the bank overdraft to exceed the permitted level.

5* *Any other breach of covenant or undertaking made by the company or its directors in the debenture trust deed,* for example, a default on the repayment of the principal monies.

6 In the case of a private company, where there is one man who is vital to the success of the enterprise, it is possible to insert the following clause: If *X* dies, or is unable to carry out his duties as the managing director, the debenture becomes repayable. If *X* breaks his service agreement for any other reason, the debenture holders may wish to have the right to enforce their security. (It is possible to take out an insurance policy on *X*'s death to act as security, or part security, for the debenture, if the asset cover within the company is not sufficient in the early years to repay the debenture.[3] The premiums must be paid out of *taxed income* for the benefits to be available tax free and the policy assigned to the debenture holders; any balance not required after repayment of the debenture reverts to the company.)

Covenants

The company undertakes the following covenants:

1* To conduct the business in a proper manner, to pay all rents, rates, etc., promptly, and to observe all covenants.

2* To file all returns, etc., concerning the registration of mortgages and charges, in accordance with the Companies Acts.

3* To keep all buildings in a good state of repair, and not to dismantle any property or plant except to replace obsolete plant or equipment.

4* To allow the debenture holders to inspect the buildings.

5* To inform the debenture holders of any notice or proceedings affecting the property, and those relating to any new properties acquired.

6* To keep fully insured through a recognised insurance company all property and plant, and to pay all premiums promptly. The company will provide where required, a certificate that all assets are fully insured.

7 Where applicable, to keep up the insurance policy on the managing director, as security for the debenture.

8* To keep proper books of accounts, and to allow these to be inspected by the debenture holders. To make true and proper entries of all dealings and transactions of the company.

9* To keep the debenture holders informed of the company's business, and to furnish them with information as required. To provide them with annual accounts within four months of the year's end.

10* To make any payments due under agreements, judgements etc., *Note:* Should the company default on keeping the property in a proper state of repair or in keeping the property fully insured, the bank can make the repairs or insure the property and recover the amount from the company.

Further Covenants

The company covenants that neither itself nor its subsidiaries, except with the approval of the debenture holders, will perform any of the following:

1 Make any change of the financial year end from the existing one.

2 Acquire any shares or assets in any other business, give guarantees or credit (other than normal trade credit), or make loans or advances, except to charging subsidiaries and reasonable loans to employees.

3* Transfer, sell or dispose of the whole or any substantial part of its business, undertaking, shareholding in any subsidiary, freehold or leasehold property, or any assets, except for replacing or purchasing such assets in the ordinary course of business,[4] except from one charging subsidiary to another.

4 Make any dividend payments, repayment of capital to shareholders, except as permitted in the articles on the preferred ordinary shares, or required to avoid a short fall payment under Section 77 of the Finance Act 1965.

5 Make any increase in emoluments or pensions payable to directors, or past directors, outside those contained in the service agreements, or previously disclosed in writing.

6 Make any hire purchase agreements without the unanimous approval of the board.

Borrowing Limits

Limits are set on the level of borrowing permitted, while the debenture is outstanding, both for secured or unsecured borrowing. These limits can be set either as a fixed amount or more usually as a factor of the adjusted capital and reserves (see below), provided that the interest cover laid down is also achieved.

Adjusted Capital and Reserves

The consolidated net assets of the group, including preference capital and all capital and revenue reserves, and any increase in capital reserves resulting from a revaluation of assets are called the adjusted capital and reserves as follows:

1 The issued and paid-up share capital of the company – preference and ordinary.
2 The consolidated capital and revenue reserves, the share premium account, any capital reserves, including amounts arising from a revaluation of properties, and the consolidated revenue reserves of the group. *Note.* These figures must be adjusted to allow for any changes since the last accounts, any increases in share capital, changes in share premium account, capital reserves arising from a revaluation and any sales or acquisitions of subsidiaries.
3 The following amounts should be deducted:
   (*a*) Minority shareholder's interests in subsidiaries (charging).
   (*b*) Reserves and sums set aside for taxation.
   (*c*) Any goodwill items or intangible assets.
   (*d*) Capitalised research and development.
   (*e*) Any distribution or proposed distribution from profits, earned prior to the last accounts, except to another group member, which exceeds the amount provided for it in the last audited balance sheets.
   (*f*) After the issue of the debenture there are likely to be restrictions on revaluations of fixed assets. However, new subsidiaries will normally be allowed to revalue their assets when they become charging subsidiaries. Such revaluations must not result in the net asset value of the company's investment in the new charging subsidiary being greater

than the purchase price (i.e. a goodwill item on consolidation). Any increase in asset value must be calculated, after deducting the capital gains tax liability from the total increase in value of the asset.

(*g*) Any debit balance on the revenue reserves of the subsidiaries must be deducted.

(*h*) Any other adjustments which the auditors feel are appropriate – e.g. deduction of excess depreciation above the relevant tax allowances.

This figure becomes the adjusted capital and reserves, and can be used as the standard against which the total limit for secured or overall borrowings is measured.

Capital Borrowings Formula

Where there are subsidiaries, some of which are charging and some non-charging, it is necessary to modify the figure for adjusted capital and reserves as a measure of the limit for secured borrowings as follows:

Adjusted Capital and Reserves
Add back minority interests in charging subsidiaries. Earlier on in the calculation of adjusted capital and reserves, all minority interests were deducted, now the minority interests in charging subsidiaries are added back, as for charging subsidiaries, the debenture holders rank prior to these minority interests.

Deduct the interests of the charging group in non-charging subsidiaries, including share, loan or other indebtedness, but excluding current account items. As the debenture holder's charge is only secured upon the shares owned by the holding company, the debenture holders would rank equal to any minority interests if both the holding company and these minority interests owned ordinary shares. Naturally, if one party owned preference shares and the other party ordinary shares, the preference shareholders would have the prior claim over the capital available at a liquidation.

Deduct any distribution or proposed distribution from profits to non-charging subsidiaries, earned prior and not provided for in the last balance sheets.

The total of all these amounts is the *capital borrowings formula* or net realisable assets, on which the debenture is secured. The security is greater than this figure, as the figure for adjusted capital and reserves is calculated on a 'going concern' basis, and is after the deduction of creditors and deferred liabilities, which, except for priority creditors, rank after the debenture.

Borrowings and Capital Cover

Secured borrowings, which are expressed as a proportion of the capital borrowings formula, will include the following (including any premiums payable on redemption and excluding loans in favour of members of the charging group):

1. Priority borrowings – the aggregate of any mortgages and fixed charges ranking *pari passu* or prior to the debentures.
2. Debentures – the total of debentures outstanding, including any subsequent debentures.
3. Bank borrowings – total bank borrowings ranking *pari passu* in security to the debenture.
4. Loans to non-charging subsidiaries. The company can only subscribe or purchase shares (including acquisitions), make loans or lend money to non-charging subsidiaries or other companies if the ratios for capital and interest cover are not exceeded by making these loans. Loans to non-charging subsidiaries reduce the assets of the charging group and must therefore, be closely controlled. Loans to charging subsidiaries, which become non-charging, are also included in this category.

The calculation of capital cover or asset cover, for debentures with capital priority over the ordinary shares, shows the proportionate amount of assets ranking as security for the stock in question. The tangible assets of the charging group are shown less current and deferred liabilities. The proceeds of the stock must be added to the net assets. The existing secured borrowings, which have already been subtracted, must be added back before cover can be calculated. Loans due to be repaid within four months of the issue of the new debenture are usually excluded, as they are being refinanced by the new loan.

In the following example, Case A shows the effect of raising a debenture of £200 ranking *pari passu* with the bank and the other priority borrowings. Case B shows the effect of adding a first debenture, as for Case A of £200, and in addition a second debenture of £200 ranking after all the other secured borrowings.

Example

		Case A	Case B
Net tangible assets of charging group as at (date)		£1,000	£1,000
Net proceeds of the debentures		200	400
Pari passu secured borrowings	bank	100	100
	priority	100	100
Total assets		£1,400	£1,600
Total secured borrowing (including the debenture first charge)		400	400
Capital cover		3.5 times	4 times
Total secured borrowings (first and second charge)		–	600
Capital cover			2.7 times

The total assets in Case A would have to fall to 28 per cent of their initial figure before the debenture was uncovered. In case B, if the value of total assets fell to 38 per cent the secured borrowings would still be covered.

Interest Cover and Net Profits

Interest cover is calculated by taking the total interest payable on all secured borrowing.[5] This amount is divided into the net profits, as defined below, of the charging group for the last year, or into an average of these profits over the last three years.

The net profits of the group as at the last balance sheet are adjusted as follows:

1. Deduct the profits and losses of non-charging subsidiaries.
2. Make any adjustment for the purchase or sale of any subsidiary since the date of the last balance sheet.
3. Exclude profits and losses of a non-trading nature, but including

receipts and issues for 'know-how'.

4 Exclude all profits and losses of a capital nature.

5 Charge all expenses, including proper depreciation and amortisation, overseas taxation, emoluments of directors and past directors, and any allowances for losses on contracts or bad debts.

6 Make full deduction for research and development expenditure unless it is fully charged to a third party. The act of capitalising these expenses increases net profits by the amount capitalised. This action therefore increases the interest cover for the first year. The subsequent effect on interest cover depends upon the policy adopted for amortising this expenditure. Thus, the improvement in interest cover might permit the company to justify further secured borrowings, although its overall position has not improved.

7 Deduct interest on all borrowings, secured or unsecured, and deduct UK taxation.

8 Include dividends and interest receivable from non-charging subsidiaries, investments and holding company management charges recovered from non-charging subsidiaries. Dividends from non-charging subsidiaries can only be included, provided that they do not exceed the profits earned. Dividends from overseas subsidiaries are also included.

9 Make such other adjustments as the auditors feel are appropriate.

Priority Percentages[6]

Interest cover for debentures and the earnings cover for preference and ordinary dividends can either be expressed by showing the number of times the interest or dividend was covered by the last net available earnings, or by the priority percentage method. This system shows the cost of interest or dividends on the various classes of stock, as percentages of total net earnings in order of priority. It does not exaggerate the interest cover as the simple cover method does, and it takes into effect, therefore, capital gearings.

Example

A company earning £70,000 after deducting corporation tax, depreciation and loan interest charges, must add back the loan interest as it is allowed as a charge against profits for tax purposes. The net effective cost to the company, however, is the gross interest, *less the corporation tax saved.* To compute the sum available to cover the cost of servicing the various classes of capital, the *net* amount of any debenture interest should be added to the company's earnings after tax which are available for dividends.

If the gross interest on a debenture is £50,000 and the rate of corporation tax is 40 per cent, then the net cost to the company would be £30,000. This sum should be added to the net earnings above, of £70,000, making a total of £100,000 available for interest and dividends.

	Cost (£)	*Available after prior charge (£)*	*Percentage of total available £100,000*	*Simple cover times covered* A	*Cumulative basis* B	*Priority (%)*
Debenture stock interest (net)	30,000	100,000	30	3.3	30 = 3.3	First 30% = 0-30%
First preference stock dividend (gross)	30,000	70,000	30	2.3	60 = 1.66	next 30% = 31-60%
Second preference stock dividend (gross)	20,000	40,000	20	2.0	80 = 1.25	next 20% = 61-80%
Ordinary stock dividend (gross)	10,000	20,000	10	2.0	90 = 1.1	next 10% = 81-90%
To reserve	10,000	10,000	10	–	100 = 1.0	next 10% = 91-100%
	£100,000		100%			

On the simple earnings basis the ordinary dividend is covered twice, but on the priority percentage basis it is covered 1.1 times as 90 per cent of the net profits are distributed. A fall of 11 per cent in earnings would uncover the ordinary dividend, and a fall of over 20 per cent would uncover the second preference dividend which appears to be covered twice by the simple method.

It is advisable to project forward the company's earnings over the next three years to assess the interest cover for the debenture and the remaining earnings which are available to pay any preference or ordinary dividends. Normally, the interest cover required is between four and five times. Therefore, for secured borrowings, the gross interest payable must not exceed 20-25 per cent of net profits, as defined above.

Overall Borrowing Limit

The aggregate amount outstanding of all borrowed monies of the company and its subsidiaries, including any fixed premium on final repayment (excluding inter-company borrowings and any borrowings about to be repaid within four months), must not exceed a factor of the adjusted capital and reserves as defined above. This figure covers all borrowings, secured or unsecured, for the whole company including the charging and non-charging group, and including any premium payable on redemption.

Borrowings are defined as follows and exclude loans made within the charging group:

1 Debentures.
2 Bank borrowings.
3 Priority borrowings – mortgages and fixed charges.
4 The nominal amounts of any paid up share capital (other than ordinary shares) of subsidiaries, which rank in priority for dividends or capital to the subsidiaries ordinary share capital, and which are owned by non-members of the group; i.e. preference shares in subsidiaries owned by minority interests.
5 The borrowings made to any subsidiary or those made by the company, if the debt ceases to be owned by the company.
6 Guarantees given by the company or its subsidiaries in sterling or in foreign currency including any investment dollar premium payable.
7 Hire purchase indebtedness.
8 Acceptance credits. } The principal amounts owing
9 Factoring.

Note. The debenture holders, as they have a floating charge, are able to prevent the company's book debts being pledged as security for block discounting, acceptance credits or factoring. The finance company will therefore rank after the debenture holders. If the company wishes to have their book debts available for block discounting or factoring, the floating charge should be adjusted to exclude these items.

Example: Overall Borrowing Limit

Factor	*1 times*	*%*	*1½ times*	*%*	*2 times*	*%*
Adjusted capital and reserves	£100 =	50	£100 =	40	£100 =	33⅓
Borrowings	£100 =	50	£150 =	60	£200 =	66⅔
	£200 =	100	£250 =	100	£300 =	100

Perhaps it would be fitting to end this chapter by paraphrasing some remarks on fixed and floating charges by Lord Macnaghten, quoted in Palmer's Company Law:[7]

A fixed charge is specific and ascertainable and is secured on specific property so that the security can be clearly defined.

A floating charge is an equitable charge on the assets of a going concern which floats with the property, until some act or event causes it to settle and fasten on the subject of the charge. It is therefore dormant until the undertaking ceases to be a 'going concern' or until the person, in whose favour the charge is, intervenes. When this event happens it becomes a fixed charge.

SCHEDULE FOR A DEBENTURE TRUST DEED

1. *Parties*
2. *Recitals* – subsidiaries – resolution to borrow – service agreements.
3. *Principal* – Amounts – how and when drawn – further loans if any.

4 *Purpose* – Application of loan – working capital.
5 *Repayment* – Dates and amounts – right of early repayment.
6 *Interest Rate* – Dates of payment.
7 *Security* – Type of charge – priority and limits to other *pari passu* charges.
8 *Charging Subsidiaries* – Existing subsidiaries – new subsidiaries.
9 *Immediate Repayment.*
10 *Assignment of insurance policy* – Security – undertaking to keep it in force.
11 *Bank's right to appoint receiver* – When principal becomes payable.
12 *Conduct of receiver.*
13 *Covenants by company.*
14 *Further covenants* – Except with bank's approval.
15 *Borrowing limits* – Secured (capital/interest cover) – overall (capital cover) – definition of cover – definition of borrowings.
16 *Payment of all legal costs* – Present or future.
17 *Service of notices.*
18 *Definitions.*
19 *Joint and several warranties* – Representation by the directors and the company in respect of the company and its subsidiaries.

CONCLUSION

The next chapter is devoted to examining how the company should apply these principles to assess its own capacity to borrow.

Note. In the Appendix to this Chapter will be found an explanation of flat yields, redemption yields and sinking funds.

APPENDIX 1: DEBENTURES AND LOANS

The following are three terms which apply mostly to publicly quoted companies but which should be explained.

Flat Yield: Gross

The yield at the current market price or issue price before payment of tax.

Flat yield. Gross =	Interest rate	x	Par value	÷	market or issue price
8.16%	8%	x	100	÷	98

Redemption Yield: Gross

The gross yield to redemption of a stock, standing below, or issued below par (£100), makes allowance for the capital lost or gained on redemption.

Stocks with different interest rates, standing at different prices, can be compared by means of their redemption yield. The sum required to offset the gain or loss to redemption is calculated by an actuarial formula, and an adjustment is made to the flat yield to allow for this. There are published tables giving redemption yields (Investment Memoranda, 1971/2, p. 48).

Sinking Funds (Investment Memoranda 1971/2, p. 54)

Sinking funds can be used to partly or wholly redeem a stock. Starting some time after redemption, sinking funds provide annual or semi-annual drawings at a fixed price. They are expressed in pounds or as a percentage of the amount of stock issued. The company can also have the right to purchase stock in the market, under or at the drawing price. There are two types:

1 Non-cumulative: a 2 per cent sinking fund will redeem a stock in 50 years.
2 Cumulative: the fixed percentage set aside for redemption is increased by the amount of the interest saved on the stock already redeemed. The annual or bi-annual drawings get bigger as the redemption is accelerated.

For example, two per cent sinking fund: non-cumulative redeems in full in 50 years; cumulative (assuming a four per cent stock) redeems in full in twenty-eight years.

REFERENCES

1 Companies Act, 1948, Section 319.
2 Companies Act, 1948, Section 223, Definition of inability to pay debts.
3 Repayment might not be able to be made without liquidating the company.
4 This would exclude a sale and lease back arrangement.
5 Interest on loans repayable within four months of the issue of the new

debenture are normally excluded, as it is assumed they are being refinanced of the new loan.

6 Investment Memoranda, 1971/2, Cazenove & Co., London 1971, p. 59.

7 C.M. SCHMITTHOFF and J.H. THOMPSON, *Palmers Company Law,* 21st Edition, Stevens & Sons, London, 1968, p. 395. See also Part 4C Borrowing Powers & Debentures.

15

Company Evaluation of Borrowing Capacity

BORROWING LIMITS

In the previous chapter, the debenture trust deed was examined and examples given of how various borrowing limits are calculated. The following operations should be carried out to assess the company's borrowing capacity, prior to any negotiations for raising a loan.

Adjusted Capital and Reserves

From the last balance sheet (*date*):

Total issued share capital – preference and ordinary		£1,000
Total consolidated – capital and revenue reserves		500
		£1,500
Changes since last accounts:		
Add or subtract		
Loan and share capital – increase	+	50
Revenue reserves – additional earnings or losses	+	50
Capital reserves – revaluation	+	200
Share premium account	+	30
Sales or acquisitions of subsidiaries		–
	+	£1,830

Subtract		
Minority interests in subsidiaries	–	150
Reserves for taxation	–	100
Interim dividends not allowed for in the last accounts	–	30
	–	£ 280
Adjusted capital and reserves	=	£1,550

Capital Borrowings Formula

To be calculated when there are non-charging subsidiaries and charging subsidiaries with minority interests.

Add		
Adjusted capital and reserves	+	£1,550
Minority interests in charging subsidiaries	+	100
Subtract		
Share and loan capital interests in non-charging subsidiaries	–	250
Capital borrowings formula		£1,400

Before making these figures final:

1 Examine existing borrowing limits for secured or unsecured borrowings permitted by the articles, and change the limit if necessary. *Note.* A resolution amending the articles requires the approval of 75 per cent of the members votes of each class of share[1] – preference and ordinary.

2 Decide which subsidiaries are to be included in the charging group. List charges already registered for the charging group and any limitations on further borrowings.

3 Where subsidiaries have minority interests, negotiate with each class of shareholder to pass resolutions to charge the subsidiaries assets, as security for the loan; obtain proxies where possible. If permission is not given, arrange separate banking facilities, and where possible, call in or refinance any loans made to non-charging subsidiaries. Make appropriate management charges for all functions performed by the group for non-charging subsidiaries.

4 Revalue any assets, prior to raising the debenture, as the right to revalue is usually limited afterwards. Add the net value of the revaluation after deduction of any capital gains tax liability.
5 Decide if any changes are required in the financial year end of the holding company or any of its subsidiaries.
6 Decide on the disposal or purchase of any major assets, the sale of interests in subsidiaries or the purchase of any companies.

Secured Borrowings Cover

Capital borrowings formula	£1,400
Secured borrowings	
Debentures – new and existing stock	200
Pari passu secured borrowings – mortgages, bank	200
Loans to non-charging subsidiaries	——
	£400 = 28.57%

Secured borrowings are just under 29 per cent of the capital borrowings formula, well below the $66\frac{2}{3}$ per cent limit for public companies. (40 per cent loan – 60 per cent equity.) For private companies, a limit for secured borrowings can be as high as 100 per cent. (50 per cent loan – 50 per cent equity.)

The maximum amount of stock that can be issued, is governed by the asset and interest cover limitations, imposed by the borrower.

Capital cover is calculated by taking the net tangible assets – the adjusted capital and reserves – and adding back the total loans and the proceeds of the new debenture stock, as in the example in the previous chapter.

Overall borrowings Cover

List all borrowings for *all* subsidiaries, charging and non-charging as follows:

Total secured borrowings at (date):	
Charging subsidiaries	£ 400
Non-charging subsidiaries	100
Minority holdings in non-charging subsidiaries ranking in priority to the debenture holders for dividends or capital; e.g. preference shares	50

Guarantees:	
sterling	10
foreign currency (+ investment dollar premium)	–
Hire purchase indebtedness	140
Acceptance credits	100
Factoring	–
Total overall borrowings	£800
Adjusted capital and reserves	£1,400 = 57.14%

Total overall borrowings are expressed as a percentage of the adjusted capital and reserves, as these borrowings relate to the whole group and not just to the charging group. The capital borrowings formula *cannot* be used, as it excludes the assets of the non-charging subsidiaries.

INTEREST

Interest Rate (Coupon Rate)

1 Find out the current interest rates charged for similar loans to other companies by the bank. (*Note.* Charges have to be registered and therefore this is not confidential information.) The bank overdraft rate can be taken as a guide, but remember it fluctuates according to changes in base-rate.
2 Find out what the bank pays for its money (x% above bank rate), and negotiate a rate as close to this figure as possible (normally convertible stocks have lower coupons than straight loans). Use this argument where the bank has an equity option.
3 Argue hotly for a lower interest rate, if the company can offer good interest cover, as the poorer the security, the greater the risk and the higher the interest rate to justify the loan.
4 Find out the expected trend of interest rates over the next few years from your bank.

Interest Cover for Secured Borrowings

1 Calculate the net profits of the charging group, as outlined in the previous chapter. Ensure that all transactions between the charging group and non-charging subsidiaries are at 'arms length',

and that non-charging subsidiaries bear the true costs of any management functions carried out for them by the group.

2 Calculate the interest cover by dividing the gross interest payable, including that of any new debenture stock, into the adjusted net profits pre-interest and tax as follows:

	Last year	Average last 3 years	Forecast average next 3 years
Add			
Net profits pre-interest and tax at (*date*)	+300	+250	+400
Receipts for know-how	+ 30	+ 10	–
Dividends and management charges from non-charging subsidiaries	+ 20	+ 20	+ 20
Dividends from overseas subsidiaries	+ 10	+ 10	+ 10
	+360	+290	+430
Subtract			
Net profits, pre-interest and tax; non-charging subsidiaries	–100	– 80	–130
Net profits of a charging subsidiary – sold	– 20	– 10	–
	– 120	– 90	– 130
Total	240	200	300
Interest gross	60	50	70
Times covered	4.0	4.0	4.3

3 Calculate the priority percentages, as in the previous chapter, before and after issue of the new stock. Decide the minimum level of profits possible over the period of the loan, and see whether any other dividends payable, preference or ordinary, are properly covered.

The Profit Contribution of the loan

Provided that the new loan money earns more than the company pays in interest, equity earnings are increased. The effect is called 'gearing' (leverage in the USA), and the degree of gearing depends upon the relationship of loan to equity capital.

Should profits fall sharply after interest is paid, there may be little left for the equity dividends. Therefore, the degree of gearing must depend upon the likely fluctuations in profits, and the calculations of priority percentages should be made on a 'worst case' example.

The same applies to any cash flow projections, showing the profits available for repaying the loan at maturity.

The following points have been abstracted from an article in *Management Today.*[2]

'A company with no loans outstanding and paying out all profits in dividends must earn 17 per cent on capital employed to yield, after corporation tax and income tax at the standard rate, the same that can be obtained at present from a building society. Naturally a higher yield than this would be required from the higher risk investment.

'If an all equity financed company earning 20 per cent, doubles its size by debt financing, and if it borrows at 10 per cent and earns 15 per cent on the new capital, the return on equity rises to 25 per cent but the overall return falls to 17½ per cent pre-interest, and 12½ per cent after interest. This represents a fall of 7½ per cent from the previous return.

'Always insist on an overall return on loan capital, as high as that required on shareholders funds, otherwise debt can be used to finance marginal projects.

'If a business is unable to generate sufficient cash for its needs, it either requires management action or the company's requirements for expansion to legitimately exceed its existing means. However, such investments for expansion will only increase the company's long term vulnerability if they lower the overall return on capital.'

SECURITY AND PRIORITY

Decide what security to offer in relation to the interest and capital cover available; the better the security, the less the security that needs to be given. An unsecured loan stock, ranking after the creditors but well covered, is a better investment than a poorly covered debenture.[3]

Secure any debenture by a floating charge and avoid, if possible, giving a fixed charge. Try to retain the right to mortgage for purchasing new property up to a limit expressed as a percentage of the total secured borrowings. For public companies, this limit is usually 20 per cent of total secured borrowings.

Negotiate the priority of the existing loans, i.e. bank loans etc., in relation to the debenture and the limit to be placed on these loans.

Exclude book debts from the charge given, if these are to be given as security for financing debtors (factoring or block discounting). Note the cost of this finance against loan finance.

Banks tend to ask for all the security available. The company, however, should give as little security away as it can, in order to maximise the borrowing potential of the company, in case of unforeseen set-backs.

If the security offered is not adequate, and the company is a 'one man' company, consider offering an insurance policy on this man's life as security for the loan.

REPAYMENT

Decide from forward, conservatively based, projections of cash flow, when the loan can be repaid. Negotiate repayment terms, preferably at the end of the period.

Ask for the right for early repayment, in case interest rates fall.

FURTHER FINANCE

In most cases it is unlikely that the existing shareholders will have more money to invest in the company's equity. If the bank has power to prevent the company from raising further loans, it may insist that further finance is obtained by subscribing more equity. Thus, the original shareholders' position of control can be whittled down, until the bank's original 30 per cent shareholding becomes a controlling interest. To avoid this position:

1 Negotiate the right to raise more loans, provided that the interest and capital limits are maintained.
2 If the bank requires a complete veto on further loans, negotiate the right to buy the bank's shares at a valuation based on an agreed formula prepared by the auditors, if the company can find finance elsewhere.
3 Allow further equity subscription by the bank, but restrict the voting rights of these shares, provided the company achieves a certain level of profits. This level of profits can be average net profits of over a certain amount, in a certain period,

representing a reasonable return on capital. Define net profits very carefully.

4 Obtain an assurance in writing, that the bank will not use any position of control to make changes in the company's capital structure or in the composition of the board, or to enable it to sell its shares to an outsider, without the existing shareholders' permission. Provided, of course, that the company achieves a certain level of profits.

Note. The time to negotiate these terms in writing is before the bank invests and not at the time new money has to be raised.

COVENANTS, WARRANTIES AND FURTHER UNDERTAKINGS

Examine these conditions, and list any items which are inconsistent with these warranties. For example, bad debts, stock losses etc.

Rectify any problems, wherever possible, for example, ensure that the file at Companies House is up to date; review insurance cover to see that it is adequate, and check properties for any planning disputes, possible compulsory purchase orders, or non-observance of property covenants.

Decide what covenants can be given, which must be qualified and which are totally unacceptable, for example, restrictions on loans and long term credit.

CONCLUSION

In conjunction with the auditor and company solicitor, prepare a written brief, outlining clearly what the company's objectives are in each section of the debenture trust deed under negotiation. List facts and figures to show the required borrowing limits, interest and capital cover, priority percentages etc., and debenture terms required.

REFERENCES

1 Companies Act, 1948, Section 141.

2. ROBERT HELLER, 'What debt does to profit', *Management Today,* July 1970, pp. 99-101.

3 Companies Act, 1948, Section 322. Limitations on debentures issued within 12 months of a Winding Up.

16

The Board of Directors

THE BOARD

General

After investment by a financial institution, the board of directors becomes an important organisation, to which the new investor normally has the right to appoint a nominee as a non-executive director to watch over its investment, and to help the company achieve the agreed objectives.

In the public company sector, where ownership and management control are in separate hands, inefficiency is usually self-correcting through a takeover bid. In the world of the private company, ownership and management are so closely linked that the board is in danger of becoming a passive and inactive body rather than a vital force which reviews continually the objectives of the company and the efficiency of the management; the only self-correcting factors being death, liquidation, a forced takeover or the arrival of an outside investor.

For this reason, the functions of the board need to be defined and the duties of a non-executive director, understood, both in the private and in the public company sector. Since the board of directors, when properly organised, provides a review body for all companies, private company managements especially can be helped by a well balanced board to overcome problems outside their experience which arise during a period of rapid expansion.

The Responsibilities of the Board[1]

The board is a committee chosen by the shareholders, and it is responsible and accountable to them. It directs the company, approves and monitors the achievement of objectives, and guides the management. It manages the managers, but it does not manage the company on a day to day basis. This is the responsibility of the executive management, which implements the policy laid down by the board. While the board will guide and counsel management, it has the responsibility for the whole business in both the long and the short term. It therefore tends to be forward and outward looking, rather than concentrating on the past performance of the company to the exclusion of all else. A long and balanced view is needed of the company's strategic plan for the next five years, and of any factors which may frustrate its achievement. The board needs to have members with qualities such as sound judgement, analytic ability and wisdom – men who will steer the company onto the correct path for the future.

Legal Functions

The board has certain legal functions to perform, which it is unable to delegate, as these are powers which, under the Companies Acts, it is required to exercise. Directors also have responsibilities to their shareholders to ensure that the business is properly managed and that the assets are properly safeguarded.[2] These legal functions are as follows:

1 Powers under the Companies Acts.
2 Powers under the articles of the company; for example, Article 80 of Table A; the powers and duties of directors.
3 Special powers not able to be delegated; for example, recommendations to shareholders on the declaration of dividends, increases in share capital, acquisitions etc.
4 The directors must report to the shareholders and recommend any action required for the long term survival of the company.
5 The directors have a fiduciary responsibility to the shareholders,

as trustees of the assets, earnings and monies of the company.
6 The directors are collectively and individually responsible for breaches of duty, negligence, default or for any breach of trust.[3]

Planning Functions

Strategic Plans

As the board is responsible for the long range profitability and the continued existence of the enterprise, it has therefore to approve the long and medium range plans of the company. These duties are as follows:

1 To carry out the annual review, and approval of the revised company strategic plan. The period of the plan depends on the industry concerned.
2 To approve the strategic goals and objectives for the company and to see that all objectives are quantified, so that performance can be measured against the objective set; for example, the objective should not be to maximise profits but to increase profits by x per cent per annum for each of three financial years from 1972 to 1974. The information and recommendations supplied by the executive management will allow the board to decide on the following courses of action: – the return on investment required, and the projected growth rate and market share, depending on whether the company is aiming for growth and increased profits, or for stability and survival.
3 To decide on the economic function of the company, how to give greater value to the users, as profits are a reward for serving society better than other competitors. A short term objective to maximise profits could be achieved by cutting product development and completely ruining the long term competitive position of the company.
4 To review the present position of the company in product quality and performance, reliability, service, price, and customer confidence.
5 To decide whether growth will be achieved by new products, diversification, increased market share at home or abroad, by acquisition, or by a combination of all or some of these methods.

External Factors
The board should consider and anticipate the long term impact of the forces of change in the environment on the company, and how it can profit from any opportunities, or avoid any potential threats. The directors should examine the effect of these conditions on the strategic plan (see Chapter 6); especially the effect of public and national goals on the company's plans (i.e. social and political pressures).

Budgets
The board will approve the annual budget, which is prepared from the long term plan, and see that it is both realistic and in line with the long term objectives laid down. The budget will be firm for one year and should also have forecasts for periods up to three or five years, or longer in some industries.[4] The following points will be considered:

1 The figures for order intake, costs and profits for the next year will be looked at to see if they are realistic or too optimistic.
2 The cash flow over the next three years or longer will be examined to establish the capital requirements of the company and to decide how these demands should be met. If the profits are not sufficient to raise new capital, capital expenditure may have to be cut.
3 The board may wish to set expenditure as a percentage of forecast sales and to approve contingency plans if the planned level of profits is not achieved.

Direction

Although the board will delegate to the executive management the powers necessary for running the business, certain key decisions will be reserved for approval by the board. These are as follows:

Corporate policy
The board will lay down the general policy required to implement the strategic plan by issuing guide lines and practice, covering such fields as finance, marketing, staffing etc. Once these decisions have been made, their execution is in the hands of management, who are in close touch with the day-to-day operations of the company. They

are therefore the body best equipped to decide how to carry out these policies within the short term, so as to achieve the long term goals of the company.

Products and Markets

The following decisions are likely to be reserved to the board for their approval:

1 Diversification.
2 Closing down old products.
3 Launching new products.
4 Entering new markets, especially international markets.
5 Acquisitions.
6 Sales of subsidiary companies.
7 Licensing existing products or taking licences from other companies.
8 The sale or purchase of patents.
9 The research and development programme.
10 Advertising policies.

The board should also be alert to external market conditions, which can affect the company, and to any opportunities and threats that arise; for example, changes in exchange rates can alter the competitive position of the company, so that a revision in the long term plan may be required. Changes may also have to be made in the objectives set for market shares, sales volume, profits, the return on investment, and in the economic function of the company, in the light of current market conditions.

Finance

Any changes in the financial policy of the company should be approved by the board, who are responsible for supervising and controlling the finances of the company. The board have a duty to see that there is always sufficient finance for the company, at its current and future volume of trading, and also for any long term commitments. They alone are responsible for deciding the balance between fixed and working capital, and for approving the levels of stocks to be held, and the length of credit allowed to customers.

The shareholders look to the board for a fair return on their investment. The directors have therefore to decide what dividend policy to adopt, after considering the overall financial needs of the company.

Changes in current market conditions and in future expectations may make it prudent that the rate of capital expenditure is reduced, postponed or increased, while changes in technology may require a faster or slower rate of depreciation of plant or equipment.

Public Accountability

The continuing success of the company in the future, will depend on the image it enjoys with its customers, the Government, suppliers and overseas distributors. The board has, therefore, to balance the demands of customers for better products or services, at lower prices, against the needs of employees for good working conditions, security and pay. These demands have to be reconciled by the directors with their responsibilities to the shareholders for the long term existence and profitability of the business and for a fair return on their capital. Although these interests appear to conflict, they are, in fact, interdependent. A successful company needs satisfied customers and employees, and also satisfied shareholders who are prepared to provide further capital. Without this new capital, the company will be unlikely to expand and thus maintain or improve its market position. In this case, the long term security of employment for the staff must be uncertain.

Organisation, Management and Staffing

The directors are responsible for seeing that the existing organisation, management and staffing of the company will allow the company to carry out its long term plan in the most efficient and economic manner. The directors will need to make policy decisions on the following matters:

Organisation Structure

The directors will have to decide whether the organisation will be on divisional lines (i.e. by product or customer group), or on functional lines (i.e. by production, marketing etc.). Although the board may help to design the middle management structure, it should not try to become involved in operating that machinery.[5] The efficiency of the organisation structure should be monitored regularly to see what changes need to be made, if any, to meet changing conditions.

Delegation

The board has then to decide what powers to reserve to itself, and what powers it will delegate and to whom. The composition of the board has next to be considered, as the company needs a sound, efficient and balanced board, representing management and shareholders. The board should also have the correct breadth of experience, from both inside and outside interests, so that sound decisions can be taken on the business of the firm.

Chief Executive

A chief executive has then to be chosen, and his responsibility and authority agreed. Although the directors will wish to approve how he proposes to delegate powers to his subordinates, any decision on how these powers are to be exercised must be the responsibility of the chief executive. Nevertheless, the board will want to make sure that proper policies and procedures exist for delegating functional authority, which are backed up by an adequate system of control.

Management

The board will want to approve any key appointments and also the compensation offered, because the company objectives may not be achieved unless there is a high quality of management. The directors are also vitally interested in seeing that there will be no management gaps on the resignation or retirement of the present management. The board will also wish to make sure that there is a programme of management training and development to develop competent executives, and thus allow for an orderly planned succession in all parts of the management structure.

Personnel Policies

The personnel policies of the company are of great interest to the board. Unless the salaries, benefits and working conditions are sufficiently attractive, the company will not have the right calibre of staff to achieve its objectives, both long and short term. The level of morale in the company is very important, as low morale will certainly affect the efficient working of the company. High morale will produce, within the company, a pride in achievement, which will drive staff at all levels to overcome obstacles and to achieve objectives set.

Union negotiations and union relations should be regularly reviewed by the board, because without good human relations and good communications with the staff any objectives set may be very hard to achieve.

Reporting and Control

As the board has delegated the function of managing the company to the chief executive, it will want to know how well the actual results measure up against the planned objectives, since the chief executive is accountable to the board for achieving the results planned. The directors, however, are still responsible for advising management how they can make the best use of the company's assets and thus increase the efficiency and the profits of the company. The purpose of the control system is as follows:

Timely Information
To furnish the board with control information which will give early warning of any failures to achieve planned objectives. The system should also allow the directors to supervise the execution of major policies.

Return
The return on capital invested in any new project should be available to measure performance against the planned return. In this way, the board will know the efficiency of management in forecasting profits from capital expenditure. Without this information, the board is not able to take action to correct any failures to achieve the planned return and thus to use the resources of the company in the most profitable manner.

Quality of Reporting
By insisting on receiving relevant, reliable and comprehensive information, the board will be more able to make decisions based on facts not guesses. Furthermore, the executive management will always be aware that their performance is being compared with competitors in market share, return on capital, output per man etc. They will therefore make sure that action to correct bad performance is taken long before the matter comes to the attention of the board. Thus, a comprehensive management information system usually ensures self-supervision by the management. Where the performance of the company is poor, there is temporary safety for the management if no

one knows what is wrong and who is responsible: 'Keep the stick stirring the pond, there is safety in a mess up!' The shock usually comes when the annual accounts are audited and presented to the board for approval.

BOARD MEMBERS AND THEIR RESPONSIBILITIES

Having defined the duties of the board, it is now necessary to define briefly, the duties of the chairman, the chief executive officer, the executive and the non-executive directors.

The Chairman

The chairman[6] is the elected head of the board, and like the chairman of any committee he is responsible for the effective and efficient conduct of their meetings. He should ensure that the business is completed as expeditiously as possible, and that the necessary decisions are obtained. But he must guide and not dominate the meeting, or he will not be using the experience of the board to the best advantage of the company. An ineffective chairman will either produce an ineffective board, or a 'second' chairman will emerge. In one company, the chairman was found to be speaking for 50 per cent of the time. This problem was solved by ensuring that he prepared a written report, issued well in advance of the meeting.[7] The chairman represents the majority board opinion and acts as an agent of the board between meetings. Acting as a catalyst, he can see that the qualities, abilities and the potential of the company are used to the best purpose in the long term interests of the shareholders.

Composition of the Board
The chairman should ensure that the composition of the board is such that all the skills the company requires are present at each stage of the company's development. Any gaps in knowledge or experience should be filled by recruiting outside directors. In representing the majority of the board, he is the natural person for other directors to consult when they feel a change is required in the policy of the company or in its management. He should eliminate any disunity or conflict by resolving the issue. If necessary, he should request the dissentients to resign in the overall interests of the company, for a divided board is little use to a company.

Adviser
In between meetings, he is available to advise the managing director as an impartial second opinion. He can often avoid mistakes being made, if and when a busy chief executive makes decisions too fast and without proper consideration of their consequences.[8]

Company Image
As the most senior officer of the company, he should act as the voice of the company. For this reason, the public image of the company, its relations with the Government, its customers and the press should be his overall concern.

Policy
He should play an important part in the formulation of policy, by seeing that new ideas are discussed and not pigeon-holed. He should not only make it his concern to see that a proper planning organisation exists, but should take a part in studying the future direction of the company: possible acquisitions, new products etc. As well as being an agent for change, it is his duty to make sure that the policy decisions of the board are being carried out by management.

Finance
He should keep a weather eye on the financial position of the company and take an active part in any negotiations for raising new capital.

Management Selection
The selection and appointment of the executive team, especially the appointment of a new chief executive, is a very important function of the chairman. The board will require the independent view of the chairman on any new appointments to the executive team.

There are good reasons for the separation of the duties of chairman and chief executive officer, even though both roles have been successfully combined. The chief executive looks inward within the company, and is principally concerned with the operations and day-to-day problems of the company. The chairman, being divorced from the routine administration, tends to look outside the company to see future difficulties and opportunities, and the relations of the company with other organisations. Furthermore, where the chairman is also the chief executive, it is difficult to approach the chairman about firing the chief executive! When the chairman is not free from executive responsibility, he is not impartial, since any criticism of the company is a criticism of his management. The fiduciary principle is thus violated, and the management tends to become a 'one man' band.[9]

The qualities a chairman needs are vision and courage. He should be a risk taker, and not so prudent that he stifles all new ideas. In addition, he needs to have good judgement and a talent for diplomacy, which will assist him to put over new ideas to his colleagues.

The Chief Executive Officer

The chief executive officer or managing director is responsible for carrying out the policy laid down by the board. He is, as his name implies, the head of the executive, and thus the head of the managers. Provided he achieves the objectives laid down, he should be left to run the company, within the agreed policy, without interference from the board. His principal duties are as follows:[10]

Meeting Objectives
The chief executive officer is financially responsible for the efficiency of the company, and for achieving the profits and objectives in the strategic plan. He must be resolute in reaching these objectives and should identify and demolish any obstacles in the way of their completion.

Leadership
He must be a leader, who will inspire confidence and enthusiasm in his subordinates, but must also be capable of being resolute, decisive and tough.

Management Selection
He should be able to choose good subordinates, to whom he can delegate certain duties without having to intervene, so that he can keep apart from, and not get too involved in, the routine administration.

Judgement
He should be able to judge in a balanced manner all parts of an evolving situation and set priorities for action.

Forward Looking
He should be forward-looking, setting goals, developing strategy, and imbuing the organisation with a sense of urgency and the drive to achieve the targets set.

Profit Improvement
He should liaise with the chairman in putting up to the board proposals to increase and to optimise profits for the company.

Executive Directors

The executive managers are full-time staff who are subordinate to the chief executive officer, as they have departmental or functional duties. However, in the board, all directors are in theory equal. Not all managers make good directors, as they are unable to throw off their departmental bias and think of the total interests of the company. The following points should be watched when considering managers as potential directors:

General Policy
Whether or not the person under consideration is able to think of the overall problems of the company, or whether his views are too specialised to allow him to play a part in formulating general policy: 'Time and again at board meetings, I have seen directors who regard themselves as specialists switch off when general policy is being discussed.'[11] Departmental managers are naturally deeply involved in the problems of today – getting orders, producing, delivering, collecting debts etc. They are tactical leaders who need to make quick decisions and implement them often on the inadequate information available. They are action orientated, and therefore may find it difficult to take an overall strategic long term view.

Parochial Attitude
As the executive directors are closely involved in the administration of the company, they may resent their own departments being criticised. In addition, as they have to live with their fellow directors, they may feel chary of criticising them. A conspiracy of silence can result, with everyone backing up everyone else, until the final crunch comes. Here the critical factor is the executive director's relationship with the managing director and their ability to act as independent advisers.

Shareholders' Interests
Because of their own involvement in the management of the company, they are prone to forget the interests of the shareholders, where these conflict with their own continued enjoyment of office.

Short Term View
Where executive directors are paid a commission on results, they are sometimes, especially if they are close to retirement, more interested in maximising their short term earnings rather than the company's long term profits.

A directorship should not be regarded as a prize for long service with a company, in the same way in which a gold watch is awarded to those further down the line.[12] In the USA, the principal executive officers are given the title of vice-presidents, which confers distinction and rank, without having to appoint them as directors. This avoids the contradiction which occurs in this country of appointing a man to be a director in charge of production, etc. when a director should have an overall and not just a departmental view.

Non-executive Directors

Two recent studies on the use of non-executive directors in the USA and the UK have revealed the following facts. In the USA, a survey of 1,500 companies has shown that 64.4 per cent of companies have more non-executive directors than executive directors on their boards.[13] In the UK, a smaller survey of 77 companies revealed that 62 per cent of the companies had a majority of executive directors.[14] The situation in one country is therefore totally the reverse of the situation in the other.

Non-executive directors have had a bad name in either country when they have been appointed for the wrong reasons. Selecting directors for prestige or cosmetic reasons is only one stage better than giving a job to some useless member of the family, who can make no contribution at all. Even when appointing a watch dog to represent a large shareholding, a person should be found who is not just a 'no' man, but one who can make a contribution to policy making.

Once the function of the board has been agreed and the company objectives clarified, the board will be aware of the principal problems that lie ahead, and the directors will then know which qualities are lacking on the board. Boards of directors need different qualities at each stage of growth, and the appointment of a suitable non-executive director can make good any such deficiency.

The function of a director is to ensure that the purpose and value of an enterprise is maintained and expanded, by setting objectives and policy, then checking overall progress towards the fulfilment of these aims.[15]

Internal versus External Boards

In government, the importance of the separation of powers, especially between the executive and the judiciary, has been recognised since the eighteenth century. However, in the field of company direction, this has tended to be forgotten in the last 50 years. In the Victorian era and in the early part of this century, the board was composed of mainly local shareholders, whose principal function was to choose a general manager to run the company, and then to check on his performance. In public companies, where ownership is nearly always divorced from control, there has been a trend towards a so-called professional board, composed of full-time executive directors. There is now recognition that non-executive directors have an important part to play and, in fact, the New York Stock Exchange now requires two such directors on the board of every newly quoted company.[16]

Professionally managed boards, which have to approve their own decisions, can hardly be expected to be objective about their own performance. They find it difficult to take corrective action when things go wrong. In addition, board meetings can become an extension of the management committee, where the historical performance of the company is discussed, rather than the future, and the strategy required to achieve growth. These criticisms have been expressed as follows:[17] 'Every board continues in its state of rest or uniform motion along a straight line unless it is impelled by some force to change that state.' Boards also tend to be self seeding: 'United we stagnate, divided we are out.'

A completely internal board, especially where the chairman is also managing director, is so closely involved in the management and performance of the company that the directors may find it difficult to take objective decisions on the company. They are unable to approach the chairman to suggest a new chief executive is required, and may only wish to preserve a very unsatisfactory status quo. The chairman in turn may feel dependent on the executive directors, and has, anyhow, authorised, approved or directed their actions, and is thus responsible for them. It is into this atmosphere that the non-executive director brings a breath of fresh air by his impartial assessment of management, the problems of the company and the interests of the shareholders, which may have been conveniently forgotten by an internal board. It may be he, and he alone, who can tell the chairman, like the boy in Hans Andersen's story, that his wonderful clothes do not exist.

APPENDIX 1: FUNCTIONS, POWERS AND DUTIES OF A BOARD OF DIRECTORS AND ITS OFFICERS

The objective of this appendix is to clarify the responsibility of directors, both individually and collectively in law, with special reference to the position of chairman.

Extracts have been taken from two publications, both prepared under the authority of the Council of the Institute of Directors. These are *The Company Director, His Function, Powers and Duties,* and *Standard Board Room Practice,* which will be referred to in the following as CD and SBP respectively.

Collective Responsibility of Directors

General

The executive authority in a company is vested in its board of directors collectively. This is clearly defined (CD p.36) in Section 80 of Table A of the articles of association, which lay down that the business of the company should be managed by the directors who may exercise all such powers of the company not vested in the shareholders. The duties of the board are deciding policy, safeguarding the shareholders, ensuring the progress of the company, checking up on progress and exercising an enlightened employment policy. They must further ensure (CD pp.10,11) that capable managers are employed and that there is a continuity of management (SBP p.15).

The directors must see that the company's business is operated at maximum efficiency and yields adequate return for its shareholders. They, therefore, have a responsibility for the long term efficiency of the company in order to carry out their obligations to the shareholders.

Policy Decisions

The board cannot and should not seek to escape responsibility for policy decisions made either by themselves or by an employee in their name. The board as a whole is responsible for approving policy and ensuring that it is carried out (SBP, p.15).

The powers delegated by the articles to the directors of a company must be exercised by them collectively, not individually, and the company is entitled (CD, p.40) to the benefit of their combined wisdom and experience. Every member of the board must be allowed to express his ideas freely even if these may be unpalatable to other members. (CD, p.89).

The individual director has no authority to interfere in the management or operations of the business except as a member of the board or where the board has conferred upon him the right to do so.

Delegation of Powers

Certain delegations are permitted under the articles of association. However, it is generally held that in law a delegate is not empowered to delegate his authority to others. For this reason the delegation of powers should always be done by minute of the board and the authority conferred should be defined with reasonable precision. Ambiguity only causes subordinates either to act with extreme caution or to exercise powers normally reserved to the board (CD, p.43). The board, having laid down responsibility, must check that the duties delegated have been properly carried out.

Nothing is more destructive of initiative and interest than constant interference with the way in which delegated actions are carried out (CD, p.43). The person to whom authority and responsibility have been delegated must be given freedom of action within the sphere entrusted to him.

Individual Responsibility of Directors

Breach of Duty

Every director is in a fiduciary position in respect of the shareholders, employees, the company's creditors and his fellow directors, regardless of whether he was appointed to represent one special interest or not. Any director who infringes this position and trust damages the system by which he exists (SBP, p.18).

Directors are jointly and severally liable to make good losses suffered by the company owing to any breach of duty on their part. They must show reasonable care (CD, p.62) in the performance of their duties. The degree of care must be such as a prudent man would exercise in the conduct of his own affairs. A director is not liable for a mere error of judgement or for not having more skill and experience than he in fact possesses (CD, p.63). A director will not be penalised for not having more skill and experience than he in fact possesses. However, if he is responsible for managing a company it may be held that having undertaken such a project he should exercise the skill and care that it is reasonable to expect for performing such a function. Non-attendance at board meetings does not constitute negligence (CD, p.63) unless this is so persistent as to amount to neglect of duty.

A director is generally entitled to believe his colleagues and subordinates are doing their duty and is not expected to act unless he suspects all is not well. For certain legal offences under the Exchange Control Act and other acts, once it is proved that a company has committed an offence, every director is presumed guilty unless he can prove it was committed without his knowledge or consent. In certain cases he must prove that he exercised due diligence to prevent an offence (CD, p.65).

Remedies by Directors

As a director is in a fiduciary position, he must require that any action which could appear to be illegal is referred to the company's legal advisers. He has a responsibility also should he think the action proposed could be disastrous for the company, in which case he should insist that such a matter is brought up at the annual general meeting of the company or referred (CD, pp. 91, 93, 94) to the Department of Trade and Industry for investigation, which is permitted under the 1948 Companies Act.

The DTI may order an investigation into a company's affairs on the application of not less than 200 members or members holding not less than one tenth of the issued capital. In addition, the board must order an investigation if the company by special resolution or the court by order declares that a company's affairs ought to be investigated. In addition, the Department may on its own volition appoint an inspector to investigate the affairs of a company to decide if a company's affairs are being conducted in a fraudulent or oppressive manner. It will be seen, therefore, that the powers of investigation possessed by the DTI are extremely wide.

Liabilities as a Trustee

The position occupied by a director is similar to that of a trustee but not so strict. However, a director is obliged to account to the company for any benefit he obtains from his position additional to the remuneration prescribed in the articles, regardless of whether the company has suffered any injury by the transaction or not. The company can recover the entire amounts from the director concerned (CD. p.52).

Contracts

With regard to contracts, any director having a personal interest in a contract that his company is negotiating with a third party must declare his interest at a board meeting under section 199 of the Companies Act. The right to vote on a contract in which a director is interested depends upon the articles of association, but a director is expected at all times to exercise good faith (CD, p.57).

Directors must remain in a position whereby the advice they give is not affected by personal motives (CD, p.55).

Chairman

The chairman has only one legal function, that is the presiding at board meetings and at annual general meetings. At both annual general meetings and board meetings the chairman has a casting vote unless this is removed by the articles of association.

The function of the chairman varies from one company to another, and it should be remembered that as most of the Council of the Institute of Directors are company chairmen, there is no doubt that they have not failed to emphasise the importance of this position.

According to the Institute of Directors, a chairman can be held to have the following duties:

1 He may have to decide whether a particular problem is a

management matter, a board matter or a question which cannot await the full meeting of the directors. However, he must avoid the temptation of interfering in matters which are strictly the province of the executive. The effective chairman knows what executive problems are and leaves managers to settle them. He is, in fact, the leader who acts as a link between the managers and the board itself.

2 At board meetings he must be an effective chairman who steers the meeting away from wasting time and trivial matters so that the board concentrates on important matters of policy. He must not seek to impose his will on the rest of the board because he has preconceived ideas on matters coming up for consideration. He must obtain the best advice from the accumulated wisdom of his colleagues for the collective direction of the business.

3 He should take a direct and personal interest in the renumeration structure of the top executives.

4 A chairman who gets on bad terms with the press adds neither to his own nor to his company's prestige. A difficult chairman does a great disservice to his company.

5 On expense accounts, the exemplary conduct of the chairman can hardly be exaggerated for he can set by his own behaviour an example to the rest of the board.

6 He should spend considerable time outside the company on industry and trade association committees and should keep his nose well above the grindstone.

The chairman must ensure that the right men are 'waiting in the wings' to take over the executive positions when the need arises. However, as the executive authority in a company is vested in its board collectively, the functions of the chairman, apart from his legal duties, are at the discretion of the board which must lay down his duties and see that he carries these out properly. He has no legal right to assume powers which should be exercised either by the board as a whole or delegated by the board (SBP, pp.45-49).

Managing Director

The managing director's duties should be laid down precisely and he should not be bound by irksome restrictions. It is a key appointment, requiring the complete confidence of the board in the man selected. If he cannot justify that confidence then the board cannot justify the appointment. The choice is clear cut (SBP, p.50).

Oppression of minority interests

Under the 1948 Companies Act, Section 210, an action can be brought by the shareholders of a company against the directors for not conducting the business in the best interests of the shareholders. In certain cases it might be more beneficial to the shareholders who bring the action for the company to continue in existence rather than be wound up.

If the court finds that certain directors have been using their voting power for their own ends and not for the general good of the company, the court is able to deprive these directors of their voting rights and to order that no amendment is made to the articles of association unless it is approved by the court. The result is, of course, that the offending directors are then able to be dismissed from their posts by the remaining shareholders.

The directors of a subsidiary could well be included in this suit, especially if it forms the major interest of the company.

REFERENCES

1 See also J.E.V. TYZACK, 'The Role of the Board and the Director', *Management Decision,* September 1967, pp. 4-8.
NILS C. SALANDER, 'The Business of the Board', *Management Today,* June 1970, p.95.
LYNN A. BRUA, 'How 1500 American Companies run the Board', *The Director,* October 1971, pp. 102-5. The principal functions of the board were placed in the following order of priority by industrial companies:

	%
Setting policy	37.6
Counselling management	21.6
Auditing management performance	19.8
Making decisions required by law	17.2
Participating in operating decisions	2.8
Other	1.0
	100.0

2 *Financial and Accounting Responsibilities of Directors,* special issue for the Institute of Directors by the General Educational Trust of the ICA, London 1970.

3 A. READ, *The Company Director*, Chapters 3 and 4.
4 In the oil or chemical industries, which have massive capital investment programmes, a 7-10 year cycle would be normal.
5 D.L. NICOLSON, *The Role of the Company Director,* An address at the Manchester Institute of Science and Technology, 13 February 1968.
6 SIR CHARLES HARDIE, 'The Non Executive Chairman', The Report of the speeches at the Institute of Directors and Financial Times Conference on the Role of the Non Executive Director, London 1971. *Standard Boardroom Practice,* p. 45.
7 T. McAULIFFE, 'There's no Management Technique Like Commonsense', *The Director,* July 1971, p.75.
8 TED LEATHER, 'The Role of the Non Executive Director', *The George Cohen 600 Group Magazine,* October 1971.
9 See Parker's Second Principle, 'The most effective division of responsibility between the board and management of the company can be achieved if the position and duties of chairman and managing director are separate and distinct and each assigned to one individual, HUGH PARKER et al, *Effective Boardroom Management,* McKinsey & Co. Inc. and the B.I.M. London 1971, p.25.
10 See also G.D. BOND, *Financial Aspects of Industrial Management,* Chapter 2, Butterworths, London, 1955.
11 DAVID MONTAGU, 'The Non Executive Director at Work', A speech given at the Conference on the Role of the Non Executive Director, sponsored by the Institute of Directors and the Financial Times, London 1971.
12 *Standard Boardroom Practice,* The Institute of Directors, 1971, p.53.
13 LYNN A. BRUA, 'How 1500 American Companies run the Board', *The Director,* October 1971, p.102.
14 *A Survey of Current Practice in the Employment of Non-Executive Directors,* The Director and MSL, June 1970, London, p.10.
15 The definitions of Direction have been combined from the following books. JOHN SEYMOUR, *Company Direction,* Chapter X. *The Relation between Direction and Management,* MacDonald & Evans Ltd, London, 1954. E.F.L. BRECH, *The Principles and Practice of Management,* Longmans Green, London 1963.
16 Sir Brandon Rhys Williams MP introduced a Bill entitled 'The Companies Bill, presented to Parliament on 24th May 1972.
17 REX MALIK, *What's Wrong with British Industry,* Penguin, London 1964.

17

The Importance of Monitoring

THE EXISTING SITUATION

General

The management of a private company has to recognise that the acceptance of outside finance is the first step towards public accountability. Whereas before the directors and the shareholders were often the same people, there is now an outside shareholder who will insist that the company is operated for the interests of all the shareholders. In addition, the board is responsible for seeing that the conditions of the agreement between the bank and the company are carried out in full. Problems may have been detected, during the investigation by the bank or its advisers, which will need to be put right. However, many of the problems may still be undiscovered, and others will certainly arise in a period of rapid expansion.

Personalities

The bank is now entering what was formerly a private world. The principal shareholder and chief executive of a private company is captain of the ship; he holds over his subordinates the power of life and death within the organisation. His managers are completely dependent on his bounty and goodwill and, for this reason, they will jockey with one another for position and power. The controlling director has had, in the past, to answer to no one, except the tax inspector, his bank manager and perhaps his auditor. He has led a lonely and energetic life with, perhaps, little criticism from his managers. How will he react to the new partnership? Will he welcome the additional experience his new shareholder will be able to offer him, or will he seek to carry on just as he did before? One thing is certain, unless everyone realises that the situation has changed for ever, it is unlikely that anyone will profit from the association.

The controlling director should recognise the change and work freely and openly with the bank in achieving the company's goals.

The Agreed Objectives

It is unlikely that there will be a profitable relationship between two parties unless their objectives are the same. The principal shareholders may see the company as a vehicle for making money, or it may be their aim to set up a dynasty of family management. The bank, on the other hand, will also want to assist the company to expand and to achieve the objects set out in the long range plan. Some banks wish to realise their investment by means of a flotation or merger within a defined period. Others are prepared to hold shares on a long term basis in an expanding company, provided that they receive an adequate return on their capital.

The company objectives must therefore be defined and agreed by all prior to the investment. Once these have been set, the company has to decide how to achieve them, given the restricted sources of capital available. The effects of growth, size and the increasing complexity of a larger organisation should be assessed against the existing skills and managerial competence of the company. Finally, the reporting system, needed to measure performance against the objectives set and to indicate any danger signals, has to be agreed and implemented.

THE NON-EXECUTIVE DIRECTOR

Before examining some of the special problems that the non-executive directors have to contend with in private companies, it is useful to examine their general function in all companies, whether public or private.

The Advisory Function

The principal role of the non-executive director is to act in an advisory and consultative capacity to the board, by looking at the whole business in the interests of all concerned. The argument that boards should consist only of those who are skilled and experienced in the particular industry in which the company is engaged, is beginning to be very seriously questioned:

'As well as having executive directors with specialised knowledge, boards should contain men who look out through many windows on the world and on the world of business.'[1]

'It is an illusion to think that the contribution of a part time director is related to his technical understanding of its production or other processes. Successful policies are born of a far wider knowledge of industry, finance, commerce and economic trends than is usually found in those whose lives have been concerned solely with one industry and often only a small part of it.'[2]

Although no two businesses are the same, the non-executive director can provide an objective and detached viewpoint, which may not be available from those who are more closely involved in the company.

Limitations

The limitations of a non-executive director were defined in a letter in the *Financial Times.*[3] These limitations should be recognised before the true functions of the non-executive director are examined. The limitations of a non-executive director are as follows:

Growth
He cannot present plans for corporate development by means of organic growth, acquisitions, disposals, diversification into new markets, the establishment of overseas operations etc., as he does not have the staff and experience. He can comment on the wisdom of the plan, but can often lack the detailed knowledge.

Time
He cannot probe too deeply on the facts presented as he may not have the time.

Management Selection
He cannot choose the senior executives reporting to the chief executive officer as this is the responsibility of the chief executive.

Cash Flow
He cannot improve the cash resources of the company as these depend on a variety of factors such as profitability, credit control, stock investment, development policies etc., as all of these except possibly development, are management responsibilities under the chief executive.

Independence

The greatest contribution that a non-executive director can bring to a board is an objective view of the operations and the problems of the company. Not being involved in management, he can take a detached view on any problem, undistorted by personal ambition, preconceived ideas, or involvement with long established practices, methods or procedures. Because he is not a subordinate of the chief executive, he can be sceptical where management has been too optimistic. He can ask penetrating questions on company problems and the actions of management which others might find it hard to raise. He will be most effective if he concentrates on objectives rather than becoming too involved in methods and detail. By bringing to any discussion an outside opinion on the company and its future, he can draw attention to the external conditions, economic, political etc., which need to be considered. Without this questioning, boards tend to become introspective, and may be more interested in rubber stamping and safeguarding their positions than in doing their best for the shareholders.

A non-executive director with the right qualifications can see that the right points are discussed at board meetings. He can see that the board guides, controls and approves the actions of management, and does not attempt to manage the company.[4] As long-term interests can be forgotten in the hurly-burly of dealing with immediate problems, he can focus the attention of the board on these matters.

The Specialist Function

The non-executive director can supply knowledge and experience which is not available to the company from its executive directors.

In a period of rapid growth, the company may require advice in any of the following fields:

1 Finding sources of finance
2 Public issues
3 Acquisitions and mergers
4 Setting up overseas operations
5 Taxation
6 Marketing and exporting
7 Research, development and licensing
8 Personnel relations and communications

Some of these skills can be supplied by non-executive directors, provided the company has carefully analysed the skills it needs.

Planning and Policies

The non-executive director can insist that the company has a three to five year strategic plan which is reviewed annually by the board. He can see that the company's position in five to ten years time is discussed by the board. By raising matters such as the growth and survival of the company and its position in the present and future environment, he can make sure that the present problems of the company do not prevent discussion on the future.

On matters of policy, the non-executive director can assist in deciding policy, by giving his opinion on recommendations from the executive. He can question whether policies have been adopted and can be available to help the chief executive in carrying out policy by providing, where he is qualified, specialised advice.

Budgets

He can examine the budgets prepared, and see that there is sufficient information on order intake, sales, costs and profits to make the forecasts seem possible. He can ask the marketing director, as well as the chief executive, to jointly and separately endorse these projections and explain their bases in open meeting, to ensure that they are not just guesses.[5]

Organisation and Management

The effectiveness of the non-executive director at board meetings depends on how well he is briefed in advance. Unlike the executive directors, who are in close touch with the business, he will need, prior to the meeting, reports, figures, as well as the agenda, outlining the proposals being made and the decisions required. Only by briefing himself fully can he make an effective contribution to any discussions.[6]

In management matters, he can see that there is a competent executive management, headed by the chief executive and supported by sufficient well qualified executives. Being outside the management team, he can advise on the appointment, promotion and remuneration of other directors and senior managers, and see that any management changes are only made after the board has had the opportunity to approve the terms.[7] He can also advise the chairman impartially on the organisation structure, and make sure that problems of succession are not conveniently forgotten, especially when the chairman or the chief executive are due to retire or in case they have to be replaced.

Monitoring and Reporting

The board cannot audit the performance of management, unless it has the key operating information properly presented, on a monthly or quarterly basis, showing the actual figures against the forecast. This information should be up to date and available to the board, prior to any meeting. The non-executive director depends on an efficient control system for his information. He is therefore very concerned that this system will highlight any operating weaknesses in time for corrective action to be taken before the matter becomes too serious.

The information covered should enable unfavourable trends in order intake, sales, deliveries, costs and profits to be recognised in time for effective action to be taken. In addition, the forecast cash flow should cover at least a three year period so that action can be taken in time to avoid a liquidity crisis, either by raising additional finance, or by postponing capital investment. Where there is an uncritical executive board, it may be necessary for a non-executive director to insist on effective action to remedy poor operating performance. For the existing management may feel unwilling to tackle the problem, if it reflects badly on them and could upset their position.

Finally, proper appraisal of investment proposals is one of the important functions which operating management can forget to monitor if the figures are not satisfactory. The non-executive director can ask for detailed reports to be prepared to justify capital expenditure, including all relevant costs. These estimates should show the output, sales and profits to be generated by the investment and the long term growth expected. The board should be presented with periodic surveys to compare the actual performance against the estimates, together with the reasons for any shortfall.

Shareholders' Watchdog

Especially in a private company, a non-executive director can represent large outside interests, or hold the balance between two major interests. But his most important function is to remind the executive directors of their responsibility to the various outside interests, especially the shareholders, which can be conveniently forgotten in the short term.

Qualities Required

The qualities required by a non-executive director, and in fact all directors, are as follows:

Personal Qualities
He should be an eager, vigorous person whose honesty and loyalty to the company are recognised by all his colleagues.

Experience
He should have broad experience of industry, combined with specialised knowledge and skills in certain fields, especially in modern management methods.

Knowledge
He should show a real interest in the company and make time to build up his knowledge of the company, its markets, organisation and problems. He should ensure that he is well briefed and know what is happening to the company.

Decision Making
As well as being informed and mature, he should be financially astute with a knowledge of external financial conditions. Sound judgement and analytical ability are required to assist the board in making fast but good decisions. Although he should be critical, except on points of principle, he must be prepared to support group decisions after his views have been fairly considered.

Personal Relationships
A compatible person is required who has an interest in people, is able to evaluate senior staff and is trusted by them; he should be compatible, not comfortable.[8]

Initiative
He should have the initiative to define his role in the best interests of the company. He should recognise the contribution of each member of the board, but possess the independence to see that his views are given due attention.

SMALL COMPANIES

Special Problems

Before examining the functions of the non-executive director in the small company, it is only logical to consider the special problems which these companies face and where they differ from public companies.

The Board
The board, especially in the very small private company, tends to be confined to carrying out the legal functions defined in the Companies Acts. It meets once a year to approve the annual accounts and the agenda for the Annual General Meeting. An ineffective board tends to be passive and inert, consisting of docile and submissive shareholders, both family and friends, as well as some well-drilled managers. For it is cheaper for the company to pay directors fees, which are allowable against corporation tax, than dividends. Shareholders also prefer to receive earned rather than unearned income.

Control

The controlling director often tends to identify the welfare of the company with his welfare. The minority shareholders are often forgotten or considered to be a nuisance. Therefore, controlling directors do not always act in the interests of all shareholders.

Management

In small private companies, unlike large public companies, funds are not provided by outside shareholders, but by administrative management who are the controlling shareholders. It is, therefore, frequently impossible to change or remove the top management without great internal upheaval, if at all. Furthermore, there is usually limited management talent available, both in skills and in depth. Since the company cannot afford to employ specialists, managers are generalists, performing a wide variety of jobs. The problem can be solved by strengthening the board by the appointment of outside specialists, and by ensuring that the organisation uses scarce executive time to the best advantage.

The board in a private company has to decide whether the management, and especially the chief executive, has the capacity to expand with the company. Managers have to be able to meet their greater responsibilities over the next few years in a far more sophisticated organisation. Unless satisfactory steps are taken to fill these gaps in knowledge or in staff, vital matters affecting the future of the company are being left unresolved.

Planning and Policy

As directors and management are usually the same people, they tend to become preoccupied with day-to-day problems on production, sales, etc., which absorb all their time and energy. Management's horizon is often limited to the four walls of the business, as internal problems are both pressing and immediate. Therefore, management can be unaware of external conditions, which can affect company policies, as internal problems nearly always push policy decisions into the background. Even when efforts are made to assess the changing external conditions, they tend to be sporadic rather than continual.[9]

Monitoring

When a company expands, the chief executive often feels that he is completely *au fait* with the current position as he was when the company was smaller. However, as he has delegated responsibility to an operating management, he needs control over the way these functions are being performed. Lack of adequate control is the principal reason for the failure of small businesses.

The Non-Executive Director

As well as carrying out the functions already described, a non-executive director can often smooth out some of the problems a small company faces in an expansion. He can draw the attention of management to the effect of change on the company, and to the important long term decisions which have to be taken, despite the more immediate operating problems for which solutions have to be found today. Management may not be aware that conditions both inside and outside the company have changed the duties that they should perform. Old functions may have become unimportant, and new vital ones are being left unattended. An effective non-executive director can train management to adapt to the challenge of expansion.

Board Organisation

The chairman should ensure that an efficient board is set up and organised, which can guide, approve and control the operations of the company. Regular monthly meetings will normally be necessary because in small companies problems can become serious in a very short time. Agendas and reports should be issued in advance of any meeting, as this discipline in itself requires a decision on what items should be discussed, and in what order of priority. It is often said that: '80 per cent of the effort is often devoted to achieving 20 per cent of the results'. The board should be so organised that it spends a large proportion of its time discussing the future. A report should be presented by the chief executive on last month's operations, together with any reasons for any performance falling below target, and the solutions recommended. However, the board should not operate as a management committee.

A board does not need people who always agree with management, but those who see things differently, disagree and question the assumptions on which management acts. The non-executive director, being remote from day-to-day problems, looks for the overall pattern, sees broad objectives and plans, and questions concepts, principles and the validity of management's assumptions [10]. The functions and objectives of the board should be clearly defined, for without this the company is not equipped to handle the problems of growth. The controlling director should seriously consider whether the non-executive director appointed by the bank is suitable to act as chairman of the company for a limited period of say, one, two or three years. The period can of course be indefinite and at the discretion of the board. If he is not overcome by the unintended slight to his self-esteem, the controlling director may realise the very great contribution that an experienced outsider can make to the efficient operation of the company. During a period of rapid expansion, and before the company is large enough to afford a full management team, the chief executive must be the driving force for growth. He is therefore deeply immersed in operating detail. An outside chairman can see that the board is efficiently organised, that it has the right information for decision making, and that the right matters are discussed. In addition, it is in the interests of the shareholders that the chairman and the chief executive are not the same person. After this period, and when there is a full operating management, the controlling director can take over the position of the chairman. He can then concentrate on the future of the company and on controlling its performance. Sometimes the interests of the controlling director as a shareholder may conflict with his position as chief executive. Then a decision should only be taken after considering the long term interests of the whole company, for he and his family have the greatest financial stake in its success.

The bank, as a minority shareholder, will be jealous of the rights of all minority shareholders, as the institutions and their nominees have reputations for fair dealing and integrity. In addition, directors are required by law to act in the interests of all shareholders. Therefore, when matters of dividends and the salaries of directors are raised, they must act impartially and not just in the interests of the controlling directors and the management. For this reason, non-executive directors can act as arbiters and provide a detached and impartial view in family squabbles between rival factions over salaries, promotion and other critical matters.

Organisation and Management

Professor Mace has pointed out the difference between the jobs of the chief executive in a large corporation and in a small corporation. In a small company, the chief executive has to manage the company and formulate policy for approval of the board. Having few trained executives, he will also have the responsibility for putting the policies into effect and seeing that they are carried out correctly. The chief executive of a small company needs a wide knowledge of the various specialised functions of the business.[11] He must be able to sell, sort out production problems, take decisions on development, and often act as his own financial director when negotiating for further finance. He must be an all rounder and any lack of specialised knowledge can be fatal.

Since it is unlikely that all the knowledge required will be found in one man, any gaps can be filled by appointing non-executive directors to advise on these matters. This becomes even more necessary in the case of the owner manager, as it is usually not possible to change the incumbent. Therefore, the chief executive should be trained to use his time to the best advantage, so that he can cope with the increased responsibility resulting from expansion. The functions to be performed by him, and those to be delegated, have to be decided upon. The organisation structure required should be drawn up, each job defined, and then staffed either from the existing executives or by selecting new managers. Executive performance has to be measured, and training programmes organised to enable executives to grow with the company, and to perform their expanded responsibilities in an efficient manner.[12] Someone from outside the company, who has no interest in gaining increased job responsibility, is the best person to raise these delicate matters and even more so in the case of management succession. All small companies are to a greater or lesser extent 'one-man' concerns. However, as the value of the business to the shareholders must depend on there being an adequate successor to the chief executive, this important decision cannot be left until the inevitable happens. The qualities required and the duties to be carried out should be agreed upon and a successor selected and trained. This is a problem which no director is justified in ignoring even if raising the matter will cause an emotional outburst.

Planning and Policies

A strong and effective board of directors will insist that the chief executive, despite the pressures of day-to-day operations, should make sufficient time available to plan for the future. The alternative is to drift without any fixed course in the hope that the company will not be overtaken by external events.

The non-executive director can bring up the subject of planning and the effect of external events on the company over which the management has absolutely no control. The whole process is discussed in Chapter 6, but some of the points that should be discussed are as follows:

1 The economic conditions – credit squeezes, interest rates.
2 Government policy and its effect on the company.
3 Changes in markets and in customers demands, and opportunities developing and ending in home and export markets.
4 New materials or processes.
5 Technical developments and shifts in competitive strengths.

Once the plan is agreed, policy making is another important board function, as the plan and policies are communicated to the company staff through policy statements. In addition, the management is relieved of much detail work if repetitive decisions are sanctioned in advance, and can thus be carried out by subordinates without reference to top management. On the other hand, management in a small company can believe that they are reacting to changing operating conditions when they are in effect making significant changes in policy. For instance, a decision to enter new markets, to launch new products, to make for stock, or to allow special terms to a customer should be considered in relation to the overall company plan and not just on its own.[13] The company should only alter its objectives after considering all the implications involved, otherwise the new objective may be inconsistent with the existing objectives or beyond the resources of the company; in this case a new decision must be made on the objectives of the company. Small companies cannot afford to commit scarce resources to projects which they are unable to complete.

The board should also check up periodically that the policies agreed upon are being implemented to find out if the chief executive is making sure that the policy of the board is being carried out.

Monitoring

The non-executive director, being uninvolved in routine operations, will want to make sure that information the board is receiving is timely, complete and accurate. Unless the board has up-to-date information on the following matters, he cannot report progress accurately to the bank.

Operating Performance

The reporting system will have to give early warning of any failure to perform to budget in the following fields:

1 Orders received, on hand and the future trend.
2 Sales and production.
3 Profit by product and total net profits to date.
4 New product developments.

Cash and Liquidity

The preparation of regular forward cash flow statements and the examination of the key financial ratios will show if the company is overtrading and concentrating on sales rather than profits. The use of funds should be examined to see if there is likely to be over-investment in stocks or fixed assets which will reduce working capital below an acceptable level. Contingency plans should also be agreed in case the expected sales do not materialise, as the forecasts were over-optimistic.

Capital Investment

The completeness of proposals for capital expenditure ought to be examined to see if all the relevant factors have been included (e.g. the working capital needed for stocks, work in progress, debtors and the investment required in jigs and tools). The board should also examine why the investment is being made, the return, the output expected, the market potential and duration, and the labour and factory space required. Sometimes it will be more economic to buy the product out rather than manufacture it. Production-minded directors may be so enthusiastic about new gleaming machine tools that they do not fully consider what is in the overall interests of the company.

Staff
The level of morale in the company, relations with the unions, and labour turnover and supply in all ranks of the company should be discussed by the board.

Management Techniques
As the company expands, the techniques it uses will need to be examined to see if improvements are required, for example, improvements in management accounting, budgeting, mechanised accounting, production control etc.

Qualities Required

The qualities required by a non-executive director of a small company are of course broadly the same as for any director. In addition to these attributes, he needs the following qualities: [14]

Small Companies
The knowledge and understanding of small company operations and the ability to solve their problems with the resources available to them.

Training Ability
The ability to train and coach management to eliminate any weak spots in their knowledge or experience.

Changing Conditions
The ability to evaluate rapidly changing conditions and to take a long-term point of view; this is the major weakness of small company managements, who are often weighed down by the problems of today.

Personal Qualities
He needs courage and the spirit of enterprise, as without this a small company will not prosper. He must also be a stable person and be able to cope with emotional outbursts and bitter family quarrels. Firmness will also be wanted, together with the ability to ask discerning questions. He can only work through management and therefore he must build up good relations and trust between the management and himself. Any proposals he presents must be able to be seen by

all as the best course for the company.

The management will be aware that their reputation with the bank will suffer if they do not have valid reasons for ignoring his warnings. They can make a mistake once, but after that their actions may be seen as either obstinacy or lack of judgement.

BANK MEETINGS

The non-executive director will be responsible for briefing the bank on the progress of their investment and on any requests for further finance. It is useful for the directors to visit the bank, even if matters are going well, at least once a year to discuss their future plans for the company.

IMPROVEMENT PLANS

Before a new investment is made, the parties should discuss and agree not only the objectives for the company but also the means whereby these aims are to be carried out. If the parties can agree in advance on any weaknesses that need to be corrected, a programme can then be drawn up to outline how these problems should be tackled (see Appendix to this chapter). These points should be incorporated into an improvement plan, together with a timetable, showing when they will be dealt with and when completion is expected.

Most of the potential weaknesses, it is hoped, will already have been discovered during the investigation process by the bank, the solicitors and the reporting accountants. These points should be added to any problems which management feels will need to be solved in the next few years. The plan should be regularly audited by the board to find out the progress being made within the timescale laid down.

When a company fails to achieve its targets, the process needs to be started again from the beginning. The checklists contained in the previous chapters should be consulted so that management can recommend a solution of the company's problems to the board and the bank, rather than vice versa.

The company can be adequately protected from 'Acts of God' by insurance to cover factory fires, loss of profits etc., and against the unexpected death of the chief executive in a car crash. However, the most likely reason for failure is management error, and errors can be either due to internal or external matters. Internal matters have already been discussed in Chapter 3 and cover such problems as faulty estimating of costs leading to lower profits, through production or design problems, or bad credit control etc. (see Chapters 3 and 4). External problems arise because the company has not correctly anticipated the market for its products and for those of competitors, in respect of timing, price, quantity and specification (see Chapter 6). Whatever the reason, the whole procedure of appraisal should be carried out to find the key points which need to be identified and solved.

The bank will also want to know the reason if their non-executive director has failed to warn them of these problems well in advance. On the other hand, the board may have disregarded such warnings, and in this case there will have to be a clear agreement between the parties on what steps must be taken, especially if new money is required to be invested in the company. Small companies are volatile, and provided that the illness is not fatal such reverses are sometimes a necessary process of growing up. Any feeling of infallibility on the part of management will have been washed away. Dr Johnson might well have said in the circumstances that 'the prospect of a receiver, wonderfully concentrates the mind!'.

APPENDIX 1: SAMPLE IMPROVEMENT PLAN (DRAFT OF LETTER TO BE SENT BY THE BANK TO THE COMPANY)

The plan for the company, agreed between the directors and the bank, has as its main objective an expansion of profits of over 250 per cent over the next three years. This expansion will bring with it problems of management, staffing and control, which the company has not yet experienced. Furthermore, the increased size of the company may make it subject to greater competition from larger competitors.

Therefore the main responsibilities of the directors will change from supervising operations to deciding on the direction in which the company is going to develop, and in planning and controlling its operations. In addition, a team of managers will have to be selected and trained to supervise the operations of the company.

After discussions with your directors, and with our advisers, we consider that the various matters which need attention are as follows:

Planning

A Strategic Plan
A strategic plan should be drawn up to incorporate the objectives agreed upon and the means by which the expansion will be carried out. The markets for the company's existing products should be analysed, to find out the present and the future requirements of its customers, especially in quality, specification etc. Decisions on new products, needed to preserve the company's competitive position, should also be made, whether they are to be developed by the company, or licensed from outside. Plans for implementing the expansion plan by the various departments (i.e. marketing, production etc.) have also to be drawn up and agreed. Then a policy statement should be issued to outline the way in which the company should achieve its objectives.

Budgets
Budgets should be prepared for revenue, expenses and profits, in detail for the next year, and in less detail for the next two years and revised annually. As a check on the budgets, the staff and floor space required to achieve the output forecast should also be calculated.

Cash Flow
A cash-flow statement should be prepared, showing the cash position and the cash requirements over the three year period, in detail for the next year and by quarters for the following two years. The position should be reviewed quarterly and any changes reported to the board.

Capital Investment
The company's programme for capital investment should be drawn up and updated at least annually, or sooner if any material change becomes known. The projects should show the working capital requirements, as well as the investment required in plant and machinery. The DCF return should be calculated over the expected life of the project, to make sure that the resources of the company are used to the best advantage.

Organisation and Staffing

Organisation Plan
The organisation plan for the company, which has been proposed in

the report to the bank, should be implemented.

Job Responsibilities
The responsibilities of the various levels of management should be defined in writing, to ensure that authority is correctly delegated. As far as possible, top management should be freed from making routine repetitive decisions, which can be delegated to lower levels of management.

The Management Team
The existing managers will have to be appraised to find out their potential for additional responsibility. We are in agreement with you that the immediate gaps that need to be filled are a second in command to the managing director and a cost accountant.

Training
A simple training scheme within the company's resources should be set up to train management and the labour force.

Staff Budget
The company should estimate its needs for staff over the next three years. Within a year, we agree that there will be a need for more work study staff.

Direction

Policy Implementation
The company policies, especially in selling, pricing, purchasing, and in personnel should be made known to the company by means of an operating manual in a loose leaf folder.

Facilities
New factory space is required within 18 months. This matter is urgent, and a decision on this and on the new plant needed is required in the very near future. The existing factory will be sold.

Distribution
In the UK an economic and fast distribution organisation system is required to handle the increased turnover. Distributors are required for the company's existing product line in Germany and Italy, and

for the new range of products throughout the principal markets in Europe.

Sales Promotion, Publicity and Advertising
An effective low cost sales promotion campaign should be drawn up to support the company's sales operations.

Buying
The company should consider the possibility of negotiating purchasing agreements with its major suppliers, which will give it the best possible terms for price, delivery and payment.

Credit Control
The credit control and collection organisation must be able to handle the increased business without delays in checking credit or in the collection of overdue debts.

Production Control
The production control system should be revised to make sure that it can cope effectively with any increased output. Machine loading schedules should be set up and revised weekly. The present system of scheduling work through the shops does not enable the foremen to be held responsible for delays.

Stock Records
The stock records must be kept up to date and orders and requirements should be booked daily against each part number to show the free stock held. For stock items, maximum and minimum stock levels should be set up and adjusted when the usage for the part fluctuates.

Reporting Accountant's Recommendations

Insurance. In paragraph 123 of their report, it is recommended that the insurance cover is examined to make sure that the sums assured cover the full replacement cost of the factory, plant, equipment, stock etc.
Depreciation. In paragraph 144 it is recommended that depreciation rates are re-considered and that the rate on plant and machinery is raised to 15 per cent per annum on a straight line basis.
Plant asset register. In paragraph 141, it is recommended that a

plant asset register is set up and kept up to date.

Excess and obsolete stocks. In paragraph 150, it is recommended that obsolete and slow moving stocks should be written off at the end of each year. A sum of £5,667 should be written off immediately, in respect of items which were in this category at the end of the last financial year.

Reporting

Costing

The costing system needs to be revised so that standard costs can be measured against actual costs for each cost centre. All costs directly applicable to a certain job should be charged directly to the job and not recovered through overheads, e.g. tooling, replacement and scrap costs etc.

Machine hourly rates also need revising and should then be used for both estimating and costing. There must be a fast feedback from the costing system to the estimators, to ensure that estimating standards are in line with actual costs.

Overhead Recovery

The overhead rate used for estimating should enable the company to recover all overhead costs incurred in a year. Therefore, every quarter the overhead recovered must be compared with the actual overheads incurred in the period under review.

Stock and Work in Progress

The value of stock on hand should be kept by part number to allow control to be kept over investment in stock. This is very important for high-value items such as X, Y and Z. Stock-turnover figures should also be available. Work in progress should be valued quarterly at cost or net realisable value whichever is the lower. The costs to completion should be estimated every quarter and any losses written off (see also accountant's report[15]).

Mechanisation

Consideration should be given to mechanising stocks, work in progress, costing and debtors.

Monthly Reports

Monthly operating reports should be prepared for the board, showing the profitability of the company, and profit by cost centre. The actual figures should be compared to budget.

Half Yearly Accounts
Half yearly accounts should be prepared and audited.

Cash Flow
Every month the cash-flow statement should be examined and any major variances reported. A revised cash-flow statement should be presented quarterly. The key financial ratios should also be calculated.

We would like to discuss these matters further with you at an early date, to agree a programme and a timetable. Although the list appears formidable, we consider it advisable to tackle these problems while there is time to resolve them and before they become serious. The company has forecast a considerable expansion over the next three years. Many problems will arise, some foreseen and others unforeseen. We should, therefore, attempt to resolve in the best interests of the company, any outstanding or potential weaknesses of which we are aware, to make the future progress of the company's expansion as smooth as possible.

REFERENCES

1 Lord Chandos, in the Presidential address at the Annual Conference of the Institute of Directors in 1956.

2 A letter by A.F. Frodsham, Managing Director of the P.E. Consulting Group in the *Financial Times* on 3rd January 1966.

3 A letter from H. Smallwood to the *Financial Times* on 10th July 1971. Mr. Smallwood goes on to comment on how non executive directors can advise in fields of long range planning, budgeting, reporting and management selection.

4 J.E.V. TYZACK 'The Role of the Board and the Director', *Management Decision,* December 1967, p. 14.

5 A letter from H. Smallwood to the *Financial Times* 10th July 1971.

6 See also SORREL M. MATHES, *Smaller Company Board of Directors,* The National Industrial Conference Board, New York, 1967.

7 A letter from H. Smallwood to the *Financial Times,* 10th July 1971. It is also suggested that the board should insist on the appointment of an able finance director, and that board approval be required for any change in this appointment.

8 HARRY ROFF 'The Non Executive Director: How to motivate and find the right man'. A speech at the Conference on the Role of the Non Executive Director, London 1971.

9 MYLES L. MACE, *The Boards of Directors in Small Corporations,* Harvard University, Boston 1948, pp. 29 and 37.

10 P.F. DRUCKER, *The Practice of Management,* Heinemann, London, 1955, p. 156.

11 MYLES L. MACE, *The Boards of Directors in Small Corporations.* Harvard University, Boston 1948, pp. 9 and 48.

12 *ibid.* p. 49.

13 *ibid.* pp. 14 and 16.

14 *ibid.* p. 73.

15 See also *Accountant's Report,* paragraph 13(i), Admission of Securities to Quotation, The Stock Exchange, London, 1969, p. 14.

18

Public Issue

ADVANTAGES AND DISADVANTAGES

A company may wish to obtain a public quotation for its shares on the stock exchange for the following five reasons:

Family Reasons

The family may wish to realise part of their investment so as to spread their finances more widely, or to provide for retirement or for the payment of estate duty.

A quotation on any recognised stock exchange provides a yardstick for fixing the price of the shares for an estate duty valuation and also avoids the possibility of an asset valuation under the Finance Act, 1940.

A controlling shareholder of a private company can be faced with an asset valuation for his shares, if within five years of his death, he controlled the company, owned over half of its shares and/or debenture capital, or received over half its dividends. Furthermore, the shares of a quoted company can be sold to raise the money required to discharge any estate duty liabilities.

Close Company Status

A company whose shares are quoted on the stock exchange, provided that 35 per cent or more of its shares are in the hands of the public, is no longer classed as a close company under the Finance Act, 1965. The company is therefore no longer subject to the possibility of a shortfall assessment under the Act, which may in certain circumstances result in 60 per cent of the earnings of the company being forced to be distributed as dividends.

Additional Finance

When a private company's financial needs exceed the funds available from retained earnings, from its existing shareholders and from the bank, further permanent capital is required. At this stage, the company should examine if it can raise money on more advantageous terms by means of a public issue, than by selling a minority equity holding to a financial institution. As a public company it can raise further capital provided its performance is up to the expectations of the market.

An increase in the issued equity of a public company widens the borrowing base and allows it to fund further expansion by issuing fixed interest loan capital. Institutions will always value the shares of a private company below those of an equivalent public company for reasons of non-marketability etc. (see Chapter 2, p. 12). The return required is higher to compensate for this risk, and, in addition, minority investment in private companies is limited to a fairly small number of specialist institutions.

Acquisitions

A publicly quoted company can make acquisitions of other companies by issuing shares and/or loan stock to the shareholders of the company they wish to acquire. Private companies are limited to using their cash for acquisitions, unless they use an existing publicly quoted company as a shell.[1] In this case the shell company acquires the private company and issues its own shares in exchange for those of the private company. This process is called a reverse takeover if the shareholders of the private company end up as the controlling shareholders of the public company.

Publicity

The image of a company can be improved by having a quotation for its shares. The company name will not only be seen in the financial press, but it will also have a much wider spread of shareholders than before. A good reputation among institutional shareholders, such as insurance companies, pension funds, investment and unit trusts, and banks, can be of great assistance when further equity or loan finance is required by the company (as these institutions are potential shareholders and underwriters).

The publicity can work the other way, however, if the performance of the company is not up to expectations. The directors have to be prepared to face criticism not just from a few family shareholders but from the public and the financial press. Public company status requires a very high level of performance from the directors. They have either to show a rising level of profits, even in difficult periods, or face the possibility of an acquisition by another company, especially if the family no longer have control.

METHODS OF ISSUE

The principal methods of obtaining a quotation for a company's shares are as follows:[2]

A Prospectus Issue or an Offer for Sale

In a prospectus issue, a company offers new shares to the public at a fixed price by means of a prospectus, which is advertised in at least two newspapers. The company will be obtaining new capital as the shares being subscribed for by the public will be new shares. A sponsor, either an issuing house or a broker, will underwrite the subscription, to make sure that the company receives the capital it needs, even if there is a downturn in the market. In the event of an undersubscription, the underwriters have to subscribe for the shares they have underwritten.

Where the shareholders of a company wish to sell some of their shares to the public, an offer for sale is used. The sponsor buys shares from the vendors and sells them to the public at a fixed price in the same manner as for a prospectus issue. Unlike a prospectus issue this type of issue produces no new capital for the company. However by using an offer for sale, a sponsor can market both new and existing shares. Most issues are made by these two methods as they offer the widest opportunity for the public to subscribe for shares. For this reason the majority of equity issues are made by means of an offer for sale rather than a prospectus issue. Effective publicity at the time of flotation should ensure a good initial demand for the shares if the issue is fairly priced. Provided the shares are allocated to a large enough number of shareholders, there will be the basis for a proper market. Interest thereafter will depend on the company's future performance.

Offer by Tender

This method of issue is the same as for a prospectus issue or an offer for sale. Either the company or the sponsor offers shares to the public, but only a minimum price is fixed. The applicant has to decide the price he is prepared to pay as well as the number of shares he wishes to purchase.

Starting at the top price bid, sufficient bids are accepted in descending order of price to fully subscribe the issue. However all bids are accepted at the price which is the lowest price required to satisfy the issue. This is called the striking price. In practice, the striking price is usually fixed at a lower level than this so as to give a wide spread of shareholders, and thus an orderly market. To achieve this, some of the larger applications at the higher prices have to be scaled down. Sponsors dislike this method as disappointed applicants tend to criticise the method used for scaling down applications.

The advantage of this method is that the company gains where the market makes a higher valuation of a company's shares rather than the 'stags'.[3] In a fixed-price issue the stags can often sell their shares at a premium over the offer price within two to three days of when dealings begin on the market. An offer by tender has been used where no comparable company exists to provide a basis for valuing the shares of a new company. However, it can result in the share price going to a discount after the issue, where the striking prices have been forced up by the stags. They are prepared to bid a very high price to obtain the shares, but are relying on larger investors to bid at a more realistic price. If the striking price is too high there are no buyers to match the sellers and the market price will fall.

The short-term advantages of an offer by tender of achieving a higher issue price can be outweighed by the long-term disadvantages if the company receives poor publicity. For should the shares fall below the offer price, further equity financing may be only possible on very adverse conditions. An issue price, fixed by an experienced issuing house after a careful investigation of the company, its past record, and its future prospects, gives the market a useful guide as to the value of a new company. In the long run, market knowledge and company performance will fix the share price, but in the short term a gradually improving share price is the sign of a well managed offer and good market acceptance.

Placings

A placing officially is only permitted by the Stock Exchange where there is likely to be little public interest in the share being offered, and where the total value of the shares being issued is not above £250,000. The sponsor purchases or subscribes for shares and then places them with institutions or private clients. At least 35 per cent of the issued ordinary share capital must be placed and at least 25 per cent of the shares being placed must be made available to the public through the market. No shares are, however, offered direct to the public, who can only buy shares after dealings have begun. The price they pay will usually be above the placing price and is, of course, then subject to the normal extras, such as the jobber's turn and broker's commission. The Stock Exchange will not permit large issues to be made in this way, as it is unlikely that there will be sufficient shareholders after the issue to make an orderly market. In addition, if public interest is likely to be aroused, there may be very bad publicity if the institutions are given priority over the ordinary investor. The advantage to the company is that the costs of the issue are lower, as the advertising required is less than for a prospectus issue or for an offer for sale, and in addition no underwriting is required.

Introduction

An introduction raises no money for either the company or its shareholders but it provides a market quotation for the shares. This method can be used to obtain a quotation for the shares of a foreign public company. Private unquoted companies whose shares are already widely held can obtain a quotation through an introduction. An introduction may be permitted by the stock exchange if not more than 65 per cent of the ordinary share capital is in the hands of five or fewer persons, and the balance of at least 35 per cent is in the hands of the public. The company is expected to have in all about 200 shareholders. However if large blocks of shares are being offered at the same time, then a full prospectus issue may be required to ensure an orderly market. In order to make a satisfactory market and to match supply and demand, a supply of shares from the existing shareholders is normally made available to the market. This is, of course, unnecessary if a supply of shares is freely available from another stock exchange. This method is the cheapest way of obtaining a quotation as no new money is being raised for the company or its shareholders.

Rights Issues

A company with an existing quotation for its shares can raise further capital by making a rights issue to its existing shareholders (see Chapter 12, p. 167). The offer price is normally made about 15–30 per cent below the current market price for the existing shares. The issue is normally underwritten to ensure that the company receives its money, if there is a sudden break in the market. Permission to deal in the shares has to be obtained from the Stock Exchange prior to the issue.

Other Issues

Securities are issued by companies for the following reasons, and permission to deal in these shares must be obtained from the Stock Exchange:

1 A capitalisation issue to existing shareholders (see Chapter 11, p. 161).
2 Where shares are issued in consideration for assets acquired or in exchange for the shares of another company, either public or private.
3 In the exercise of options or to satisfy conversion rights (see Chapter 8, p. 134).

DIRECTORS' RESPONSIBILITY

The directors of a company seeking a public quotation for its shares should be aware of their responsibilities to the public. Under the 1948 Companies Act, directors are personally liable for the accuracy of any statements made in a prospectus and for any damages to any shareholder resulting from any untrue statement; there is also the possibility of a criminal prosecution. For this reason, the directors need the best qualified advisers to protect them from making any mis-statements and to guide them through the procedures prior to a quotation.[4]

ADVISERS

Issuing Houses

An association with an issuing house provides the following advantages for a private company which wishes to make a public issue.

Advice
A decision on the timing of a public issue depends on two factors, the conditions within the company and the external market conditions. The issuing house will make itself familiar with the company and its management, the company's position in the industry and its strong and weak points. A plan can then be prepared to put right any weaknesses prior to the issue.

Even if the company is ready for an issue, the timing may not be right, as the prospects for the industry may not be considered favourable by the market. So until the time is right, an issuing house can usually provide finance, if required, to bridge this gap. In a broader sense, an issuing house is also in a position to advise on external conditions, such as expected movements in exchange rates, in interest rates, and in the supply of credit. This is a very valuable service to the management of an expanding company, who are often too busy and are also perhaps inexperienced in reading the economic omens. A close relationship often develops where the bank has a minority equity interest in a private company and has, in addition, a director appointed to the company's board. In any event, a company is well advised to establish a close working relationship with an issuing house, a year or two in advance of a public issue.

Sponsor

Unless the prospects of the company look sufficiently good, an issuing house will not risk its name and reputation by sponsoring the issue. In addition to choosing a favourable time for the issue, the issuing house will aim to fix both the terms and the issue price so that an acceptable premium is achieved immediately on the initial dealings. In the case of a successful initial issue for an expanding company, the shares will gradually improve as investors begin to appreciate the company's prospects. This process will be accelerated if the profits forecast for the financial year end after the issue is exceeded by an acceptable margin.

If a company's share price goes to a discount on the offer price immediately after dealings begin, it may suffer a bad investment image which may take years to live down. The issuing house will also be at risk financially as, in the case of an offer for sale or a prospectus issue, it will either be purchasing the shares or underwriting them. The clients of the issuing house will also be at risk as sub-underwriters to the issue. A poor record of issues will therefore make it very hard for a bad issuing house to find sub-underwriters; in addition its name can become a liability to a company rather than as asset.[5]

Prior to sponsoring an issue, the issuing house will require an independent accountant's report. The past performance of the company and its future expectations will be examined in the light of the growth prospects for the industry, competition at home and abroad, and future technical developments. The level of pre-tax profits at which an issuing house is prepared to sponsor an issue can vary between £250,000 and £350,000. However, some issuing houses which specialise in financing smaller companies float companies which have achieved pre-tax net profits of £150,000. The Stock Exchange requires the market value of the company to exceed £250,000 and the value of any one security quoted to exceed £100,000.

Issuing houses are looking for a good past record which demonstrates management's ability to achieve profitable growth, but with sufficient stability of earnings to be able to overcome a temporary setback. Normally the flotation is timed to take place after the first six months' accounts are available, so that only the second half year's profits have to be estimated. The profit forecast is always pitched on the conservative side so that it is almost certain to be exceeded. Finally the cash position is more accurately forecast for the next two years to make certain that there are sufficient cash resources to avoid the possibility of further fund raising during this period.

Coordinator

The issuing house acts as coordinator of the team of advisers and experts who are required under section 40 of the 1948 Companies Act to state that they have given and not withdrawn their consent to any statement made by them in the prospectus. A timetable has to be drawn up for drafting and proofing the prospectus, printing, holding the press conference etc, and also for the actions to be taken after the issue has taken place, such as issuing share certificates, etc.

THE STOCKBROKER

Where the issue has a low market capitalisation or when an issuing house is not being used, the broker to the issue also acts as sponsor. Even where there is an issuing house as a sponsor, the broker's name is connected with the issue and therefore with its success or failure.

In the initial period, the broker acts as the link between the issuing house and the quotations department of the Stock Exchange. The principal matters which the broker has to settle with the quotations department are:

1 The letter of application for a quotation, giving the method of issue to be used. If an introduction or a placing is required, proper reasons have to be given explaining why this method has been chosen.
2 The proof of the prospectus has to be passed by the department to see that a full and fair picture is being given of the company's present position and of its future prospects.
3 The department requires assurances that the company has sufficient working capital and facilities for its immediate needs.
4 The broker will liase with the government broker on the timing for impact day, which is the day on which the terms of the issue are first made available to the market. If the issue is over £3 million, Bank of England approval must first be obtained, so that large issues can be carefully spaced out and an orderly new issue market can be maintained.

The broker also has an important part to play in deciding with any issuing house the terms of the issue. These terms must be sufficiently attractive to obtain the sub-underwriting required, or in the case of a placing for the shares to be placed. The broker is responsible for managing the market in the initial stages after the issue, and it is his responsibility to find a permanent shareholder for any shares sold by the stags as otherwise the issue may go to a discount. Prior to the issue the broker will have seen the jobbers and informed them about the company, its products, prospects, etc. He will also have placed sub-underwriting with his institutional clients and thus should have generated institutional interest in the issue. In this initial stage he has to sell the issue, build up confidence in the company and manage the market. After the issue, the broker acts as a link between the jobbers, the institutions and the company.

Qualities Required

The qualities required in a broker are as follows:

1 He must know the industry, its future and any prospective developments, and be able to understand the company, what it does, why it is unusual, and what its future is likely to be.
2 He must be able to compare the company and its prospects with other similar quoted companies and be able to explain how and why, at the issue price, it represents a good buy. Unless the prospective merits of the company are understood the issue can be wrongly priced. He must believe in the company's future and be able to justify the price earnings ratio for the issue. He must also satisfy himself that the forecast profit can be achieved and relate it to the past performance. This understanding is essential for the broker to be able to 'sell' the issue.
3 Where the broker also acts for a much larger firm in the same industry which could be interested in making an offer for the company's shares, it will not be possible for the broker to act for both firms. The smaller firm should ensure that the information given in confidence to the broker cannot be used unwittingly against their interests.

Most of these points could also apply to the selection of an issuing house. While a broker probably charges less initially than an issuing house, the latter can provide a far wider range of services and advice than a broker can offer.

AUDITORS AND REPORTING ACCOUNTANTS

Two firms of accountants will frequently be involved in the issue, and both names will appear on the prospectus or on the advertisement, the company's auditors and the accountants reporting to the issuing house or sponsor. The issuing house may wish to use an accounting firm which is familiar with their method of working and is thus well known in the new issue world. Where the company's auditors also act as reporting accountants, and in particular where the auditors are acting alone in this capacity, another partner unconnected with the audit will have to conduct the investigation, so that the report is impartial and unbiased.

Normally two reports will be prepared: one a private report to the directors of the company and the sponsoring house, giving detailed background information on the company, on past profits and assets and liabilities, and commenting upon the directors' profits forecast and the company's financial position.[6]

They would also report on any weaknesses in accounting control which should be remedied prior to the issue.

The report will provide the sponsors with sufficient information for them to judge whether they will wish their names to be associated with the issue.

Secondly the accountants would prepare a formal report on past profits and net assets which would be included in the prospectus itself.

SOLICITORS

Again two firms may be required, the company's solicitors and those reporting to the issuing house. The issuing house may wish to use a firm which is well known to them and which is very well acquainted with new issue work. The company's solicitors on the other hand may not be very familiar with new issue work, but they should know the background history of the company which will be needed for drawing up the prospectus.

The solicitors have to draft the issue documents, the prospectus, the revised memorandum and articles of association, and any scheme for capital reorganisation, etc. They must also investigate the title of the properties. Solicitors have to preserve a balance between a selling document and one that presents a true and fair picture of the company's present and future position. But, above all, they must protect the directors from any possible charge that they permitted an untrue statement to be made in the prospectus. For this could lay the directors open to unlimited damages and even imprisonment.

THE RECEIVING BANKER

The new issue department of a clearing bank or a merchant bank may be used to handle the paperwork of the issue; this involves receiving applications, clearing cheques, eliminating multiple applications, and in the case of an oversubscription, operating a ballot or scaling down applications. Cheques have also to be returned to unsuccessful applicants, while allotment letters and finally share certificates have to be sent to successful applicants.

The bank can also act as registrars and transfer agents for recording subsequent purchases and sales of the company's shares. They will maintain a register of shareholders, send out dividend cheques and annual reports, and handle capitalisation and rights issues.

PUBLIC RELATIONS

The presentation of the company to the public should take place well in advance of the flotation to make sure that the public are aware of the company, its products and its record. For this reason, a financial public relations firm will often be appointed to work in close coordination with the issuing house and the brokers. A press conference for the financial press in usually held just before the advertisement appears in the London newspapers, and a director of the company should be present to answer any questions. Visits to the company by interested large institutional investors can also be arranged at this time.

REPORTING ACCOUNTANTS

The Formal Report

The Accountants Memorandum in 'Admission of Securities to Quotation' (commonly known as 'the Yellow Book') outlines certain information which must be contained in a report by the auditors in connection with a new issue. Where, in addition to the auditors, another firm of qualified accountants acts as reporting accountants, a joint report is made. The report must deal with:

Profits and Losses

The Stock Exchange requires a statement in respect of profits and losses for the last ten years or since incorporation, if this is for a shorter period. The report should, where appropriate, also show and explain the profits trend and the influence of changes in financing, borrowings, share capital and acquisitions on this trend.

Assets and Liabilities

A statement of assets and liabilities at the last accounting date is required.

Directors' Emoluments

The level of emoluments paid to directors in the most recent financial year must be stated. The amount that would have been payable under the arrangements in force at the time of the prospectus has also to be stated. It often happens that the board is increased in size and strengthened just prior to a public issue.

Dividends

The rate of dividend for each class of share during the five financial years preceding the prospectus date must be given together with details of any waivers; i.e. the agreement by major shareholders not to receive dividends on their shares for a stated period.

Other Matters

The reporting accountants should include any other matters which they consider relevant to the purpose of their report.

Ancillary documents to be supplied to the quotations department by the reporting accountants are their statements of adjustments and their letter concerning certain accounting matters. The method of setting out the statements of adjustments is given in the memorandum – its objective being to reconcile the reported profits and losses with the audited accounts from which they are derived and to disclose in detail the adjustments made. The reporting accountants will be seeking to ensure that the results contained in their report have been arrived at on acceptable and consistent bases throughout the period under review. The letter to be submitted to the quotations department concerning certain accounting matters must deal with the following specific items:

Stocks and Work-in-progress
The reporting accountants will make particular reference to the availability of records and their completeness. Their report will confirm to what extent these assets have been brought into account annually on bases in accordance with generally accepted accounting principles, which have been consistently applied.

Depreciation and Amortisation
They will indicate their satisfaction with the rates adopted for all assets after considering the assets, which the company does not or will not in future depreciate. They are also required to comment upon the rates for any assets which have already been or are about to be revalued.

Tax Equalisation
The report will indicate if this is material, and, where the position is not covered by a deferred tax account, the difference between the tax and the book values of fixed assets, which are eligible for capital and industrial buildings allowances.

Disclosure of further accounting or financial matters may be required either in the body of the prospectus document or within the accountants' report itself. Examples are:

Overseas Interests
The geographical situation of assets and profits must be disclosed where these overseas interests are material. An explanation of the level of taxation, any restrictions on profit remittance and capital repatriation, and the bases of currency conversion adopted, must also be stated.

Long-Term Hire of Plant
Where this is material in relation to the company's business, this may have to be disclosed.

Accounting Policies
Where building, contracting or similar finance companies are the subject of the issue the accounting policies must be stated. In the case of building and contracting companies, the method of taking credit for profits and that used for arriving at stocks and work in progress should be defined.

The memorandum specifically states that its requirements are not exhaustive and that further information will be required where it is relevant.

Forecast Profits

The sponsors will normally require that the basis of the directors' forecast of profits for the next year is examined by the reporting accountants. They will examine the working papers prepared by the management, the assumptions made and their reasonableness, and will also consider the accuracy of the previous forecasts made.

The reporting accountants, when deciding on the validity of the forecast profits to be published in the prospectus by the directors, will consider any particular uncertainties attaching to the company and the trade in question, and also the period of time covered by the forecast. The difficulties of forecasting are of course reduced if interim accounts are available, covering a part of the year for which the forecast is to be made.

As it is a serious setback for a company if the profits forecast is not achieved, the figure actually published will normally include a suitable margin to cover unforeseen contingencies.

Working Capital Requirements

The sponsor is required to provide a letter to the quotations department, confirming that the company has sufficient working capital for its present requirements and that the company's bankers have confirmed in writing the facilities available to the company.

It is usual for the sponsor, before providing such a letter, to call for a detailed cash forecast by the directors not only for the period covered by the published profits forecast but for the following financial year as well. This of course requires a profit forecast for the second year as well. The sponsor will normally instruct the reporting accountants to review and report on these forecasts. A new company would not normally be expected to raise further capital within, say, one and a half to two years of its market debut.

Accounting Records

The Accountants Memorandum[7] contains the following warning: 'A report which contained any significant qualification or reservation as to any of the profits or losses reported upon or as to the assets and liabilities would not be regarded as acceptable by the department'.

The company should therefore take steps to maintain adequate accounting records which will make any investigation as straightforward as possible. The following records should be kept and maintained at a standard which would permit reporting accountants to investigate the ten year record required by the quotations department.

Books of Account – private and nominal ledgers.

Working papers – all working papers and supporting schedules used for preparing the annual accounts.

Audit working papers – these are the property of the auditors but the company should obtain an assurance that these papers will be kept for the necessary ten year period.

Fixed asset register – the existence of such a register will make the investigation process very much faster.

Tax records – complete tax files should be kept for the period. Clearance should be obtained from the Inland Revenue on surtax and shortfall assessments for the period relevant to the report (usually for the last six accounting periods).

The relative importance of particular records will of course vary with the type of business, the above list being generally appropriate to a manufacturing, wholesaling or retailing concern. Other or additional records would be relevant to, for instance, finance companies, insurance brokers, property investment organisations and agency businesses.

PROSPECTUS

Content[8]

The regulations in the Companies Act and those applied by the Stock Exchange are designed to protect investors from fraud and to make sure that there is an orderly market in the shares being issued.

Accuracy

The directors are responsible for seeing that sufficient and accurate information is made available for the public to make an informed decision on the merits of any security. A full and fair and balanced picture of the financial and trading position and the future prospects of the company must be given in the prospectus. It is true that the experts concerned have to give their consent for their report to be published in the prospectus and that their reputation will suffer if a mistake is made. However, the full financial responsibility falls on the directors, and this cannot be avoided by consulting the Stock Exchange. In the final analysis the court will decide on the evidence whether a statement was untrue or not. It is even harder for the directors to decide, where certain matters are open to interpretation. For instance, all material contracts entered into in the last two years which are not in the ordinary course of business, have to be disclosed. In addition, the Stock Exchange requires the directors to disclose the financial and trading prospects of the company, together with any relevant information, including where known to the directors, special trade factors or risks (if any) which are not mentioned elsewhere in the prospectus and which are unlikely to be known or anticipated by the general public and which could materially affect the profits.[9]

A file should be kept on all factual information such as figures, statements and source data, on which all opinions stated in the prospectus are based. This file should be updated throughout the drafting of the prospectus and should provide a record of why the directors felt that the statement was true at the time the prospectus was issued.[10]

A Good Market

Even if all the statements are true, the investor will not be able to sell his shares freely unless there is a 'good market' in the security. The Stock Exchange always wishes to avoid a false market in the shares, which can happen, if there is a shortage or an excess of stock, especially in the early stages immediately after an issue. In offers for sale or prospectus issues, normally 35 per cent of the issued ordinary share capital must be offered to the public, unless the issue is very large, to make sure the market has an adequate supply of stock. In a placing, 35 per cent of the issued ordinary share capital must be placed, and of the amount placed, one quarter has to be offered to the market. The Stock Exchange restrictions of a minimum market capitalisation of £250,000 for the company or £100,000 for any one security are not meaningful for the London market, as most issues are much bigger.[11]

Warranties and Indemnities

Warranties are required by the Stock Exchange from the directors that the accounts presented give a true and fair picture of the company's financial position and that all liabilities have been disclosed. The directors and shareholders are required to give the company an indemnity against any undisclosed tax and estate duty liabilities, relating to former years.

Terms

The actual method of valuing a company has already been described in Chapter 9. A final decision on the terms is left as late as possible in case any adjustments are needed to bring them into line with current market conditions. The shares will normally be offered at a discount on the prevailing market price if the company's name and reputation are unknown to investors. In fact, a study[12] by Merrett and Newbould found that market discounts averaged 17.7 per cent on a sample of 24 offers for sale, and 26.8 per cent on a sample of 19 placings. Market discount was higher for smaller issues, but the samples were not large enough for any strong inference. The price of course must be such that the sponsor can underwrite the issue. In addition, it is wise to aim for a reasonable premium (up to 15 per cent) when dealings begin, to allow for a deterioration in market conditions and/or to provide an incentive for the market to deal. At all costs a discount on the offer price should be avoided as it damages the market image of the company. Thereafter it may find that it can only raise capital from its disgruntled shareholders on very uneconomic giveaway terms. For this reason, the record of the issuing house should be studied, before a client makes his choice, to determine its efficiency in pricing an issue.

Timetable

The timetable for an issue depends on three factors: the time taken for the company to show it is ready for a public issue, the market conditions needed for a favourable reception for the issue, and the time taken in the new-issue queue, and in completing the prospectus requirements.

The Company
In previous chapters, the methods of reorganisation which are sometimes required have been described, such as restructuring the share capital, acquiring minority holdings in subsidiaries and associated companies, and satisfying the problems raised by reporting accountants. In addition the brokers and sponsors should be given time to understand the company, its strengths and weaknesses and its prospects.

Market Conditions
The market conditions must be right for the issue, or the shareholders will not be selling at a reasonable price; the prospects overall and those for the industry concerned must also be favourable. In addition, unknown companies have to be priced at a larger market discount than established ones. If the company is expecting a faster growth in earnings than the existing quoted companies, a public relations exercise may be needed to make the public aware of any significant strengths over competition.

New Issue Queue and Prospectus Requirements
There is at present a queue of about three months for large new issues. The timing for issues of £3 million or over is controlled by the Bank of England so as to maintain an orderly market. The sponsoring broker has to apply to the government broker for impact day, which is the day on which the market is made aware of the terms of the issue.

The timetable in *Company Share Quotations* shows[13] that the actual process of drafting the prospectus and the other documents required should begin about 40 days before impact day. This assumes that the issue is a viable proposition and that no snags arise. This period does not include any time for an accountant's report which would have been prepared previously. The time taken for this depends on the state of the company's past records and those of its auditors. Bearing in mind the potential liabilities the directors assume when their company issues a prospectus, sufficient time should be taken to make sure that the picture given is a correct one.

Costs

The costs of a new issue are normally borne by the company, except where existing shareholders are offering their shares to the public. In this case, they must bear a proportion of the costs of the issue, including underwriting, as Section 54 of the 1948 Companies Act does not allow a company to purchase its shares either directly or indirectly. The main costs are, advertising, printing, accountants and solicitors fees, quotation fees, commissions to sponsors, stockbrokers, underwriters and the receiving bankers fees. As many of the fees are fixed regardless of the amount raised, the larger the issue the lower the costs as a percentage of the amount raised and vice versa.

Fielding Newsom Smith and Co. quote[14] figures of average costs as a percentage of the average amount raised on the London market in 1969 (see Figure 18.1).

Group	Number of issues	Average amount paid by public	Costs as percentage of amount raised
Placings up to £200,000	3	£142,417	15.0%
Placings £200,000 – £500,000	8	£319,161	6.7%
Offers £200,000 – £500,000	13	£372,248	9.3%
Offers £500,000 – £750,000	12	£623,275	7.0%
Offers £750,000 – £1,250,000	10	£951,537	5.2%
Offers over £1,250,000	13	£3,374,854	3.1%

Figure 18:1 Costs as Percentage of Amount Raised

These figures should be taken as a guide only as costs have risen since publication.

RESPONSIBILITIES AFTER A PUBLIC ISSUE

The directors and the company are required as a condition for the quotation to enter into a listing agreement with the Stock Exchange as laid down in their regulations.[15] The objects of this agreement are to protect the position of the existing shareholders, as the company agrees to observe certain practices. Among other matters, there are regulations on:

The Protection of Ordinary Shareholder Rights
On issuing further equity except to the existing shareholders; a restriction on the amount of preferential share offerings to employees to 10 per cent of the amount offered; the issue of options to employees is restricted to five per cent of the issued share capital.

Directors' Service Agreements
These agreements have to be disclosed and in certain cases approved in general meeting.

Information
Certain information has to be made available in an approved format and presented in a manner to avoid a false market in the shares. The regulations cover half year and annual statements and accounts, both preliminary and final, dividends, bids and offers.

Companies should remember that the Stock Exchange has the power to withdraw a quotation already given if the company does not follow the regulations laid down. For this reason, the directors of any company contemplating a public issue should make themselves well acquainted with these regulations.

REFERENCES

1 A shell company is a company with a quotation but with a low asset value and or low earnings into which can be injected the assets and earnings of a private company. Defunct rubber estate companies whose estates have been nationalised have often been used for a shell operation.

2 The contents of a prospectus are defined in the Fourth Schedule of the 1948 Companies Act. In addition, the Stock Exchange issues its requirements for quotations in *Admission of Securities to Quotation,* Memorandum of Guidance and Requirements of the Federation of Stock Exchanges in Great Britain and Ireland, The Stock Exchange, London, 1969.

3 Stags – short term speculators who apply for new issues which they feel will reach a premium over the issue price directly after the issue. Where there is an over-subscription for an issue, those who do obtain shares can often sell at a profit in the initial days of new dealings.

4 See also *Financial and Accounting Responsibilities of Directors,* a Special Issue for the Institute of Directors by the General Education Trust of the Institute of Chartered Accountants of England and Wales, London 1970.

5 The record of new issues can be examined by obtaining a copy of *New Issue Statistics,* issued by Singer & Friedlander Ltd. which gives the performance of new issues over a two-year period, together with the levels of premium or discount over the offer price for the period; the figures are updated quarterly.

6 The Institute of Chartered Accountants have issued new instructions on profit forecasts. The Stock Exchange now tends to require both the issuing house and the reporting accountants to accept responsibility for a profit forecast.

7 *Admission of Securities to Quotation,* p. 11, Section 1.

8 Companies Act, 1948, 4th Schedule and *Admission of Securities to Quotation,* Schedule 11, Part A, p. 64.

9 *Admission of Securities to Quotation,* p. 66.

10 'Going Public 1971', *Accounting Age,* p. 30, London 1971.

11 *New Equity Issue Statistics,* Singer & Friedlander Ltd.

12 A.J. MERRETT and G.D. NEWBOULD, 'The Comparative Efficiency of Methods of Issue', The Manchester School, January 1966, p. 2.

13 *Company Share Quotations,* Fielding, Newsom-Smith & Co., London, pp. 30-31.

14 *ibid.,* p. 19.

15 *Admission of Securities to Quotation,* Chapter 2.

19

Takeovers and Mergers

INTRODUCTION

A private company may decide that its future prospects would be improved by merging with another company or by joining a large industrial group. If the company can obtain a quotation for its shares prior to a merger, it is often possible to obtain better terms for the shareholders, firstly because the market price establishes a minimum price for the shares, and secondly because a second bidder may enter the market and offer a higher price.

In this chapter, no reference will be made to the mechanics of making a public offer for the shares of a quoted company. Many mergers fail for the much more fundamental reason that both sides have not fully thought out how the two companies will operate as one unit. Often each partner has a completely different idea of the role of his company to that of his new partner. Both sides assume that they will manage the new group and often fail to understand their new partners' aims, ambitions and objectives. Boards of directors should first decide the reasons for merging, whether they are valid, and whether the merger will further both companies' long term objectives. The mechanics of the offer can be left to the company's advisers, once the board has decided the value they place on their company or on the company they wish to acquire.

ATTITUDE

Both parties should realise that, after a merger, life will never be the same again. There is rarely any point in merging and remaining completely separate units. For a 'sea change' will take place, especially when a private company joins a large industrial group.

The entrepreneur who has built up a private company, has been his own independent master. Like a privateer, he can sail in any direction he chooses; he can sell what product he wants, to whatever customer will reward him best. If he is the controlling shareholder, he is the master of the ship with the power of life and death within his organisation over all those he employs. In the outside world, he suffers few constraints provided he cherishes his customers, has good relations with his bank manager and his auditors, and pays his taxes and his bills within the time allowed. However as part of a group, he is only the captain of a ship of the line. He is subject to sailing instructions and limited perhaps to operating in a defined sector. His authority will be limited and he will be required to report in a prescribed manner at certain times. From time to time, his company will be inspected by his superiors. Even worse, he will be advised by a host of experts that he is not observing group policy. He may begin to think that this preoccupation with means may not allow him to achieve the objectives he has for the company. For some the transition from chief executive of a private company to managing a group subsidiary is too hard to bear.

Inter-Group Politics

An industrial group, with a mass of different departments and subsidiaries is a complex political entity. The managements of these units are all competing for group resources and for individual advancement. Any new company is fair game to be hunted and broken up so as to expand the existing empires of the present line managers. The new entrant is at a disadvantage, as he does not know group methods and procedures, and especially the short cuts. All large organisations tend to have 'civil service' structures and procedures, but those who have worked together for long periods are usually able to short circuit the system. Those who are unfamiliar with the system can find out the *de jure* power matrix, but the *de facto* structure is harder to determine. Who are the managers that can make decisions and do so, and who can decide, but won't?

OBJECTIVES

'An ambitious company seeking growth through acquisitions must preserve the balance between earnings per share, assets per shares, borrowing, liquidity and the issue of new shares if it is not to court disaster.'[1]. As the market expects to see real growth in earnings and assets per share, over-borrowing and a lack of liquidity can place a company in a dangerous position if profits turn down unexpectedly. Furthermore, a rapid increase in share capital, as in the case of many conglomerates, can make for an unstable market for the company's shares,[1] especially if the company being bought does not achieve a sufficiently impressive expansion in earnings to justify the holding company's high share price and price earnings ratio.

An acquisition should only be contemplated as a means of achieving an overall corporate objective. Any difference between the future earnings from existing and new products and the overall corporate objective in earnings per share can only be filled by making an acquisition.

Example

Earnings per share
An overall expansion of 10 per cent per annum in earnings per share is acquired, of which only 3 per cent will come from the existing business.

Issued Share Capital
The issued share capital cannot be increased by more than 10 per cent per annum.

Purchase Price
The share capital available for acquiring companies must be related to the company's overall borrowing and its borrowing limit after considering the company's forward capital requirements. Any substantial goodwill element[2] in any purchase price will have an adverse effect on the overall borrowing capacity of the group.

Current Ratio
The effect of any purchase on the company's liquidity should not be forgotten, in case unforeseen events could place the company in a

serious financial position. The acquisition by one company of another one which is illiquid, has overstated earnings or unrealisable assets priced too highly can cause a serious setback to any company. Where the purchase is financed by equity, a failure to reach an earnings forecast can seriously affect the company's earnings per share and share price (Figure 19:1).

	Earnings		Issued share capital (number of shares)		Earnings per share	
Pre purchase						
Company	100.0		25.0		4.0	
1st purchase year						
Company	103.0	(3%)	25.0	(- -)	4.12	(3%)
Acquisition	18.0		2.5	(10%)	7.20	
Group	121.0	(21%)	27.5	(10%)	4.40	(10%)
2nd purchase year						
Company	106.1	(3%)	25.0	(- -)	4.24	(3%)
Acquisition	26.5	(47%)	2.5	(- -)	10.60	(47%)
Group	132.6	(11%)	27.5	(- -)	4.82	(11%)
Increase (1st to 2nd year)						
Company	3.1	(27%)				
Acquisition	8.5	(73%)				
Group	11.6	(100%)				

Figure 19.1 Earnings per Share

Therefore in this case, 90 per cent of the equity is producing 27 per cent of the increase in earnings, while 10 per cent of the equity is producing 73 per cent of the increase in earnings. This objective of expanding earnings per share is dependent on the acquisition maintaining a 47 per cent increase in earnings in the second year. If, in the second year, the earnings of the acquired company fall by 17 per cent from the previous year's level, i.e. by 3.1 and the earnings of the original company rise at the budgeted rate of 3 per cent per annum, i.e. 3.1, then, overall, the company will have achieved no growth.

The failure will have consequence for all, including the company acquired, as the group may face a takeover or may be unable to obtain the funds it needs for expansion. For this reason, both parties should examine carefully the plans and future prospects of the other party.

The company being acquired should study the group's corporate plan to see whether the objectives of both companies are similar. They should then find out the following:

1. Why does the group wish to acquire their company?
2. What can the group contribute to the company's future prosperity benefits – how and when?
3. How will the two organisations fit together and will the company being purchased be autonomous or will it be totally absorbed?
4. Does group management understand the industry's problems, the products, and the customers of the acquired company?
5. Do both companies have similar attitudes and outlook?
6. What is the minimum selling price?

The acquiring company will wish to consider the following points:

1. Does this company fit into our corporate plan and does its acquisition assist us to achieve our objectives?
2. What is our maximum price?
3. How will we integrate the company, without losing what we have bought?
4. What integration savings can be made and when?
5. Can any surplus assets be realised, or can unprofitable assets be made profitable, and if so when?

REASONS FOR BEING ACQUIRED

'In most, but not all, of the cases studied, the one single fact which characterised the decisions to sell was fear; fear about the future.'[3]

Some of the reasons for selling are given below.

Fiscal

For estate duty and family reasons, as the shareholders wish to have their funds invested in quoted securities rather than in the unquoted shares of a private close company.

Management

If the company has 'one man' management problems arising from a major policy disagreements or succession problems. Key staff may have left or be about to leave and set up in competition, especially if they are not given the opportunity to acquire equity in the company.

Failure

If the company's return is too low, if its products are obsolete or about to be made obsolete by a new technical breakthrough, or if its markets are static or declining, then it will be unlikely to be able to afford the investment required to update its product line and equipment.

Success

A small company may not be able to exploit its advantage before it is overtaken by larger groups through lack of cash, or productive capacity, or because its market coverage is too narrow. Furthermore, even if it has a good patent position, it may not be able to afford to fight an infringement by a large group in the courts, as patent actions tend to be won by the party which can afford the longest court case.

REASONS FOR ACQUIRING

The reasons for making an acquisition should always be related to the *specific objectives* in the company's overall plan, which can only be achieved by a takeover or merger. The excitement of making acquisitions with the attendant publicity for the management is not, in itself a valid reason for this course of action. The main reasons for making acquisitions are as follows:

Management

To acquire management with special technical or other skills in unfamiliar fields, or to acquire a young, successful and dynamic management. This is only a valid reason, if the new management will be given the correct level of responsibility and motivation to make it worth while for them to remain. As well as proper service agreements, the compensation of these executives should be in line with those with similar responsibilities and achievements in the rest of the group. The 'old' management must be able and willing to work with, and share the new tasks with, the 'newcomers'. Where there is an efficient and capable management, which is underemployed, it can be highly profitable for the company to acquire businesses which can be turned round and made more profitable.

Assets

The company may be able to acquire assets at an attractive price, for example, factories, land or machinery. For, if a new factory is required urgently, a direct purchase can be cheaper and more certain than putting up a new building. When assets are being acquired, which either are, or will be made, surplus by the merger, then it is wise to find out in advance their estimated selling prices. The location and specialised nature of some buildings may make them hard to sell at their book values.

Financial

The earnings per share of the group may be improved by acquiring a company at a price earnings ratio below that of the quoted company. The purchase of an asset rich company should also improve the asset base and thus the borrowing capability of the business. A generous allowance should also be made for the almost inevitable delays which occur in making any unprofitable companies or assets profitable, and in reaching the pre-acquisition profit forecasts.

Fiscal

In certain cases it may be worth while acquiring a 'tax loss' company, if the two companies are in the same field of business. When a private company management wishes to 'go public' it can make a reverse takeover for a quoted 'shell' company with few assets, so that the private company shareholders end up in control (see p. 255).

Technology

The acquisition of technology in either a new or in a related field will often save not only development costs, but may also be buying time and a reputation, which is often needed to catch up with or to surpass competition.

Integration

The company may wish to integrate backwards by acquiring a source of supply, or forward, by taking over a customer. These actions can ensure either a source of raw materials or components, or deny markets to competition. Horizontal integration normally involves the purchase of companies, serving similar markets or making similar products which can result in economies of scale, in production, marketing and even in development.

Economies of Scale

Savings can be made by amalgamating resources. However the time taken to realise these economies may be longer than forecast, unless the integration plan is prepared in great detail prior to the takeover:

1 *Research and development:* rationalising teams and projects.
2 *Administration:* lower management expenses and lower accounting costs, by centralising services and using computers if applicable. Excess computing capacity can often be eliminated.
3 *Buying:* economies from central buying and greater discounts from bulk buying.
4 *Marketing:* fewer sales offices, centralising advertising and public relations, and by centralising outside maintenance staffs. Acquiring a sales force through an acquisition can save the build-up time otherwise needed, especially in a new product field where the group has no product reputation.
5 *Working capital:* the merger may make it possible to reduce stocks and work in progress and thus to release working capital.
6 *Products:* new markets can be more easily and quickly entered by acquiring established products than by developing new ones, especially where both the technology and the market needs are unfamiliar. A 'one product' company or one with products subject to seasonal or cyclic trends or to Government control should be able to diversify for a known investment. It is well known that new product launch costs can accelerate through design and production problems and through delays in market acceptance.

Where markets and customers are related, a bigger product line and greater variety can often be serviced by the same sales force. In addition the established reputation of the group and its wider distribution network can often make a significant impact on the sales of the new company.

DANGER AND PITFALLS

For the management of the acquired company, a successful and profitable integration can give them a good position on the executive ladder of the new group. The reverse is also true even if the failure is not their fault. They should learn to recognise the group on an 'acquisition jag' which is suffering from 'auction mania'. Some managements have no integrated plan and will buy anything, regardless of price, either to inflate their ego or to make it harder to compare the results of the current year with those of the previous ones. Such managements, even if they buy the right company, may throw it all away by poor planning and execution of the integration of the company into the group.

Compatibility

A well managed private company should find a partner with the same aims and style of management, which preferably understands their business. A thrusting young and independent racehorse should not be harnessed to a sleepy, old and tired carthorse. If the management of the acquiring company does not understand the new company's product fields or markets, they are unlikely to know the criteria for success or the right type of management for the new subsidiary, if it is operating in fields unfamiliar to them. The purchase of electronics companies by engineering companies is often a failure, as the top management does not appreciate the higher level of risk-taking required in a high-technology industry.

Hotchpotch

By not acquiring according to a plan the group can become a hotchpotch of companies with unrelated markets and technologies. This lack of policy tends to cause problems of organisation and communication without any countervailing advantages. Two bad companies do not usually produce one good one. Furthermore, companies which can often exist as independent units are sometimes not able to earn sufficient profits, to absorb the higher management, accounting and publicity charges a group subsidiary has to carry.

The managements of acquiring companies which make these mistakes may be a 'soft touch', but they are unlikely to be occupying their positions for very long. For a lasting relationship will only be built up by the two managements through the successful integration of the new company, which achieves its planned objectives and by doing so plays its part in carrying out the overall strategic plan for the group.

STRATEGY

The Acquiring Company

To summarise therefore, the acquiring company should only purchase companies in order to reach the objectives set out in the corporate plan. Objectives should be set for new companies in the same way as for the rest of the group. It is only by such discipline that the company may obtain the best return on the funds at its disposal. An efficient management will only commit funds outside the group, if the long-term return is more favourable than can be obtained from investment in one of the existing subsidiaries.

The Company Being Acquired

A merger should only take place if the two long-term plans are complementary. If their overall aims are the same and if the managements are compatible in outlook and temperament then a merger may well be profitable to all. As the management of the private company will probably be acquiring shares in the new group, they should investigate the present market standing, the past record, and the future prospects for the group.

The New Group

Once the terms have been agreed, a draft integration plan should be prepared. The price agreed should be fair to both parties after considering the earnings assets and cash flow contributed by both sides, and their respective shares of the issued share capital after the merger. The price paid for the company will be related to the relative price earnings ratio for the industry and the size of company concerned. The borrowing capacity of the new group should also be calculated. This limit should be related to the present level of borrowings to find out if the balance of borrowings available will be sufficient for the group's present and future financial requirements. If not, other sources of funds should be considered, such as a rights issue, loan stock etc. The integration plan should lay down an agreed basis for the two organisations to work together – the management structure, the organisation, the location of factories and offices, the staffing, and the control system.

Advantages and Methods

Both sides should make sure that they are as concerned with ends as they are with means. They should agree why the merger makes sense industrially to each of them, how it helps them to achieve their objectives and what sacrifices they are prepared to make to achieve these ends.

INVESTIGATION

The level, direction and scope of the investigation will depend on the reasons why the company is being bought. If the company is being bought for its assets, then all that is needed is an accurate valuation of the present assets and liabilities, together with an estimate of any further liabilities that will be incurred in closing down the company. If, however, it is required as a trading entity, in whole or in part, then the assessment should be from this angle. The acquiring company will wish to discover, if the objectives it wishes to achieve by purchasing the company, are attainable or not. Therefore the depth of the investigation will depend on the level of administration of the company, and the adequacy of its past audit records etc. (see p. 269). The investigation itself however may be hampered by a requirement for secrecy and by the necessity for completing the investigation within a short time-scale.

Provided the management are selling a viable unit and are not dressing up a 'lame duck' for sale, then they should co-operate fully in the investigation. The procedures they should adopt, for placing their company in readiness for this investigation are very similar to those already described in Chapters 4, 5 and 6.

Financial

The first stage will be an investigation by reporting accountants, probably the auditors of the purchasing company, to establish whether there are any financial skeletons in the cupboard, such as undisclosed tax liabilities and substantial stock and work in progress deficiencies, which may make the whole scheme impossible. The content of the report will probably follow the lines of the Appendix to Chapter 5, but there may be variations for special industry conditions. The report will aim to show, whether the accounts for the last *X* years give a true and fair picture of the assets, liabilities, profits and losses of the company (see Chapter 5 and Appendix to Chapter 5). The report will also contain details of the company's accounting methods which may need to be altered to meet the group's accounting practices.

Non-financial

This part of the report will be written by the staff of the acquiring group or by a consultant. The content will be similar to that already described in the Appendix to Chapter 4. It will cover such matters as an evaluation of the management and staff, the products, the technological and market position of the company, the production techniques used and the level of control and administration. This investigation will aim to uncover non-financial problems that the company may face in the future, such as declining or static markets, obsolete products, management succession problems, low staff morale, out of date technology, worn out and obsolete equipment, etc. Naturally these problems, if they are left unsolved will reduce profits. Their existence however may not be evident from an examination of the company's past financial records.

Forecasts

In Chapter 6, the forward planning process was described. This same information is needed to assess the composition and prospects for the new group. The growth potential of the company to be acquired should first be assessed for at least the next three years, its probability of success and its downside potential. Then the profits of the company, as a part of the group after the merger, should be assessed after allowing for any group charges to the company for management, publicity etc. The budgeted expenses should also be adjusted for any integration savings that can be made. However any estimates should make allowances for the delays which will almost certainly occur, especially in such sensitive matters as factory closures.

Cash Requirements

The financial position of the company should then be examined, its cash flow, and the financial facilities required, after allowing for any additional capital required for new fixed assets and working capital. Finally the return on the group investment should be calculated.

Advantages and Disadvantages

The final task is to assess whether the return on group assets justifies the operation and meets the objectives of the strategic plan. The various non-financial objectives of the plan should be re-examined, to see whether the needs of both parties will be satisfied by a merger. The buyer will need to assess the future prospects for the company against the price provisionally agreed, and after considering the pros and cons, he will decide whether to go ahead or not. The sellers will wish to establish whether or not membership of the group will enable them to fulfil the aims they have for the company. If the answer in both cases is 'yes', a deal will probably be made, provided the difference between the buyers maximum price and the sellers minimum price is sufficiently close for negotiation. The bargaining position of the private company will depend on its ability to exist as an independent unit. A company with no financial, managerial or product problems, with a good past record and good expectations for the future is naturally in a strong bargaining position. A purchaser who needs to acquire profits, management, new products and technology, and who cannot allow the company to be acquired by a competitor, is naturally in a weak position. In the interests of their shareholders, both parties should carefully assess their bargaining position. Each should determine how far he can push the other side in the direction he wants them to go, without causing the other party to break off negotiations.

The role of each man taking part in the negotiations should be carefully laid down in advance, as well as the maximum and minimum aims which are to be achieved. Bacon advises using fair spoken men for persuasion, crafty men for inquiry and observation, and bold men for expostulation; but all should be experienced men who like negotiating. The negotiations should be used to find out about a man so as to manipulate him. Men show their natures in anger, when unawares or when they are trusted. They can be led by knowing their nature and how they react, or persuaded by knowing their ends both for themselves and for their company. They can be awed by playing on their weaknesses or disadvantages, and by understanding the aims of those that have influence over them and govern them, i.e. their superiors. Lastly, business should not be hurried but carefully prepared and ripened by degrees.[4]

The vendors should therefore carefully consider the position of the bidding company and also the political situation of the management, prior to any negotiations. Full disclosure in the negotiations should apply to both parties equally. The vendors need to examine the group's future plans to know where they will fit in and how much assistance they will receive as a group member. The vendors have a duty to their shareholders and to their staff to expose any weaknesses in their opponent's thinking. Specific plans and written agreements limit the future freedom of action of the group management, while vague indefinite arrangements leave the initiative in the hands of the group, to be determined by inter-group politics.

AGREEMENTS

Equity Holding

The purchasers may intend operating the company they are acquiring as a separate entity rather than integrating it into another division of the group. The vendors can test the validity of this intention and also obtain some protection for their independence by retaining a small equity stake of over 10 per cent in the company.[5] Where minority shareholders exist, the company has to deal on an 'arms length' basis with the rest of the group. Furthermore, the existing executive directors, who continue to hold shares, can benefit from any expansion in earnings over the period as it will increase the value of their shares. An undertaking would certainly be required from the vendors to offer their shares first to the purchasers at a certain valuation and within perhaps a fixed time limit. The vendors also need a 'put' option which requires the purchasers to acquire the minority holding at a certain price and at certain dates within a set period.[6] Otherwise the original shareholders have no way of realising their investment, if they are dismissed or if they dislike the way in which they and their company are being treated. The vendors should also obtain undertakings that if their company is offered for sale at a later date they will be given first refusal to purchase the equity at the agreed selling price.

Price: Straight or Incentive

The method of valuing a company has been described above in Chapter 12. The sale can either be at a fixed price for all or part of the equity or at a variable price depending on future performance. There will nearly always be an argument on price. The vendors will always want to use projected earnings and a price earnings ratio which allows for the anticipated future expansion in profits. The purchasers, on the other hand, will wish to work on last year's earnings and on a lower price earnings ratio, which is consistent with the past record. If the purchasers pursue this line of argument, the vendors should negotiate an incentive payment over the existing market price, based on actual future profits achieved. The incentive can be based on average annual profits earned above the level expected over the next, say, three to five years. This amount can be multiplied by a factor to arrive at the capital sum which will be distributed to the former shareholders *pro rata.* To be able to calculate the incentive the company must be treated as a separate entity from the rest of the group. The vendors need protection against the group adding loss-making products or transferring profitable lines to other parts of the group. The level of interest charges (X per cent above the base rate), management charges and the level of research and development spending should all be fixed. Any reorganisation within the incentive period would have to be approved by the vendors if it could affect the incentive payment.

Payment Method

If an outright payment is made in cash, capital gains tax is payable by the vendors on any gain from the disposal. If, however, the vendors receive shares or loan stock, no gains tax is payable on the transfer. Loan stock is not usually attractive unless it is convertible into ordinary shares. Permission from the Stock Exchange to deal in the shares and for a quotation should be obtained prior to the transfer. Having decided the acquisition price, the number of shares to be issued by the purchaser in exchange for the vendor's shares is fixed. Alternatively, a price is taken for the purchaser's shares at the middle market price on a certain date, and this figure divided into the acquisition price gives the number of shares to be issued. The new shares should rank *pari passu* (equal) with the shares already quoted, and should enjoy in full all future dividends, rights, etc. Unless the shares are freely negotiable, the vendors will not have the option of realising part of their investment if they so wish. (Permission from the Stock Exchange to deal in the shares and for a quotation must be obtained prior to the transfer.)

Restrictions on Disposal or Transfer of Shares

Any restrictions on the disposal or transfer of quoted shares issued to vendors in consideration for an acquisition should be viewed in two ways. Firstly, by how much do these restrictions reduce the value of the shares, and secondly how far do these restrictions negate the family's legitimate wishes to avoid death duties? Even if a period is agreed upon, the vendors should have the right to transfer shares within their immediate family or between the various shareholders. There is no objection to agreeing to consult the group's stockbroker, when a substantial line of shares is to be sold, as he may be able to place the shares without unduly upsetting the market price.

Non-Competition Undertakings and Service Agreements

If the major shareholders are also active in the business, the purchasers will usually require them to give an undertaking not to compete with the company for a certain period. They may also have to enter into an agreement to give their services to the company for a definite period. In the case of major shareholders, this undertaking can be treated as having been given in return for part of the purchase price. Damages may therefore be payable if any of these undertakings are broken. For ordinary working directors with few shares, the restrictions should not be such that they are unreasonable and could prevent a man from seeking other employment in the field he knows best. Agreements which are over-restrictive are contrary to public policy and may be set aside by the courts. The vendors should understand the restrictions placed on them by these covenants, if they are dismissed by the group. If the executive is dismissed without due cause (i.e. for a drop in profits below a certain level), or if the company breaks its part of the agreement (i.e. reduces a man's responsibilities without due cause), then these restrictions should be void. It might save arguments if the test for unfair dismissal was the same as that used in the Industrial Relations Act.

Warranties and Indemnities

The indemnities and warranties required have already been described (see Chapter 9). The period for which these undertakings stand should be fixed. Most of them will relate to matters which should be able to be resolved after the next group audit or at the most within one year from the date of acquisition. Any liabilities imposed by the purchaser should be shared in proportion to the purchase consideration received by each of the vendors.

THE LETTER OF OFFER AND THE AGREEMENT

As in the case of an offer to acquire a minority holding in the equity of a private company, the first step is a letter of offer from the acquiring company to the shareholders of the company being purchased (see Chapter 7, pp. 127-130). The offer will probably be subject to the following conditions:

Acceptance: to acceptance by all the shareholders (or to a proportion of over *X* per cent of the issued equity capital).
Inspection: to an inspection of the company's books disclosing no material change in the company's state of affairs to that already disclosed.
Service agreements: to Mr A and Mr B entering into service agreements for *X* years, expiring on — at a salary of £ — at the company's standard terms and conditions.
Non-Competition: to Mr A and Mr B entering into an agreement not to compete with the company being acquired in its present field of activity (or the exact fields specified) as agent, director, employee, for *X* years from the date of this agreement. An attempt to restrict the person concerned from competing with the company for *X* years from the date of leaving the company's employment might be unfair, if the employment had been terminated by the company.
Loans: there may be loans outstanding from banks, other financial institutions and from individuals, which would reduce the company's need for further finance. If this factor has been taken into account in

arriving at the total capital required (the purchase amount and any other long term capital required), the offer may be conditional upon the continuance of these loans.
Agreement: the offer is always made subject to the signature of a formal agreement, which will include the necessary warranties and indemnities.

The letter of offer which will be sent to all the shareholders as well as to the board will also probably contain the following points:

Share capital: authorised and issued.
Shareholders: a list of shareholders, showing the number of each different class of share held by each member.
Shares to be purchased: the number of shares to be purchased of each class will be stated. This is usually all the issued share capital, to avoid complications with minority shareholders. The shares are purchased with all rights attaching to them including any dividends due after completion and must be free of all liens, charges and encumbrances. The shares are described as being fully or partly paid. Any call outstanding on partly paid shares should be stated.
Consideration: in the case of a cash offer, the purchase price is stated and when it is to be paid. For a share exchange, the number of shares to be exchanged for each of the vendor's shares is stated. The letter must also contain details of the shares being offered, their rights, especially as to future dividends, and whether or not there will be a public quotation for these shares.

Costs

The costs of the offer, such as legal costs etc., must be borne by the vendors, as no company can purchase its shares either directly or indirectly (see also Chapter 18, p. 273). The vendors should decide at the time of the offer how the legal costs are to be apportioned. Each shareholder may decide to pay his own costs. If however one solicitor represents all the vendors, they should decide in advance whether the costs are to be shared *pro rata* to their shareholdings or on some other basis.

Announcements and Publicity

The press releases to be made should be agreed by both parties and the release date decided upon. However, of greater importance is how the matter is to be announced to the employees of the company being acquired. This event should take place before the official announcement is made and should normally be made by the directors at a meeting, where they can explain the reasons for the takeover, and the advantages and disadvantages to the staff of being part of a larger group.

THE BOARD OF DIRECTORS

Compensation for Loss of Office

Certain existing members of the board may be required to resign as they are not required in the new group. If these members are also executive directors, the problem of compensation needs careful consideration. The purchasers may require all those required to resign to do so, without receiving any compensation. However, a director who is only a small shareholder may not be prepared to give up any rights he may have against the company. This matter should therefore be settled before the letter of offer is sent out, as any compensation will usually have to come out of the purchase price. At present up to £5000 can be paid tax free in compensation for loss of office.

Service Agreements and Non-Competition

Service agreements and clauses relating to non-competition have already been discussed (see above and also the Appendix to this Chapter and Chapter 13, pp. 182-184). The most important function is to define how the executive concerned is to operate in the future, his authority and responsibility and the performance on which he will be judged.

The Board's Function within the Group

The function of the board and the new duties of its members will largely depend upon the relationship of the new company to the rest of the group. The company may cease to exist as a separate entity and may be absorbed into one or more divisions, or it may exist as an independent unit. Whatever its function is, however, the board will no longer be the ultimate arbiter of policy and practice, as it will be subject to group policy. The method of control will also decide how active the board will be in the future. Control may be exercised through a management committee, which meets monthly to review the performance of the company and to discuss progress with the executives concerned. In this case, a formal board meeting will only be needed to meet the requirements of the Companies Acts, i.e. to pass the annual accounts, etc. This decision will determine not only who remains on the board and who joins it from the group, but also how frequently the board meets.

INTEGRATION

Objectives and Time Scale

A plan should be prepared for implementing the objectives of the takeover according to a timetable agreeable to both parties. The extent of the plan will depend on the level of integration of the new company with the rest of the group. A new company will either be left on its own, or swallowed, wholly or in part. Whatever the objectives, the plan should define the company's relationship with the other parts of the group. It should also be acceptable to both sides so that total commitment is obtained from all for the new entity. Unless the group management is able to generate this feeling in the management and staff of the new company, it may find that all that is left are some buildings and the least gifted staff. The rest will have gone to reinforce their competitors' operations, with a determination to show how foolish the group was, not to recognise their talents.

Organisation and Rationalisation

The organisation and scope of the new company needs careful definition in the early stages to avoid future misunderstandings. The decisions to be made are as follows:

Management authority. What authority is the management to be given, what limits are to be imposed on it, and what broad objectives is it to achieve? Will the company operate as a separate unit or be a part of another division? Will it be controlled by a board or will it report directly to a specific person?

Products and scope. The scope of the company and its product range should be defined and especially how problems of competition with other parts of the group will be resolved. Will there be restrictions on extending the company's product range and on the type of customer it serves? Will the company be permitted to use its own method of distribution, at home and abroad, or not? Will the group impose restrictions on pricing and discount policies?

Manufacturing. If there are to be factory closures, where will the factory be located? Will the scope of the factory be restricted to assembly work, with machine shop and foundry work being carried out elsewhere?

Research and development. Will the company retain a development team and if so will its operations be restricted to a certain field? In some cases considerable savings can be made from centralising R & D.

Central Services and Overheads

Certain economies will result if the company uses central services rather than continuing to use its own advisers. The group will want the company to use its own auditors, legal department, patent department, and some part of the company's administration may well be carried out by the central computer department, e.g. the payroll. The pension fund will probably be handled centrally, and the group will usually operate a group bank account rather than individual ones for each subsidiary. Advertising, publicity and exhibitions may also be handled by the group. In the case of the buying function, a subsidiary should be free to buy in the best market, to allow it to obtain the quality, service and delivery it requires, but to give it, where possible, the advantage of benefiting from any group discounts. Centralisation should not be treated as an end in itself to increase the power of the central group management, but it should be judged on the effect it has on the group as a whole and on its subsidiaries. Centralisation, as in buying, can reduce the efficiency of subsidiaries and their ability to meet the targets set for them. Any disadvantage must therefore be carefully matched against any possible savings.

Staff and Human Relations

Apart from any problems of redundancy, there may be problems in resolving the differences between the group and the new subsidiary, in salary scales and fringe benefits, such as pension rights, holidays and especially company cars. Within their profit targets, the management should have the right to fix their own wage and salary rates, rather than have to accept group rates, which may not be suitable to attract the staff they need. This should also extend to salary increases.

Selection, promotion and dismissal should normally be in the hands of the local management subject to overall group policies. However, the group management will usually want to approve any top management appointments over a certain salary level. Those held responsible for meeting a profit target must be allowed to build up the work force they need to achieve their objectives. Promotion opportunities within the group should be given to staff of the new subsidiary. They will then see that they are considered on their merits and not treated as second class citizens. The group management should show the staff of the new company that they have a future which is as good as the original employees. Especially in high technology fields, the acquisition of management and technology is frequently given as the main reason for an acquisition. How often does management take any effective action to retain what it has spent so much to acquire?

Reporting and Profits

The new company may have to alter its accounting periods and year end to fit in with those of the group, as well as its accounting methods, practices and their reporting system. Where management has been given an incentive on profits achieved over a period, the accounts for comparison purposes will also have to be prepared on the same basis as before. The management of the new company will, therefore, be very sensitive to any attempt to make it contribute to group overheads for services which it may not need, or which it thinks are performed inefficiently. The use of group services or group products should be optional and dependent on their relative efficiency as against competition. During the incentive period, the company, as a profit centre, should remain separate and no attempt should be made to add or to subtract any functions which can affect the level of profitability.

Dangers

After an acquisition there can be dangers from extremes of independence or of centralisation. In the first case, the local 'Mafia' may try to prevent anyone from outside from finding out what is going on. In the second case, there may be attempts to impose group policy, regardless of how applicable it is. Our ancestors often decorated their castles, especially those they captured, with their arms and crests. Their servants were required to wear their livery. Nowadays, there is little change in human attitudes: the new company must sport the group livery on its writing paper and on its literature. If this is a sign that there will be equal prospects for all the group staff regardless of origin, then all will be well. The newcomers will only have total commitment to the aims of the group if they have an equal opportunity for advancement based on merit and not on origin. It is easy to acquire a company and to retain only a shell, as the living part has gone elsewhere. Acquisitions are easy to make, but very few managements are successful in building a greater whole from the sum of the two parts.

APPENDIX 1:
AGREEMENT TO ACQUIRE A COMPANY'S SHARE CAPITAL

Parties
The vendors and the purchaser.

Share Capital
The authorised share capital is £*xx,xxx* which is sub-divided into ordinary shares of £1 each of which *xx,xxx* shares are issued and fully paid.

Shareholders
The vendors, as beneficial owners, agree to sell the shares and the purchasers agree to purchase the shares listed in the attached list of shareholders. These shares must be free of any lien, charge or encumbrance and with the benefit of all rights both present or future.

Consideration
The consideration will either be:

1 A cash payment per share.
2 *X* ordinary shares of £*x* par value of the purchaser for *Y* ordinary shares of the vendor.
3 A combination of 1 and 2, or part payment in a loan stock.

The shares allotted will be fully paid and will enjoy the same rights as the existing ordinary share capital of the purchaser. Prior to allotment, the Stock Exchange will have granted permission to deal and quotation for these shares.

Transfer

The vendors will deliver signed transfers in favour of the purchaser, together with relevant share certificates and any other documents required to enable the shares to be registered in the purchaser's name. The vendors agree on receipt of the stamped transfers, to register the purchaser as the owner of the shares.

The purchaser will deliver a share certificate to each vendor for the number of shares to which he is entitled. The vendors are also required to warrant that they are not resident outside the scheduled territories nor are they acquiring the shares as a nominee of someone who is resident outside these territories.

Incentive

An incentive payment can be made *pro rata* to the original shareholders, provided the annual average of net profits, as defined, for the period of *X* years ending *(date)* when multiplied by a stated factor, exceeds £*P*. It is also possible to allow for repayment by the vendors, if the average profits at the end of the period when multiplied by the factor were below the purchase price by more than *x*%. In the event of an incentive payment, the shares to be allotted would have their par value defined and would be allotted at the middle market price on a fixed day after the end of the period.

Adjusted Net Profits

The definition of net profits would be the same as that quoted in Chapter 8 with the following additions:

1 To prevent the group from siphoning profits away from the company, the interest rate for monies borrowed from the group would be fixed at *X*% above the base rate, and any charge over

this level would be deducted when calculating the incentive.

2 Management charges can either be limited to a certain level or confined to charges for work carried out for the company.

3 To prevent profits from being artificially inflated, the level of annual private venture R & D spending may be fixed as a percentage of net sales. In addition, some limitation may be placed on taking profits on partly completed fixed price contracts, prior to final delivery. Adjustments agreeable to both parties must be made if the character of the business has been changed after completion and during the incentive period. If profitable activities are transferred from the business and/or if loss-making activities are taken on by the company from the group, then the incentive profits will have to be adjusted. The profits used for the incentive must be attributable to the efforts of the management in running the business activity acquired by the group at completion.

Completion

The date and place for completion will be fixed. Certain actions will be required to be carried out prior to completion as follows:

1 Any changes in the board required by the purchaser will have to have been made. Any director required to resign must agree to do so without receiving any compensation.

2 New articles shall be adopted as laid down by the purchaser.

3 The vendors will sign the deed of indemnity attached.

4 The following directors will sign service agreements with the purchaser in accordance with the schedule attached to this agreement.

The purchaser will have the right to rescind the agreement without any liability if any of these actions are not carried out. In addition the purchaser may withdraw if there is any breach of the warranties given or if any matter arises between the date of signing the agreement and completion, which is not in accordance with these warranties or which could reduce the company's agreed value.

Non-Competition

Any restrictions on any vendor not to engage in direct competition for a certain period from the date of the agreement or from *X* years from leaving the company are defined. These restrictions are applied only to the existing business carried on by the company at the time of completion (not to the group's business) and cover acting as an adviser, a principal or as an employee.

Period
The period of the agreement is defined.

Disclosure
Any matter either inconsistent with the warranties given or which can affect the value of the shares must be disclosed to the purchasers by the vendors between the date of the agreement and completion.

Inspection
The purchaser is given the right to inspect the books of account, documents, premises, machinery etc. from the date of the agreement.

Warranty and Indemnity
The vendors warrant that the recitals of the agreement are true and correct. They also indemnify the purchasers from any breach of warranty or from any breach of the indemnities given.

The indemnities and warranties required by purchasers are in most cases very similar to those already discussed in Chapter 9, (warranties p. 144 and indemnities, p. 148).

REFERENCES

1 C. St.J. OHERLINY, 'Management for the Boardroom: 5. Real growth from acquisitions: the rules for a dangerous game', *The Director,* September 1971, p.371.

2 Goodwill is defined as the amount of the purchase price over and above the market value of the assets acquired: e.g. if a company with assets of £80 is purchased for £100 the goodwill is £20.

3 MYLES L. MACE and GEORGE G. MONTGOMERY JR. *Management Problems of Corporate Acquisitions,* Harvard Business School, Division of Research, Boston, Massachusetts, 1962, p.33.

4 *Of Negotiating,* No. 47. Essays by Francis Bacon, London 1625.

5 An equity holding of over 10% prevents the possibility of a compulsory acquisition under section 209 of the 1948 Companies Act.

6 A 'call' option gives the option holder the right to buy a number of shares from someone at a certain price within a definite period. A 'put' option gives the right to sell a certain number of shares to someone with similar conditions as for the 'call' option.

20

Conclusion

Government Assistance

Although the future of small business in a capitalistic society, must depend on the actions of these companies themselves, the government can provide an atmosphere which is either favourable or unfavourable to small companies. Excluding the field of taxation which has been dealt with very comprehensively in the Bolton Report,[1] there are certain actions which could be taken.

Government Purchasing Power

The government has a considerable buying power through central government, through local authorities and through the nationalised industries. Part of these purchases could be set aside for small business to supply. In the United States, 20 per cent of all government contracts have to be placed with registered small businesses. Furthermore the main contractor is not paid by the central government until receipted bills are submitted for the proportion placed with small businesses. Now that the government, especially in the field of defence procurement, has adopted the prime contractor method, small firms can be frozen out, unless this policy is adopted.

Cooperative Ventures

The government could also encourage cooperative ventures between large and small firms. The United States, in the OECD Report on Small and Medium Sized Businesses,[2] emphasises the management aid which small firms enjoy from large corporations when they are engaged on the same supply contract. The large companies will work closely with these firms to make sure they are sound and healthy, so as to avoid delays in completion dates. This type of activity happens in this country between Marks and Spencer Ltd and its suppliers. Unfortunately the only relationship most large companies can envisage with a small company is complete ownership, which frequently destroys the qualities of innovation and individuality, recognised as the 'seed bed function' in the Bolton Report.[3]

Credit Terms Required by Large Companies

Large companies frequently use their strong bargaining position to take extravagantly long payment terms as the small company is not powerful enough to resist this pressure. This practice weakens small firms and can drive them into liquidation. As the small firms are not in a position to resist, the government should take steps to outlaw this monopolistic practice. In the same way that the government imposes certain standards of behaviour on its suppliers (racial discrimination), it should require small firms to be paid promptly. In addition this practice should be recognised as a policy tending towards monopoly which should be covered by the Restrictive Practices Act.

Overseas Marketing

For the small firm that wishes to export, the hardest part is to find good distributors, which are credit-worthy, reliable and dynamic, especially if the product is highly technical. It is usually their lot to have to employ the lean and hungry firms, which are bad payers, or to have to deal direct with the territory themselves. Perhaps consideration should be given to encouraging an efficient marketing organisation, especially in the Common Market, which would be able to make the overseas exporting activity of a small firm a less costly operation. Japan appears to have a strong advantage through her very powerful and efficient export merchanting firms, which are prepared to sell and service equipment in the market concerned.

Minority Shareholders' Rights[4]

Under present conditions, a minority shareholder in a private company has very little legal protection. Section 210 of the 1948 Companies Act gives protection against oppression in theory, but the section is not frequently used and is little understood. If the public is to be encouraged to invest in private companies, there should be a clearer definition of minority rights and a quick and cheap method of redressing any grievances. This is a matter to which the Department of Trade and Industry should give further consideration.

CONDUCT OF PRIVATE COMPANIES

While they cannot of course be exhaustive, the following maxims would seem especially applicable to private companies. Success can never be assured, but the observance of these principles could add considerably to the likelihood of success:

Field of Activity
Small companies have a better chance of competing successfully with large companies if they concentrate all their resources in a few profitable fields, where there are no economies of scale in production, purchasing and marketing. They should aim to compete on design, quality, service, fast delivery, and in the adaptation of products to suit special customer needs. It is as foolish for them to try and compete in markets where volume and price decide sales, as it is for a numerically inferior guerilla force to take on regular troops in a pitched battle.

Market Research
The management of a small company should always have an accurate view of the company's markets and its customers' future needs. It should be aware of the external factors, over which it has no control, which can increase or decrease the company's future profits. A small company should be able to anticipate changes in customers' demand so as to avoid a drop in profits by entering new markets or marketing

new products. This is especially true of companies serving small specialist markets with a few customers.

Long Range Plan
A small company should draw up a long range plan and review it regularly for changes in the environment, so that opportunities can be seized and potential threats minimised. A plan allows the company to decide in advance how to apply its limited resources in order to produce maximum long term profits.

Control
An accurate and up-to-date system of internal controls, which measures actual performance against planned objectives or standards, will ensure that any deviations are quickly known. Fast action can then be taken to optimise profits and to achieve the best use of available resources.

Finance
As a small company has little capacity to borrow additional funds, the management should always know the company's present and forward cash position, so that it can anticipate and, if possible, correct any cash outflow.

Management
Small companies need few managers, but those that they have should be experienced, well trained and knowledgeable in the latest management techniques and skills which are relevant to the needs of the company. To capitalise on the advantages of a small company, the management should be flexible, decisive, fast moving, and in direct contact with the market.

Succession
Management succession should be carefully planned in advance in order to avoid a forced takeover.

Communications
Small companies should use to the full the advantage they have over large companies, of good communications between management and staff, by adopting personnel policies which will produce a high level of morale. Good morale will ensure active support for the company

from its staff in meeting its requirements faster than its larger competitors.

Balance
A small company can mortgage its future and lose its freedom, by being too dependent on the fortunes and whims of one supplier or customer. Good balance is achieved by having as wide a spread of customers as possible, covering several industrial markets and also by having some second sources for major supply items.

Marketing
If the marketing function is carried out by another company, a small company should retain design responsibility for its products, to avoid becoming a sub-contractor. It should also maintain independent contact with its markets, so that it can, at any time, reassume the marketing of its products.

NEGOTIATIONS FOR FINANCE

The executives of the financial institutions which provide long term capital for private companies have to be specialists in company investigation and in negotiating investments. For them, this is a daily happening, while for the small company management it is an unfamiliar and rather frightening experience. To avoid being at a disadvantage in the negotiations, management should hire the best advisers to make up for its lack of knowledge. Management can correct this imbalance by having a complete and exhaustive knowledge of the company and of the industries it serves, its past, its present and the future. Their opposite numbers must of necessity be generalists, they must be specialists in their own industrial field.

The following maxims are recommended for consideration by those approaching institutions for finance:

Preparation
A company should not approach an institution for finance until it has complete knowledge of its past and present record and its existing financial position. It should also have a clear and comprehensive forward plan, covering what finance is required, why and what results can be expected from the investment.

The Market

Management should always find out what can be obtained in the market and what must be given in return. It should then decide how far the company is prepared to go to obtain its financial requirements and tailor its requirements accordingly.

Timing

The best bargaining position is obtained if the financial facilities are negotiated well in advance of their requirement. Financially stretched companies usually obtain poor terms, if they obtain any at all.

Institutions

Managements should approach an institution with a good name which will make up its mind quickly whether a deal is possible or not. These firms have a reputation to lose and should therefore make a fair deal. They are also more likely to be understanding if there is a delay in achieving planned results. Others may insist on punitive clauses which remove control of the company from the hands of the directors.

Advice

Bad professional advice is very costly. Any premium paid for using the best advisers should be amply repaid by the quality of their advice and the stronger bargaining position thus obtained. The other side will certainly have the best advice available.

Managements, as they negotiate, should remember that in the minds of the institutions there is one great fear, best expressed[5] by Prospero in *The Tempest:*

> Our revels now are ended. These our actors,
> As I foretold you, were all spirits, and
> Are melted into air, into thin air:
> And, like the baseless fabric of this vision,
> The cloud-capped towers, the gorgeous palaces.
> The solemn temples, the great globe itself,
> Yes, all which it inherit, shall dissolve,
> And, like this insubstantial pageant faded,
> Leave not a rack behind.

In banks, as in other companies, the chairman or chief executive officer may play the role of Prospero himself. Those responsible for the failure may not only lose their reputations but also their jobs. But forgetting their worries, it is appropriate to finish with two maxims of Napoleon which should always be in the mind of the managements of small companies:

> The art of war consists, with a numerically inferior army, in always having larger forces than the enemy at the point which is to be attacked or defended. But this art cannot be learnt from *books* or from practice, it is an *intuitive* way of acting, which properly constitutes the genius of war.[6]

> To keep one's forces together, to bear speedily on any point, to be nowhere vulnerable, such are the principles which assure victory.[7]

REFERENCES

1 Bolton Report, pp.193-231.
2 *Problems and Policies Relating to Small and Medium-Sized Businesses,* OECD, Paris, 1971, p.8.
3 Bolton Report, paras 8.5 and 19.7.
4 Report of the Company Law Committee (CMND 1749) (The Jenkins Report) Section 209, HMSO, London, June 1972.
5 *The Tempest,* Act IV, Scene 1, Lines 148-156.
6 J.C. HEROLD, *The Mind of Napoleon,* Columbia University Press, New York, 1955, p.293 (my italics).
7 PROFESSOR L.E. HENRY, *Napoleon's War Maxims,* Number LXXVII, Gale and Polden, London, 1899.

Bibliography

Research Reports refer to the reports commissioned by the Committee of Inquiry on Small Firms

Report of the Committee of Inquiry on Small Firms, Chairman J.E. Bolton, CBE, DSC (The Bolton Report), Cmnd 4811, HMSO, London 1971

Research Report No 3, *Small Firms in the Manufacturing Sector,* J.R. Davies and M. Kelly, HMSO, London 1971

Research Report No 4, *Financial Facilities for Small Firms,* The Economists Advisory Group, directed by D. Lees, HMSO, London 1971

Research Report No 5, *Problems of Small Firms in Raising External Finance,* results of a sample survey, The Economists Advisory Group, directed by J. Dunning, HMSO, London 1971

Research Report No 12, *Dynamics of Small Firms,* Merrett Cyriax Associates, HMSO, London 1971

Research Report No 16, *A Postal Questionnaire Survey of Small Firms – An Analysis of Financial Data,* M. Tamari, HMSO, London 1972

Research Report No 17, *A Postal Questionnaire Survey of Small Firms Non-Financial Data, Tables;* Research Unit, HMSO, London 1972

Admission of Securities to Quotation, A memorandum of guidance and requirements of the Federation of Stock Exchanges in Great Britain and Ireland, The Stock Exchange, London 1969

Appraisal of Management, The, J. MARTINDELL, AMA, Harper Bros., New York 1962

Board, The, H. PARKER, October 1970, *The Director,* pp 170-179

Board of Directors, The (Management Survey Report No. 10), BIM, London 1972

Board of Directors and Business Management, The, M.T. COPELAND and A.R. TOWL, Harvard Business School, Division of Research, Boston, Mass., 1947

Board of Directors and Effective Management, The, H. KROONTZ, McGraw-Hill, New York 1967

Board Room, The, Sir W. PUCKEY, A guide to the role and function of directors, Hutchinson, London 1969

Boards of Directors in Small Corporations, M.L. MACE, Harvard Business School, Division of Research, Boston, Mass. 1948

Boards of Directors in Small/Medium Sized Private Companies, A survey of the composition of boards of directors in 289 private companies, Information Summary 149, BIM, London 1970

Britain's Small Firms – Their Vital Role in the Economy, CBI, London 1968

British Board of Directors, Rudder or Rubber Stamp, The, L.A. BRUA, *The Director,* July 1972, pp 42-46

Business of the Board, The, N.C. SALANDER, *Management Today,* June 1970, pp 95-97

Business Failures in England and Wales, R. BROUGH, Issues 2 and 3, Business Ratios, Dunn and Bradstreet, London

Business Planning, D.R.C. HALFORD, Pan Piper, London 1971

Business Policy in Growing Firms, R.B. BUCHELE, Chandler, San Francisco 1967

Checklist for Mergers, D. HARGREAVES (PA Management Consultants), *The Financial Times,* February 23rd 1968

Closer Look at the Non-Executive Director, A, G. BULL, *The Director,* December 1970, pp 512-515

Companies Act 1948, The, HMSO, London 1948

Companies Bill, The, presented to Parliament on the 24th May 1972 by Sir B. Rhys Williams, Bart, MP

Company Direction, J. Seymour, McDonald and Evans, London 1954

Company Director – His Functions, Powers and Duties, The, A. READ, Institute of Directors, London, 3rd revised edition, Jordan and Sons, London 1967

Company Share Quotations, Fielding Newsom-Smith, London, reprinted February 1972

Comparative Efficiency of Methods of Issue, A.J. MERRETT and G.D. NEWBOULD, The Manchester School, Manchester, January 1966

Conference on the Role of the Non-Executive Director, 19th January 1971, London, Institute of Directors/Financial Times

Corporate Director, The, J.M. JURAN and J.K. LOUDEN, American Management Association, New York 1966

Director's Contracts, the Vital Points to Watch, J. HANWAY, *The Director,* March 1970

Effective Boardroom Management, H. PARKER, M. BOWER, E.E.

SMITH and J.R. MORRISON, McKinsey and Company, BIM, London 1971

Efficiency Comparisons in Large Organisations, BIM and The Centre for Interfirm Comparison, London 1962

Environmental Change and Corporate Strategy, Stanford Research Institute, California 1960

Finance Act 1965, HMSO, London

Financial and Accounting Responsibilities of Directors, A special issue for the Institute of Directors by the General Educational Trust of the Institute of Chartered Accountants of England and Wales, London 1970

Financial Aspects of Industrial Management, G.D. BOND, Butterworth, London 1955

Financial and Operating Ratios, Information Note No 61, BIM, London 1971

Financial Times, 3 January 1966 – A letter by A.F. Frodsham
10 July 1971 – A letter by H. Smallwood
6 March 1972 and 9 January 1973 – re Levex

Focus the Future, H.F.R. PERRIN, Management Publications, London 1971

Going Public 1971, edited by R. WILLOTT, *Accountancy Age,* London 1971

Great Pierpoint Morgan, The, F.L. ALLEN, Harper and Bros., New York 1948

History of Warfare, A, MONTGOMERY OF ALAMEIN, Collins, London 1968

House of Morgan, The, E.P. HOYT Jr, Frederich Muller, London 1968

How 1500 American Companies Run the Board, L.A. BRUA, *The Director,* October 1971, pp 102-105

How to Move Small Firms, E.G. WOOD, *Management Today,* January 1972, pp 54-57, 118 and 122

Investment Memorandum 1971/2, p 179, Cazenove, London 1971

Investors Chronicle, 3 March 1972, p 7, 6 and 12 January 1973, re Levex

Management for the Boardroom: 5. Real Growth from Acquisitions – the Rules for a Dangerous Game, C. St.J. O'HERLINY (Urwick, Orr and Partners Ltd), *The Director,* September 1971, p 371

Management Problems of Corporate Acquisitions, M.L. MACE and G.C. MONTGOMERY Jr., Harvard Business School, Division of Research, Boston, Mass. 1962

Mergers and Takeovers, Management Checklist No 23, BIM, London 1969

Mind of Napoleon, The, J.C. HEROLD, Columbia University Press, New York 1955

Napoleon's War Maxims, Professor L.E. HENRY, Gale and Polden, London 1899

New Entrepreneur, The, *Management Today,* London, January 1970, p 10

New Equity Issue Statistics by Singer and Friedlander Ltd, London, issued quarterly

Of Negotiating, No. 47, Essays, FRANCIS BACON, London 1625

Overseas Investment – A guide to planning for U.K. Manufacturers, BIM, London 1968

Palmers Company Law, C.M. SCHMITTHOFF and J.H. THOMPSON, 21st edition, Stevens and Sons, London 1968

Planning in Business, Stanford Research Institute, California 1963

Policy Formulation for the Smaller Company, BIM, London 1969

Practice of Management, The, P.F. DRUCKER, Heinemann, London 1955

Presidential Address at the Institute of Directors Annual Conference, by Lord Chandos, London 1956

Principles and Practice of Management, E.F.L. BRECH, Longmans Green, London 1963

Private Company Today, The, A.J. MERRETT and M.E. LEHR, Institute of Directors and Gower Press, London 1970

Problems and Policies relating to Small and Medium Sized Firms, OECD, Paris 1971

Problems of Small Business, Monograph 17, An investigation of the concentration of economic power by the Temporary National Economic Committee, The US Government, Washington 1941

Problems of Small Business: The Manager, J.C. DENYER, BIM, London 1963

Problems of Small Firms, CBI evidence to the Bolton Committee, London 1970

Profile of the British Board of Directors – and comparisons with American boardroom practice, A survey prepared by Heidrick and Struggles, London 1972

Report of the Company Law Committee, Cmnd 1749 (The Jenkins Report), HMSO, London, June 1972

Role of the Board and the Director, The, J.E.V. TYZACK, *Manage-*

ment Decision, Winter 1967, pp 4-8

Role of the Non-Executive Director, The, An address by D.L. Nicolson at the Conference on the Role of the Company Director, University of Manchester Institute of Science and Technology, 13 February 1968

Role of the Non-Executive Director, The, G. BULL, *The Director,* December 1969, pp 426-429

Role of the Non-Executive Director, The, A report of the speeches at the Joint Institute of Directors, Financial Times One Day Conference, 19 January 1971, London

Role of the Non-Executive Director, The, T. LEATHER, *The George Cohen 600 Group Magazine,* October 1971

Service Agreements, T.M. ALDRIDGE, Oyez Practice Notes, No 52, 2nd edition, Oyez Publications, London 1969

Simon's Taxes, Volume D, 3rd edition, Butterworths (loose leaf edition), London 1970-71

Smaller Company's Board of Directors, The, S.M. MATHES, (Managing the Moderate Sized Company No 3), National Industrial Conference Board, New York 1967

Small Firms Survey, C. ALLEN, ICFC, London 1970

Spanners in the Works, The Institute of Works Managers, London 1963

Specimen Form of Director's Service Agreement, Institute of Directors

Standard Boardroom Practice, Prepared by a special committee under the chairmanship of Lord Tangley, revised edition, Institute of Directors, London 1971

Survey of the Current Practices in the Employment of Non-Executive Directors, A joint research project by the Institute of Directors and MSL, London 1971

The Tempest, WILLIAM SHAKESPEARE

There's No Management Sense like Commonsense, T. McAULIFFE, *The Director,* July 1967, pp 74-77

Thrusters and Sleepers, D. INSILL, Allen and Unwin, London 1965

Valuation of Shares in Unquoted Companies, A.R. ENGLISH, ICFC, London (no date)

What Debt Does to Profits, R. HELLER, *Management Today,* July 1970, p 101

What is Your Business? E.F.L. BRECH, BIM Occasional Papers (new series) OPN 4, London 1969

What Makes a Company Go to the Wall, *The Scotsman,* 20 October 1971

Questionnaire: Development and Venture Capital

The Object

To find out the broad policies of institutions with regard to development and venture capital, so that managements of private companies would be able to select those institutions whose policies best fit their company's requirements.

Questionnaires

Questionnaires were sent between 20 and 21 February, 1973 to 38 financial institutions located in London. The answers were as follows:

Questionnaires returned:		16
Refusals:		
Activity not undertaken or too early to comment	7	
Approach too flexible to complete questionnaire	6	13
No reply:		9
		38

Limitations

Some institutions were reluctant to reply as their policy was very flexible and precise answers were impossible as no two cases were ever the same; the package as to finance and advice being tailored specially for each case.

For this same reason, the answers given by those replying to the questionnaire represent their normal or typical approach. This should not be taken to mean that those institutions will not go outside these terms when an attractive situation presents itself. So much depends on the prospects for the proposed investment and the risk involved.

However these firms replying to the questionnaire have carefully thought their policies through and are prepared to table them, so that prospective clients can see how they normally operate.

By examining the questionnaire the prospective seeker of finance can gauge for each institution:

1 The type and size of company, and the growth potential required.
2 The total investment, the investment period, whether realisation is required within a fixed time limit; the size and type of equity holding and how it is acquired.
3 The hardest question to answer is that on valuation on which few were prepared to commit themselves as there are so many intangibles: size, prospects and also the external stockmarket situation.
4 On dividend yields and interest rates, there was also a reluctance to be committed, as these rates will vary with market conditions, risk etc. The base rate at the time the questionnaire was answered was 9½ per cent, so any answers have to take this factor into account.
5 The other terms of the loan, security, and period are also of vital interest to borrowers in order to find a lender who matches the timescale that they require.
6 No company wishes to be locked in with an institution which has a monopoly of providing new finance which may be on its own terms. Most organisations do not insist on an exclusive right to provide new finance but at the most require a first refusal to provide finance at competitive rates. Some will allow a company to refinance a project completely if they cannot match the terms available or if they will not back an expansion.

   Few impose a penalty for not reaching a forecast and the large majority want to maintain a minority equity position, unless of course the company goes seriously wrong and cannot meet its loan interest and capital repayments.

7 It is wise to settle any fees payable in advance. However the level of these may depend on the state of the company's records, especially in the case of the legal and accounting fees.

8 Finally the function of the non-executive Director, his fees, experience and the type of assistance he can provide, are important matters for discussion. The importance of this service will depend on whether or not managements wish an institution to make a significant contribution towards solving some of the problems of growth a company may face, during its expansion.

The management of a private company enters a negotiation at a disadvantage if it does not know what the institution's normal policy is, especially on taking a majority or minority position, and on the normal period of investment.

If the financial institution keeps all its options open, these matters may come out when negotiations are far advanced. For this reason a copy of the questionnaire is included in this book so that those approaching institutions, outside this survey, can make their own enquiries of these organisations, prior to starting serious negotiations.

Questionnaires Returned

1 Wm. Brandt's Sons & Company Limited, 36 Fenchurch Street, London EC3P 3AS, tel. 01-626 6599

Contact: Malcolm R. Bates – Director, Head of Industrial Division

2 Charterhouse Development Limited, 1 Paternoster Row, London EC4P 4HP, tel. 01-248 3999

Contact: E.G. Cox – Managing Director

3 Citicorp Venture Capital London Limited, 336 Strand, London, tel. 01-240 1222

Contacts: Ronald Millican – Managing Director; Alex Kaye – Investment Officer

4 County Bank Limited, 75 Cornhill, London EC3V 3NN, tel. 01-283 2577

Contact: R.N. Bowes – Director

5 Robert Fraser & Partners Limited, 1 Noble Street, London EC2, tel. 01-606 4010

Contact: C. Wardle – Director

6 Guinness Mahon & Company Limited, 3 Gracechurch Street, London EC3V 0DP, tel. 01-623 4611

Contact: M.J. Knight – Director

7 Hambros Bank Limited, Department of Industrial Services, 55 Bishopsgate, London EC2, tel. 01-588 2851

Contact: K.F. Dibben – Director

8 Industrial & Commercial Finance Corporation Limited, Piercy House, 7 Copthall Avenue, London EC2, tel. 01-628 4040

9 Ionian Bank Limited, 64 Coleman Street, London EC2R 5BD, tel. 01-638 5666

Contact: E. Ivan Kingston – Director

10 Midland Montagu Industrial Finance Limited, Moor House, London Wall, London EC2Y 5ET, tel. 01-638 8861

Contact: J.R. Beevor – Managing Director

11 Minster Trust Limited, Minster House, Arthur Street, London EC4R 9BH, tel. 01-623 1050

12 National & Commercial Development Capital Limited, 34 Nicholas Lane, London EC4, tel. 01-623 5478

13 Old Broad Street Securities, 39 King Street, London EC2V 8DT, tel. 01-606 7291

Contacts: E.B. Fairman – Director; E.S.O. Bishop

14 Small Business Capital Fund Limited, 88 Baker Street, London W1, tel. 01-486 5021

Contact: J.S. Laybourne – Director

15 Sterling Industrial Securities Limited, 10 St James Street, London SW1, tel. 01-930 1986

Contact: N. Warshaw – General Manager, Industrial Division

16 Wood Street Capital Limited, 100 Wood Street, London EC2P 2AJ, tel. 01-628 8011

Contacts: C.S. Taylor – Manager; G.R.T. Bateman

THE QUESTIONNAIRE

1 Institution

(a) Name
(b) Address
(c) Contact

2 Scope of Operation

(A) The year the development capital operation started
(B) Number of investments made in companies:
  (a) Since the operation started
  (b) Current number of investments held now
  (c) Average number of new investments per annum (last 3 years)
  (d) Is a list of current investments available?
  (e) Are introductions provided to these companies?

3 Type of Company

(A) Institution's investment policy on areas of operation and types of company: (if the institution makes high and low risk investments, please tick both)
  (a) *High risk* – high growth and profit potential by investing in unestablished companies or 'start ups' in volatile fields, such as advanced technology, new product ideas, films, and service industries with few assets.
  (b) *Low risk* – lower growth and profit potential by investing in established companies in non-volatile fields with good growth records.
(B) How long does it take on average (in months) for an investment

to be made?

(a) From initial contact
(b) From when an investment decision is taken

4 Size of Company Considered

(a) Minimum pretax profits (per annum)
(b) Average pretax profits (per annum)

5 Growth Potential Required

(a) Increase in level of pretax profits required (e.g. from £50,000 to £200,000)
(b) Period in years for expansion: (e.g. 5 to 7 years)

6 Investment

Total investment per company (loans and equity)

(a) Maximum level
(b) Minimum level
(c) Average level

7 Period of Investment (in years)

(a) Maximum
(b) Average
(c) Is realisation of the investment required within a fixed period?
(d) If fixed, within what period in years?

8 Equity Stake Taken in Average Sized Company (percentage of equity after investment)

(a) Maximum
(b) Minimum
(c) Average

9 What Type of Shareholding is Most Frequently Taken?

(a) Preference (pref)

(b) Ordinary (ord)
(c) Convertible Preference (conv pref)
(d) Preferred Ordinary (pref ord)
(e) Other

10 How is Equity Usually Acquired?

(a) By immediate subscription (sub)
(b) By immediate purchase (pur)
(c) By conversion (con)
(d) Through exercising an option (opt)

11 Option or Conversion Rights Taken (if 10 (c) or (d) ticked)

(a) Period in years
(b) Share price or subscription price (fixed or variable)

12 Basis of Valuation of Company

(a) What range of factors (e.g. from 5 to 7) is applied to pretax profits for companies with pretax profits of:
  (i) under £50,000
  (ii) £50 – 75,000
  (iii) £75 – 100,000
(b) Which pretax profits are most frequently used?
  Last year's (LY)
  This year's forecast (TYF)
  Next year's forecast (NYF)
  An average of the last 3 to 5 years' profits (AV)
(c) Is a penalty clause applied for not reaching a forecast?
(d) If (c) is 'yes' does it enable the bank to obtain voting control of the company?

13 Dividend Yield Required on Share Purchase Price (percentage)

(a) Fixed yield
(b) Variable yield (*X*% above base rate)

14 Loans

Are loans available without an equity stake provided they are adequately secured?

15 Security Required for Loan

(a) A fixed charge (fixed)
(b) A floating charge (float)
(c) Fixed and floating (F & F)
(d) None – unsecured (unsec)

16 Loan Interest Rate Range

(a) Fixed: from ___ % to ___%
(b) Variable: from ___ % to ___% over base rate (9½%)

17 Total Loan Period (in years)

(a) Total period in years
(b) Repayment starts in
(c) Repayment finishes in

18 New Money for an Existing Investment

What rights does the institution reserve to itself to provide the company with additional finance?

(a) An exclusive right
(b) A first refusal to provide finance provided its terms are competitive
(c) Where the institution will not back an expansion or if better terms can be found elsewhere, is the refinancing of the whole project negotiable
(d) Is additional loan capital available without equity, provided that interest cover and security are reasonable?

19 Is the Proposal for New Capital for an Existing Investment Judged:

(a) As a whole on progress to date and on the existing equity stake (to date) or is each proposal judged separately (sep)?
(b) When supplying new capital, is it the policy of the institute to gain control (control) or to retain a minority stake (minorit

20 Fees

Average fees payable by the company on investment (£):

(a) Institution's investigation fees
(b) Accountant's investigation fees
(c) Institution's legal fees
(d) Other – (market research)
(e) Total fees

21 Nominee Director

Details of nominee director:
(a) Is the right to appoint a Nominee Director required?
(b) Is the appointment always made?
(c) Status:
Employee (empl'ee)
Consultant (conslt)
Other
(d) Background:
Industry (ind)
Lawyer (law)
Banker (bank)
Accountant (acc'nt)
(e) Annual fees for x days per annum (including director's fees)

22 Functions of Non Executive Director

(a) Institutional protection. To approve plans for:
(i) Capital expenditure
(ii) External borrowing
(iii) Directors' salaries
(iv) Sale of shares
(v) Other
(b) Company: What fields covered and assistance given:
(i) Financial (accounting, costing, budgeting, reporting)
(ii) Marketing (pricing, planning, etc.)
(iii) Production (production and inventory control)

Note: The numbers in the left-hand column of the following table relate to the above questions.

VISUAL GUIDE TO SOURCES OF FINANCE

1(a)	Wm. Brandt's & Sons Ltd	Charterhouse Development Ltd	Citicorp Venture Capital London Ltd	County Bank Ltd	Robert Fraser & Partners Ltd	Hambros Bank Ltd	Guinness Mahon & Co Ltd	Industrial & Commercial Finance Corporation Ltd
2(A)	—	1934	1972	1969	Mid 1971	Long ago, but very active since 1967	1971	1945
(B)(a)	Numerous	Approx 200	2	30	8	Numerous	6	Over 2,800
(b)	35	50	2	22	5	40	6	Over 2,300
(c)	4	8	—	Only by special arrangement	Not available	8	3	—
(d)	No	Yes	No	No	No	No	Some	No
(e)	No	Yes	No	No Only by special arrangement	No	Yes	Some	No
3(A)(a)	Yes	Yes	Yes	Yes, very occasionally	Rarely	Yes	Rarely	Yes
(b)	Yes	Yes	Yes	Yes	Yes	Yes	Yes	Yes
(B)(a)	2	2	3	Say 2	1	7/8	Too varied to say	—
(b)	1	1	1½	Say 1	2-3	2½		—
4(a)	£50,000	—	£0	Say £25,000 subject to occasional exceptions	No set criteria	No minimum	Any size	No minimum
(b)	£100,000	£50,000	£50,000	Say £50,000 (as above)		£50,000		Not available
5(a)	From £50,000 to £250,000	Varies with circumstances	From £50,000 to £1 million	Impossible to generalise	From £0 to at least £250,000	—	No fixed yardsticks	No restrictions
(b)	1 to 5 years	5 to 7 years	3 to 5 years	No absolute limit but generally up to 10 years	3 to 5 years	—		
6(a)	£1,500,000	£1,000,000	£200,000	Unlimited	£500,000 normally	No maximum	£500,000	No upper limit but not normally over £1 million
(b)	£250,000	£50,000	£50,000	Usually not less than £50,000	£50,000 normally	£50,000	£50,000	£5,000
(c)	£375,000	£150/200,000	£100,000	Say £150,000	—	£150,000	£250,000	£75,000

Ionian Bank Ltd	Midland Montagu Industrial Finance Ltd	Minster Trust Ltd	National & Commercial Development Capital Ltd	Old Broad Street Securities Ltd	Small Business Capital Fund Ltd	Sterling Industrial Securities Ltd	Wood Street Capital Ltd (a subsidiary of Hill Samuel & Co Ltd)
1962	1969	Prewar	1971	1967 approx	1969	1971	Hill Samuel—many years Wood Street Capital Ltd—1969
30	20	Countless	8	50 approx	18	8	15
—	15	6	8	11	10	8	Not available
—	5	2	Not available	5 last year	6	6 in 18 months	—
No	Yes	No	No	No	Yes	Yes	No
Yes	No	No	No	No	Yes	Yes to some	—
Rarely	Yes	No	—	Yes	Yes	Yes	Yes, not usually high technology
Yes	Yes	Yes	Yes	Yes	No	Yes	Yes
2	Up to 3	3	3	1-2	3	1½	Days to months
¼	2	1	1	1	1	½	
Not applicable	No minimum	No minimum	£100,000 after injection of capital	New venture	No set limit	£10,000	Normally £25,000
£30,000	£50,000	£100,000 typical	Not available	£30,000		£70,000	—
From £50,000 to £150,000 minimum	From £0 to £250,000	Each case judged on its merit	From £100,000 to £300,000	From £30,000 to £200,000	From £0 to £100,000	From £10,000 to £250,000	— —
2 to 4 years	1 to 7 years		3 to 5 years	5 to 8 years	1 to 5 years	5 to 7 years	5 to 7 years
£250,000	£300,000+	£500,000	£300,000+ bank loans	£2,000,000	£500,000	£250,000	None
£20,000	£50,000	£100,000	£70,000+ bank loans	£20,000	£25,000	£5,000	approx £25,000
£60,000	£150,000	£200,000 typical	Not available	£100,000	£80,000	£70,000	£100,000

	Wm. Brandt's & Sons Ltd	Charterhouse Development Ltd	Citicorp Venture Capital London Ltd	County Bank Ltd	Robert Fraser & Partners Ltd	Hambros Bank Ltd	Guinness Mahon & Co Ltd	Industrial & Commercial Finance Corporation Ltd
7(a)	—	25 years	7 years	Generally 10 years No absolute limit	Loans and equity Up to 5 years	7 years	Indefinite	20 years
(b)	4	7 years	5 years	7 years	—	4 years	4 years	Not available
(c)	No	Yes, hoped for	No	No	Normally yes	No	No	No
(d)	—	—	—	—	—	—	—	—
8(a)	100%	49%	25%	49%	49%	40%	49%	Not available
(b)	15%	5%	5%	Not available	10%	5%	20%	
(c)	40%	25%	15%	Say 15%	15-30%	25%	30%	
9	Ord	Pref/ord/pref ord package varies with circumstances	Ord	Pref ord	Ord	Pref ord	Ord	Secured loans & debentures
10	Pur/opt	Sub/pur	Pur/opt	Pur/opt	Sub/pur/opt	Sub	Any	Sub/pur/con/opt
11(a)	Flexible	—	—	Up to 19 years	3 years	—	3 years	Not available
(b)	Variable	—	Variable	Normally fixed	Fixed	—	—	Fixed
12(a)(i)	5	Varies with circumstances	—	Each case to be taken on its merits without any preconceived range of factors	—	2½-4	Depends on industry, record, prospects, etc	No fixed limits
(ii)	6		—		—	3 -6		
(iii)	6		—		—	5 -7		
12(b)	AV	Varies with circumstances	TYF NYF	LY	—	TYF	All are evaluated	—
(c)	No	No	No	No	No	Usually not	—	Normally no
(d)			—	—	—	Occasionally	—	—
13(a)	—	Varies with circumstances	—	Each case considered on its merits	Depends on company's financial position	7/8%	—	
(b)	-		—			—	5-10% initially growing with profits	

nian Bank Ltd	Midland Montagu Industrial Finance Ltd	Minster Trust Ltd	National & Commercial Development Capital Ltd	Old Broad Street Securities Ltd	Small Business Capital Fund Ltd	Sterling Industrial Securities Ltd	Wood Street Capital Ltd (a subsidiary of Hill Samuel & Co Ltd)
Equity: 5-7 years Loan: 2-3 years	To early to say	5-7 (Intention)	5 years	8	—	Undated	—
—		3-5 (Typical)	—	5	5/6	3-5	—
Usually	No	No	Yes	No	Yes	No	No
As above	—	—	5 years	—	5/8	—	—
—	49%	49%	30%	49%	49% } Usually	26%	49%
10%	15%	10%	10%	5%	25% } Usually	10%	15%
25%	25%	20%	—	25%	35%	20%	—
Ord	Ord	Ord/pref ord/conv pref	Ord/conv loans	Pref ord	Ord	Ord	—
Sub/con/opt	Con	Con loan or pref	Con/opt	Opt, attached to a loan	Sub	Sub/con/opt	—
2-5 years	3-5 years	No hard & fast rule	5	5-8 years	—	3	—
Fixed	Fixed		Variable	Fixed	—	Fixed	—
—	3-4	No hard & fast rule	3 to 7	Variable	Not normally used in an evaluation of a company	Not applicable	—
—	3-5					3-5	—
—	3-6					4+	—
All 4	LY } TYF } Depends on year end date	No hard and fast rule	TYF	LY } TYF } NYF } Aver	Not normally used in an evaluation of a company	NYF AV	—
No	Sometimes	No	Yes	No	—	No	No
—	Sometimes a reward can be applied for reaching a forecast	—	Yes	—	—	—	—
—	8-10%	No hard and fast rule	Not available	No general requirement	Not applicable	No required yield	Depends on cash requirements
Related to profits	—						

	Wm. Brandt's & Sons Ltd	Charterhouse Development Ltd	Citicorp Venture Capital London Ltd	County Bank Ltd	Robert Fraser & Partners Ltd	Hambros Bank Ltd	Guinness Mahon & Co Ltd	Industrial & Commercial Finance Corporation Ltd
14	Yes but rarely	No	No	Yes, if other circumstances are right	Yes (Ansbacher)	No	On normal banking terms	Yes
15	F & F	Unsec	Unsec	Fixed float unsec	F & F	Float	F & F	Fixed/ float/ unsec
16(a)	—	8 to 12½%	7 to 10%	Each case considered on its merits & in the light of current market rates	—	—	11 to 14%	In line with current market conditions
(b)	2½ to 4%	0 to 3½%	½ to 5%		3 to 5%	3 to 4%	2 to 6%	
17(a)	Variable	Varies with circumstances	5	Generally up to 10 years	5	5/6	No fixed rules	20
(b)			2nd year	Each case is considered on its merits	3rd-5th years	2nd/3rd		No set timing
(c)			5th year		5th	5th/6th		
18(a)	—	No	No	No	No	—	—	No
(b)	—	No	Yes	Yes, this is normally understood	Yes	Yes	Yes	No
(c)	Yes	Yes	Yes	Yes	Yes	—	Yes	No
(d)	Yes	Yes	Yes	Yes, other circumstances being right	Yes	No, this is banking business	Unlikely unless good security	Yes
19(a)	Sep	Sep	To date	To date	To date	Both	To date	Sep
(b)	Minority but sometimes control	Minority	Minority	Minority	Minority	Minority	Minority	Minority

Ionian Bank Ltd	Midland Montagu Industrial Finance Ltd	Minster Trust Ltd	National & Commercial Development Capital Ltd	Old Broad Street Securities Ltd	Small Business Capital Fund Ltd	Sterling Industrial Securities Ltd	Wood Street Capital Ltd (a subsidiary of Hill Samuel & Co Ltd)
Yes	No	Sometimes	No	Yes	No	Yes	Yes
Flexible	Float	Best charge permitted by circumstances —straight banking loans secured by guarantee of 3rd party, by deposit of securities or by both	Fixed/float/ unsec	Fixed (if available) & float	Debenture with fixed charge, normally postponed in favour of the bank	F & F	Unsec (usually)
—	—	No hard and fast rule	Around cost of 5 year money	Depends on individual circumstances and conditions	10 to 12%	10 to 17%	Commercial rates
—	3½ to 4½%				—	1 to 6%	
2-3 years	5 years		5 years	10 years	4/5 years	2-7 years	Depends on company's requirements
Last year	2nd		—	1st-2nd year	2nd/3rd year usually	Either even repayments, or a fixed maturity or conversion date	
Last year	5th Depends on cash flow		5th year	10th year	—		
No	No	No	Yes	No	No	No	No
Yes	No	Yes	—	No	No	Yes	Yes
Yes	Yes	No hard and fast rule	Yes	Yes	Yes	Yes	—
No, but overdraft facilities are available	Yes		Yes	Yes	Yes	Yes	—
Both	To date	Both	To date	To date	Sep	To date	Sep
Minority	Minority	No hard and fast rule	Minority	Minority	Minority if company performance is satisfactory	Minority	Minority

	Wm. Brandt's & Sons Ltd	Charterhouse Development Ltd	Citicorp Venture Capital London Ltd	County Bank Ltd	Robert Fraser & Partners Ltd	Hambros Bank Ltd	Guinness Mahon & Co Ltd	Industrial & Commercial Finance Corporation Ltd
20(a)	—	Nil	—	Nil	Nil	Nil	—	
(b)		£500/1,500 varies with size	£500	Say £1,500		£300+	Yes if outside accountants are used	1½% on 1st £50,000 and 1% on amount in excess of £50,000 on acceptance of an offer to provide finance
(c)		£300/1,000 varies with size	£1,000	Say £500	Cost of professional services where required	£250	Yes	
(d)	Usual city fees	—	—	Valuers fees depend on property value		Rarely	—	
(e)		£1,000/2,500 varies with size	£1,500	Say £2,000+ valuers fees & company's advisers		£5/600	—	
21(a)	Yes	Yes	No—but right to attend board meetings is required	Yes, often	Yes	Yes	Usually	Yes
(b)	Yes	No		No	Yes	Yes	Usually	No
(c)	Empl'ee/ other	Empl'ee	—	Empl'ee, normally	Empl'ee	Conslt	Empl'ee usually	Other
(d)	Ind/acc'nt	Ind/law/ bank/acc'nt	Bank	Acc'nt normally	Ind	Ind	Ind usually	Ind/law/ bank/acc'nt
(e)	£1,000 for 10 days p.a.	Flat annual rate	Nil	No fixed scale often not charged	£2,500 p.a. one off projects are charged extra	£1,000 for 15 days p.a.	£100 per day. Number of days depends on each case	Negotiable
22(a)(i)	—	Yes	—		Yes	Yes		—
(ii)	—	Yes	Yes		Yes	Yes		—
(iii)	—	—	Yes	Specific powers are not generally vested in a nominated director	Yes	Yes		—
(iv)	—	—	Yes		Yes	—	Usually	—
(v)	Report progress and monitor investment	Yes	Yes		Yes—all major policy decisions e.g. disposal of assets	—		Yes

Ionian Bank Ltd	Midland Montagu Industrial Finance Ltd	Minster Trust Ltd	National & Commercial Development Capital Ltd	Old Broad Street Securities Ltd	Small Business Capital Fund Ltd	Sterling Industrial Securities Ltd	Wood Street Capital Ltd (a subsidiary of Hill Samuel & Co Ltd)
Nil	Nil	Nil	£2,000	Nil	—	Nil, unless competing with another firm—then £5 per employee hour	Nil
All	Cost	No hard and fast rule	—	Cost	—	Cost	Sometimes
All	Cost		—	Cost	—	Cost	
None	Only if agreed with company		—	Surveyors fees at cost	—	Cost	—
—	Cost		£2,000	Cost	Approx £1,500/2,000	—	—
Yes	Yes	No hard and fast rule	Yes	Yes, occasionally	Yes	Yes	Usually
No	Yes		Yes	No	Yes	Yes	No
Empl'ee	Empl'ee		Empl'ee/ director	Empl'ee	Other	Empl'ee/ consult	—
Bank	Ind		Ind	Ind/bank	Ind	Ind/law/ bank/acc'nt (all available)	—
£2,000	To be agreed		£2,000 for x days as required	Negotiable	£1,000/1,500 for support when needed + 12 board meetings	£1,200 for 24 days p.a.	On work done
Yes	Yes	Act as a normal director unless something has gone wrong or special assistance is required	Yes	Yes	Above certain limits	Yes	Sometimes
Yes	Yes		Yes	Yes	Yes	Yes	
Yes	Yes		Yes	—	Yes	—	
Yes	Yes		Yes	Yes	Yes	Yes	
—	Any change in capital structure		Yes	—	Yes	—	—

<table>
<tr><th></th><th>Wm. Brandt's & Sons Ltd</th><th>Charterhouse Development Ltd</th><th>Citicorp Venture Capital London Ltd</th><th>County Bank Ltd</th><th>Robert Fraser & Partners Ltd</th><th>Hambros Bank Ltd</th><th>Guinness Mahon & Co Ltd</th><th>Industrial & Commercial Finance Corporation Ltd</th></tr>
<tr><td>(b)(i)</td><td rowspan="3">Yes As required</td><td>Yes</td><td>Yes</td><td rowspan="3">Not specific, as to help given. But general financial advice is given when required</td><td>Yes</td><td>Yes</td><td>Yes</td><td>Yes</td></tr>
<tr><td>(ii)</td><td>—</td><td>—</td><td>Yes</td><td>Yes</td><td>Yes</td><td>Yes</td></tr>
<tr><td>(iii)</td><td>—</td><td>—</td><td>Yes</td><td>Yes Specialists available covering all functions</td><td>Yes And on general management</td><td>Yes</td></tr>
</table>

Ionian Bank Ltd	Midland Montagu Industrial Finance Ltd	Minster Trust Ltd	National & Commercial Development Capital Ltd	Old Broad Street Securities Ltd	Small Business Capital Fund Ltd	Sterling Industrial Securities Ltd	Wood Street Capital Ltd (a subsidiary of Hill Samuel & Co Ltd)
Yes	Yes	Yes	Yes	Yes	Yes	Yes	Yes
Yes	Yes	Yes	Yes	—	Yes	Yes	Yes
Yes	Yes	Yes	Yes	Yes	Yes Experienced general management support and help on recruitment	Yes	Yes

Index